Index of Initials and Acronyms

Index of Initials and Acronyms

Compiled by RICHARD KLEINER

AUERBACH®
Publishers
Princeton   New York
Philadelphia   London

Published simultaneously in Canada by Book Center, Inc.
Library of Congress Catalog Card No. 76-121868
International Standard Book Number: 0-87769-041-3
First Printing
Printed in the United States of America

CONTENTS

Dedicated, with love and admiration,
to my favorite initials —
HRK, KJK, CAK, and PRK

PREFACE

WHEN MAN FIRST began to speak, a few monosyllables were sufficient to convey what he wished to express — basic emotions such as those involving cold, warmth, hunger, fatigue, pain. As his mind became more complex, so did his speech. He needed an ever-increasing vocabulary to tell others what he was thinking. Time went on and man and his world became increasingly caught up in thinking about ideas and images. One word was no longer sufficient in many cases; now it took two or three to get across those complicated thoughts.

Man has sought ceaselessly to shorten his speech, which has sometimes become unwieldy. He invented a device he called "sound navigation ranging," which took a fairly long time to say, especially if it were necessary to use the term frequently. So he chopped off a couple of letters from the ends of the words and came up with the acronym "sonar."

Initials and acronyms have long been part of the English language. But it is only since World War II that they have become so widespread that a book such as this is necessary.

Initials and acronyms are handy language tools, especially when an initiate is talking or writing to another initiate. One doctor knows what another is talking about when he says "H-E-T-P." An engineer can understand a colleague who mentions the "SHA." An educator comprehends his fellow educator's use of the term "PSAT." But let an uninitiated layman wander unarmed into such a conversation, and he may as well be in another world; he is lost.

It is for such people — average persons who may on occasion come into contact with today's complex and esoteric fields — that this book is intended. As the use of spoken and written shortcuts increases, so does the need for a reference work that lists many useful initials and acronyms. The need for such a guide will increase as people more and more encounter technology (the space program, for example), government (a *complete* list of the initials and acronyms used by the federal government would fill several volumes), international events, and other fields.

Obviously no one volume can include every set of initials used in this abbreviation-conscious society. For example, each town and city has its PD (police department); it would be cumbersome and nearly impossible to include them all, every CPD or NYPD or LAPD. One "PD" in the *Index* is sufficient. Similarly, there are hundreds of colleges and universities and high schools in the nation, most of which are known familiarly (and usually only locally) by their initials.

I have included here only those sets of initials which in my judgment are most frequently used and which might perhaps be found by the general reader. My intention here is to include initials and acronyms which are found in reading, traveling, browsing, or simply listening to a conversation. Unexplained they can leave the reader, traveler, or browser with an unanswered question in his mind, along with a vague sense of annoyance at not knowing what is under discussion. This book should be kept close at hand, as you would a dictionary. What do those peculiar initials mean? Look them up in the *Index*.

A few words about the organization of this book. The Classification Code indicates the general field in which the initial or initials are used. It is possible, indeed probable, that a set of initials will refer to several categories of usage. If you are reading an article dealing with education, you may look in the Code and see that number 23 applies to this subject; those definitions with the number 23 after them are used in matters related to education.

In most cases letters in the definition are italicized to coincide with the letters in the set of initials. Thus "TIROS" is defined as "*t*elevision and *infra*red *o*bservation *s*atellite," with italicization of the letters that made up the set of initials or the acronym. The only exceptions are the symbols of companies listed on the New York and American Stock exchanges. Since these are often assigned arbitrarily, they do not necessarily take their letters from the actual corporate names. The names of the corporations, therefore, are given in their entirety, and no attempt is made to match italicization with initials.

In alphabetizing the initials, I have listed subjects that have ampersands (&) at the head of each alphabetical category: "A&A" — *A*rcade and *A*ttica Railroad — is listed before all of the AA listings. The purpose of this is to make looking up a term easier.

This field is so vital and constantly changing that new initials are certain to appear before this book is published. And the coinages will continue; some, of course, will die out, but there will be an overall increase. It is my hope that the *Index* will be kept up-to-date by the issuance of new editions from time to time, in which new initials and acronyms, plus any omissions or corrections, will be included.

Richard Kleiner

September 1970

CLASSIFICATION CODE

1. Transportation—airlines, railroads, ships, transportation terminology
2. Organizations—charity, college, fraternity, private
3. Industry—businesses, slogans, trademarks
4. Military—branches, ordnance, titles and ranks, units
5. Degrees
6. Government Bureaus—federal, state, and local; agencies, commissions, offices
7. Government Terms—fiscal, legislative, monetary, officials, postal
8. Common Usage—colloquialisms, slang, word coinages
9. Business and Economics—accounting, manufacturing procedures, sales, trade
9A. New York Stock Exchange Ticker Symbols
9B. American Stock Exchange Ticker Symbols
10. Associations—business and trade associations
11. Sports and Athletics
12. Foreign and International—groups, industrial concerns, organizations, political parties
13. United Nations Organizations
14. Acronyms—sets of initials that have become words in their own right and part of the language
15. Linguistics—etymology, grammar, languages
16. Religions—churches, expressions, orders, titles
17. Science and Medicine
17A. Chemical Elements
18. Pharmacy
19. Foreign Phrases
20. Professional Societies
21. Labor Unions
22. Communications—newsgathering organizations, printing, publishing
23. Education—colleges and universities, educational philosophies, recognized tests
24. Politics—movements, parties, terms
25. Entertainment—film, music, recordings, television, theater
26. Police—law enforcement, penology, terminology
27. Geography and Navigation—areas, compass directions, navigational terminology
28. Titles—awards, honors, membership in honorary societies
29. Well-known Persons
30. Chronology—dates, times, time zones

A The Anaconda Co.—9A

argon—17A

A&A *A*rcade and *A*ttica Railroad—1

AA *a*chievement *a*ge—23

*a*dministrative *a*ssistant—28

*A*erolíneas *A*rgentinas (Argentine Airlines)—1

*a*ir *a*ttaché—28

*a*irman *a*pprentice—4

*A*lcoholics *A*nonymous—2

Aluminum Company of America—9A, 9B

*A*merican *A*irlines—1

*A*nn *A*rbor Railroad—1

*a*ntiaircraft (or *a*ntiaircraft artillery)—4

*A*ssociate in *A*ccounting—5

*A*ssociate in *A*rts—5

*A*ugustinians of the *A*ssumption—16

*a*uthor's *a*lteration—22

AAA *A*gricultural *A*djustment *A*dministration—6

*A*ll-*A*merican *A*viation—1

*A*mateur *A*thletic *A*ssociation—2, 11

*A*merican *A*utomobile *A*ssociation—2

*a*ntiaircraft *a*rtillery—4

*A*utomobile *A*ssociation of *A*merica—2

AAAA *A*mateur *A*thletic *A*ssociation of *A*merica—2, 11

*A*merican *A*ssociation of *A*dvertising *A*gencies—10

AAAE *A*merican *A*ssociation for *A*dult *E*ducation—23

AAAL *A*merican *A*cademy of *A*rts and *L*etters—20

AAAS *A*merican *A*ssociation for the *A*dvancement of *S*cience—20

AAB *A*rmy *A*ir *B*ase (World War II)—4

AAC *a*ir *a*pproach *c*ontrol—1

*A*laskan *A*ir *C*ommand—4

*A*merican *A*lumni *C*ouncil—2, 23

*A*merican *C*ement *C*orp.—9A

AACS *A*irways and *A*ir *C*ommunications *S*ystem—4

*A*rmy *A*ir *C*ommunications *S*ystem—4

AAD *A*rlan's *D*epartment Stores, Inc.—9A

*A*rmy *A*viation *D*igest—22

AAE *A*merace Esna Corp.—9A

*A*merican *A*ssociation of *E*ngineers—20

AAEE *A*merican *A*ssociation of *E*lectrical *E*ngineers—20

AAF *A*merican *A*dvertising *F*ederation—10

American Air Filter Co., Inc.—9A

*A*rmy *A*ir *F*ield (or *F*orces) (World War II)—4

AAG *a*ssistant *a*djutant *g*eneral—4

*A*ssociation of *A*merican *G*eographers—20

AAHPER *A*merican *A*ssociation for *H*ealth, *P*hysical *E*ducation and *R*ecreation (of the *N*ational Education Association)—2, 23

AAIN *A*merican *A*ssociation of *I*ndustrial *N*urses—20

AAL *A*rctic *A*eromedical *L*aboratory—17

AAM *a*ir-to-*a*ir *m*issile—4

AAMA *A*merican *A*pparel *M*anufacturers *A*ssociation—10

AAO *a*m *a*ngeführten *O*rte (in the place cited)—19

*a*ntiaircraft *o*fficer—4

AAONMS *A*ncient *A*rabic *O*rder of the *N*obles of the *M*ystic *S*hrine—2

AAP Allied Artists Pictures—9B

*a*ntipernicious *a*nemia *p*rinciple—17

*A*pollo *A*pplications *P*rogram (NASA)—17

*A*ssociation of *A*merican *P*ublishers—10

AAPSS American Academy of Political and Social Sciences—20

AAR Adams Russell Co., Inc.—9B

AARS All-American Rose Selection—3

AAS Academiae Americanae Socius (Fellow of the American Academy)—28

Airport Advisory Service—1

American Academy of Sciences—20

American Antiquarian Society—2

American Astronautical Society—20

Associated Spring Corp.—9A

Associate in Applied Science—5

AASA American Association of School Administrators—20, 23

AASHO American Association of State Highway Officials—20

AASR Ancient Accepted Scottish Rite (Masons)—2

AAU Amateur Athletic Union—2, 11

Association of American Universities—23

AAUP American Association of University Presses—10, 22

American Association of University Professors—20, 23

AAUW American Association of University Women—2, 23

AAV American Automatic Vending Corp.—9B

AAVSO American Association of Variable Star Observers—2, 17

AAW antiair warfare—4

AB able-bodied seaman—1, 8

afterburner—1, 4

Aid to the Blind—7

air base—4

Ambac Industries, Inc.—9A

Artium Baccalaureus (Bachelor of Arts)—5

assembly bill—7

at bat—11

ABA airborne alert—4

American Bakeries, Inc.—9A

American Bankers Association—10

American Bar Association—20

American Booksellers' Association—10, 22

Associate in Business Administration—5

ABAD Air Battle Analysis Division—4

ABAJ American Bar Association Journal—22

ABAR alternate battery acquisition radar—17

AB&C Atlanta, Birmingham and Coast Railroad—1

ABC A Better Chance—2

Alcoholic Beverage Commission (or Control)—6

alum, blood, clay, and charcoal (sewage treatment)—17

American Bowling Congress—11

American Broadcasting Co.—9A, 25

Argentina, Brazil, and Chile powers—12

Aruba, Bonaire, Curacao (ABC islands)—12

atomic, biological, and chemical warfare —4, 17

Audit Bureau of Circulation—22

boric acid, bismuth subnitrate, and calomel—17

ABCA America, Britain, Canada, and Australia—7

ABCC Atomic Bomb Casualty Commission (of the Atomic Energy Commission)—6

ABCD America, Britain, China, and Dutch East Indies—7

ABCFM American Board of Commissioners for Foreign Missions (Congregational Church)—16

ABCP Argentina, Brazil, Chile, and Peru powers—12

ABEPP American Board of Examiners in Professional Psychology—17, 20

ABFM   *A*merican *B*oard of *F*oreign *M*issions—16

ABG   American Ship Building Co., Inc.—9A

ABJ   *A*bacus Fund—9A

ABL   American Biltrite Rubber Co., Inc.—9B

*au*tomated *b*iological *l*aboratory—17

ABLE   *a*ctivity *b*alance *l*ine *e*valuation—14, 17

ABLS   *A*rtium *B*accalaureus (Bachelor of Arts) in *L*ibrary *S*cience—5

ABM   *a*dvanced *b*ill of *m*aterials—9

American Building Maintenance Industries—9B

*a*nti*b*allistic *m*issile—4

ABMA   *A*rmy *B*allistic *M*issile *A*gency—4

ABMIS   *a*irborne *b*allistic *m*issile—4, 14

ABN   American Bank Note Co.—9A

ABP   *A*merican *B*usiness *P*ress—10

ABPC   *A*merican *B*ook *P*ublishers' *C*ouncil—10, 22

ABRES   *a*dvanced *b*allistic *r*eentry systems—4

ABRL   *A*rmy *B*allistic *R*esearch Laboratories—4

ABS   *a*crylonitrile *b*utadiene styrene—17

*a*lkyl*b*enze*n*esulfonate—17

*A*merican *B*ible *S*ociety—16

*A*merican *B*ureau of *S*hipping—1

*a*ntiseptic *b*iological *s*uppositories—17

ABT   *A*bbott Laboratories—9A

*A*merican *B*allet *T*heater—25

ABW   Associated Brewing Co.—9A

ABX   American Book-Stratford Press, Inc.—9B

ABY   A. M. Byers Co.—9B

*A*merican *B*oat and *Y*acht Council—10

ABZ   Arkansas Best Corp.—9B

AC   *a*bsolute *c*eiling—17

*a*ccount *c*urrent—9

*a*cetyl*c*holine—17

*a*ctinium—17A

*a*ir *c*ontrolman—4

*A*ir *C*orps—4

*a*lternating *c*urrent—17

American Can Co.—9A

*a*merican *c*heese—8

*a*nte *C*hristum (before Christ)—19

*a*nte *c*ibum (before meals)—18

*a*rea *c*ode—9

*A*rmy *C*orps—4

*A*ssociate in *C*ommerce—5

*a*thletic *c*lub—2

ACA   *A*merican *C*anoe *A*ssociation—11

*A*merican *C*hiropractic *A*ssociation—20

*A*merican *C*onstitutional *A*ssociation—2

ACAA   *A*gricultural *C*onservation and *A*djustment *A*dministration—6

ACAPS   *a*utomated *c*ost *a*nd *p*lanning system—9, 14

ACB   *A*ssociated *C*redit *B*ureaus of America—10

ACBL   *A*merican *C*ontract *B*ridge League—2

ACC   *a*ir *c*oordinating *c*ommittee—1

*A*llied *C*ontrol *C*ommission—6

Allied Control Co.—9B

*a*nodal *c*losure *c*ontraction—17

ACCC   *A*merican *C*ouncil of *C*hristian Churches—16

ACCUS   *A*utomobile *C*ompetition *C*ommittee for the *U*nited *S*tates—11, 14

ACD   Allied Chemical Corp.—9A

*A*merican *C*ollege of *D*entists—20

*a*rms *c*ontrol and *d*isarmament—7

ACDA   *A*rms *C*ontrol and *D*isarmament *A*gency—6

ACDC   *a*lternating *c*urrent and *d*irect *c*urrent—17

ACDUTRA   *a*ctive *d*uty for *tr*aining—4,14

ACE Acme-Hamilton Manufacturing—9B

*A*ctive *C*orps of *E*xecutives (of Small Business Administration)—6, 9, 14

*a*drenal *c*ortex *e*xtract—17

*a*lcohol, *c*hloroform, and *e*ther—17

*A*merican *C*inema *E*ditors—20, 25

*A*merican *C*ouncil on *E*ducation—23

*a*utomatic *c*heckout *e*quipment—9, 17

ACF *A*merican *C*ar and *F*oundry Co. —3

ACF Industries, Inc.—9A

ACFL *A*tlantic *C*oast *F*ootball League—11

AC&HB *A*lgoma *C*entral and *H*udson *B*ay Railroad—1

ACH The Ansul Co.—9B

ACI Atlas Chemical Industries, Inc.—9A

ACIC *A*eronautical *C*hart and *I*nformation *C*enter—1, 6

ACJ *A*merican *C*ouncil for *J*udaism—16

ACK Armstrong Cork Co.—9A

ACL Acme Precision Products—9B

*a*llowable *c*argo *l*oad—1

*A*tlantic *C*oast *L*ine Railroad—1

ACLANT *A*llied *C*ommand, At*lant*ic (NATO)—6, 14

ACLS *A*merican *C*ouncil of *L*earned *S*ocieties—20

*a*utomatic *c*arrier *l*anding system—4

ACLU *A*merican *C*ivil *L*iberties *U*nion—2

ACM Atlas Consolidated Manufacturing and Development Corp.—9B

ACN American Chain and Cable Co., Inc.—9A

*a*utomatic *c*elestial *n*avigation—27

ACNO *A*ssistant *C*hief of *N*aval Operations—4

ACO *a*ir (or *a*irborne) *c*ontrol officer—4

Ameco, Inc.—9B

ACOG *a*ircraft *o*n *g*round—4, 14

ACP *A*merican *C*ollege of *P*hysicians—20

ACR American Credit Co.—9A

AC&S *A*tlantic *C*ity and *S*hore Railroad—1

ACS *a*lternating *c*urrent, *s*ynchronous—17

*A*merican *C*ancer *S*ociety—17

*A*merican *C*eramic *S*ociety—10

*A*merican *C*hemical *S*ociety—10

*A*merican *C*ollege of *S*urgeons—20

American Crystal Sugar Co.—9A

*A*ssociate in *C*ommercial *S*cience—5

*a*ttitude *c*ontrol *s*ystem—1

ACSEA *A*ir *C*ommand, *S*outheast *A*sia—4, 14

ACSI *A*ssistant *C*hief of *S*taff, *I*ntelligence—4

ACSS *A*ir *C*ommand and *S*taff *S*chool—4

ACT *A*merican *C*ollege *T*esting—23

*A*merican *C*onservatory *T*heater—25

*A*ustralian *C*apital *T*erritory—27

ACTH *a*dreno*c*orti*c*o*t*rophic *h*ormone (pituitary)—17

ACTU *A*ssociation of *C*atholic *T*rade *U*nionists—21

ACV *a*ir *c*ushion *v*ehicle—1, 17

Alberto-Culver Co.—9A

ACW *a*ircraft *c*ontrol and *w*arning—1 *a*lternating *c*ontinuous *w*aves—17

ACWA *A*malgamated *C*lothing *W*orkers of *A*merica—21

AC&Y *A*kron, *C*anton & *Y*oungstown Railroad—1

ACY American Cyanamid Co.—9A

AD *a*ctive *d*uty—4

*a*fter *d*ate—9

Amsted Industries, Inc.—9A

*a*nno *D*omini (in the year of our Lord)—19

*a*nte *d*iem (before the day)—19

*a*ssembly *d*istrict—24

*a*ssistant *d*irector (motion pictures)—25

*a*ssociate *d*irector (television)—25

*a*utographed *d*ocument—9

ADA *a*irborne *d*ata *a*utomation—1, 9, 17

*A*merican *D*ental *A*ssociation—20

*A*mericans for *D*emocratic *A*ction—2, 24

Astrodata, Inc.—9B

*A*tomic *D*evelopment *A*uthority—6

ADAR *a*dvanced *d*esign *a*rray *r*adar—4

ADB *A*sian *D*evelopment *B*ank—12

Associated Baby Services, Inc.—9B

ADC *a*ide-*d*e-*c*amp—4

*A*ir *D*efense *C*ommand—4

American Distilling Co.—9A

ADD *A*mes *D*epartment *S*tores, Inc.—9B

ADE *A*pplied *D*evices Corp.—9B

ADF *a*ir (or *a*utomatic) *d*irection *f*inder—1

ADGB *a*ir *d*efense of *G*reat Britain—12

ADH *a*nti*d*iuretic *h*ormone—17

ADIZ *a*ir (or *a*ircraft) *d*efense *i*dentification *z*one—4

ADL *a*ctivities of *d*aily *l*iving—8, 17

Admiral Corp.—9A

*A*nti-*D*efamation League (of B'nai B'rith)—16

Arthur *D*. Little, Inc.—3

ADM Archer-Daniels-Midland Co.—9A

ADMA *A*ircraft *D*istributors and *M*anufacturers *A*ssociation—10

AD&N *A*shley, *D*rew and *N*orthern Railroad—1

ADP *a*denosine *d*iphosphate (or *d*iphospheric) acid—17

Allied Products Corp.—9A

*a*utomatic *d*ata *p*rocessing—9

ADPB *a*ir *d*efense *p*lanning *b*oard—6

ADPL *a*verage *d*aily *p*atient *l*oad—17

ADR *A*merican *D*epository *R*eceipts—9

ADS Allied Mills, Inc.—9A

*A*merican *D*ialect *S*ociety—2

*a*utograph *d*ocument, *s*igned—9

ADT American District Telegraph Co.—9A

ADU Associated Products, Inc.—9B

ADV *a*d *v*alorem (in proportion to the value)—19

American Dualvest Fund, Inc.—9A

ADX Adams Express Co.—9A

A&E *a*zimuth and *e*levation—27

AE *a*ccount *e*xecutive—9

*a*eronautical *e*ngineer—28

*a*gricultural *e*ngineer—28

*a*lmost *e*verywhere (mathematics)—17

*A*ssociate in *E*ducation—5

*A*ssociate in *E*ngineering—5

AEA *A*ctors' *E*quity *A*ssociation—21

*A*dult *E*ducation *A*ssociation—23

*A*merican *E*conomic *A*ssociation—20

A&EC *A*tlantic and *E*ast Carolina Railroad—1

AEC *A*rmy *E*lectronics *C*ommand—4

*A*tomic *E*nergy *C*ommission—6

AEDS *a*tomic *e*nergy *d*etection *s*ystem—4

AEF *A*frique *E*quatoriale *F*rançaise (French Equatorial Africa)—27

*a*irborne *e*quipment *f*ailure—1

*A*merican *E*xpeditionary *F*orces—4

AEI Arctic Enterprises—9B

AEIL *A*merican *E*xport-*I*sbrandtsen Lines—1

AEIOU *A*ustriae *E*st *I*mperare *O*rbi *U*niverso, or *A*lles *E*rdreich *I*st *O*esterreich *U*ntertham (to Austria is the whole world subject) (Hapsburg monogram)—19

AEL Anderson Electric Corp.—9B

AEN All American Engineering—9B

AE&P *A*mbassador *E*xtraordinary and *P*lenipotentiary—28

AEP *A*merican *E*lectric *P*ower Co., Inc.—9A

AEPW *a*ircraft *e*mergency *p*rocedures over *w*ater—1

AER AeroFlow Dynamics—9B

AERA *A*merican *E*ducational *R*esearch *A*ssociation—20

AES *A*pollo *e*xtension *s*ystem—17

AESC *a*utomatic *e*lectronic *s*witching *c*enter—4, 17

AET *A*etna *L*ife and *C*asualty Co.—9A

*A*ssociate in *E*lectrical *T*echnology—5

AEW *a*irborne *e*arly *w*arning—4

*A*ppalachian *P*ower Co.—9B

AEX *A*merican *E*xport *I*ndustries, Inc.—9A

AF *A*ir *F*orce—4

*A*ir *F*rance—1

*A*nglo-*F*rench—15

*A*rmy *f*orm—4

The *A*rthritis *F*oundation—2, 17

*a*udio *f*requency—17

AFA *A*dvertising *F*ederation of *A*merica—10

*A*ir *F*orce *A*ssociation—2

*A*ssociate in *F*ine *A*rts—5

AFAL *A*ir *F*orce *A*vionics *L*aboratory—4, 17

AFAM *A*ncient *F*ree and *A*ccepted *M*asons—2

AFB *a*ir *f*orce *b*ase—4

*A*merican *F*ederation for the *B*lind—2

AFBSD *A*ir *F*orce *B*allistic *S*ystems *D*ivision—4

AFC *A*ir *F*orce *C*ross—28

*a*irman *f*irst *c*lass—4

*A*ssociated *F*ood *S*tores, Inc.—9B

*a*utomatic *f*light *c*ontrol—1

*a*utomatic *f*requency *c*ontrol—17

AFCE *a*utomatic *f*light *c*ontrol equipment—1

AFCEA *A*rmed *F*orces *C*ommunications and *E*lectronics *A*ssociation—2, 4

AFCENT *A*llied *F*orces *Ce*ntral *E*urope (NATO)—4, 14

AFDC *A*id to *F*amilies with *D*ependent *C*hildren—7

AFDCS *A*merican *F*irst *D*ay *C*over *S*ociety—2

AFE United States *A*ir *F*orce in *E*urope—4

AFESD *A*ir *F*orce *E*lectronic *S*ystems *D*ivision—4

AFH *A*ffiliated *H*ospital Products—9B

AFHQ *A*ir *F*orce *h*eadquarters—4

AFI *A*merican *F*ilm *I*nstitute—20

*A*tlantic *R*ichfield Co.—9A

AFL *A*merican *F*ederation of *L*abor—21

*A*merican *F*ootball *L*eague—11

AFLC *A*ir *F*orce *L*ogistics *C*ommand—4

AFL-CIO *A*merican *F*ederation of *L*abor and *C*ongress of *I*ndustrial *O*rganizations—21

AFM *A*ir *F*orce *m*anual—4, 22

*A*ir *F*orce *M*edal—28

*A*merican *F*ederation of *M*usicians—21

AFN *A*merican *F*orces *N*etwork—4, 25

AFOSR *A*ir *F*orce *O*ffice of *S*cientific *R*esearch—4, 17

AFP *A*gence *F*rance *P*resse (French Press Agency)—22

AFPFL *A*nti-*F*ascist *P*eople's *F*reedom *L*eague (Burma)—12

AFQT *A*rmed *F*orces *Q*ualifications *T*est—4, 23

AFS *A*merican *F*ield *S*ervice—23

*A*merican *F*inance *S*ystem, Inc.—9B

AFSC *A*ir *F*orce *S*ystems *C*ommand—4

American Friends Service Committee—16

AFSCME American Federation of State, County and Municipal Employees—21

AFT American Federation of Teachers—21

American Manufacturing Co., Inc.—9B

annual field training—4

automatic fine tuning—9, 17

AFTAC Air Force Tactical Air Command—4

AFTMA American Fishing Tackle Manufacturers' Association—10

AFTO Air Force Technical Order—4

AFTRA American Federation of Television and Radio Artists—14, 21

AFUS Air Force of the United States—4

AG adjutant general—4

aerographer s mate—4

albumin to globulin ratio—17

Allegheny Ludlum Industries—9A

silver (from argentum)—17A

attorney general—7

AGA air-ground-air—4

Alabama Gas Corp.—9A

AGAC American Guild of Authors and Composers—20

AGB any good brand—8

AGC Adjutant General's Corps—4

American General Insurance Co.—9A

automatic gain control—17

AGCA automatic ground-controlled approach—1

AGCL automatic ground-controlled landing—1

AGCT Army General Classification Test—4, 23

AGD Andy Gard Corp.—9B

AGE aerospace ground equipment—1, 17

Assembly of Governmental Employees—10

Associate in General Education—5

AGER agricultural economics research—7

AGG Aguirre Co.—9A

AGI American Geological Institute—20

AGL Angelica Corp.—9B

AGM air-to-ground missile—4

The Amalgamated Sugar Co.—9A

AGMA American Gear Manufacturers' Association—10, 14

American Guild of Musical Artists—14, 21

AGO Adjutant General's Office—4

Anglo-Lautaro Nitrate Co., Ltd.—9B

AGR advanced gas-cooled reactor—17

AGS abort guidance section (or system)—17

American Geographical Society—20

Army General Staff—4

Associate in General Studies—5

AGU American Geophysical Union—20

AGVA American Guild of Variety Artists—14, 21

AGZ actual ground zero—4

A&H accident and health—9

AH Agricultural Handbook—7, 22

Allis-Chalmers Manufacturing Co.—9A

ampere-hour—9

anno Hegirae (in the year of the Hegira)—19

AHA Alpha Industries, Inc.—9B

American Hardboard Association—10

American Historical Association—2

American Hospital Association—10

American *Hotel* Association 10

American *Humane* Association 2

AHC Amerada Hess Corp. 9A

AHD American *Heritage* Dictionary of the English Language 22

AHE Associate in *Home* Economics—5

AHF antihemophilic factor—17

AHG antihemophilic globulin —17

AHMA American *Hotel* and *Motel* Association—10

AHMS American *Home* Mission Society—16

AHO American Hoist and Derrick Co.—9A

AHP American Home Products Corp. —9A

AHQ air (or army) headquarters—4

AHS American Helicopter Society—10

American Hospital Supply Corp.—9A

attitude horizon sensor—17

AHSA American Horse Shows Association—11

A&I agricultural and industrial—23

AI airborne interception—4

aircraft identification—4

Air India—1

Apollo Industries, Inc.—9B

artificial insemination—17

AIA Aerospace Industries Association—10

American Institute of Aeronautics—20

American Institute of Architects—20

AIAA American Institute of Aeronautics and Astronautics—20

AIBS American Institute of Biological Sciences—20

AIC American Institute of Chemists—20

American Investment Co.—9A

AICBM antiintercontinental ballistic missile—4

AICC All-India Congress Committee 12

AICE American Institute of Chemical Engineers 20

AID Agency for International Development 6

American Institute of Decorators 20

American Institute of Interior Designers– 20

artificial insemination donor 17

AIDS aircraft integrated data system 1, 17

AIEEE American Institute of Electrical and Electronics Engineers—20

AIFS American Institute for Foreign Study—23

AII Automation Industries, Inc.—9A

AIL Aileen, Inc.—9B

airborne instrument laboratory—17

AIM AIM Companies, Inc.—9B

American Institute of Management—10

AIMBW American Institute of Men's and Boys' Wear—10

AIME American Institute of Mining Engineers—20

Association of the Institute of Mechanical Engineers—20

AIMMPE American Institute of Mining, Metallurgical and Petroleum Engineers—20

AIMS army integrated meteorological system—4, 14

AIN Addressograph-Multigraph—9A

AIP American Independent Party—24

American Institute of Physics—20

American-International Pictures —25

American-Israeli Paper Mills Ltd. —9B

AIREA American Institute of Real Estate Appraisers—10

AISC American Institute of Steel Construction—10

AISI *A*merican *I*ron and *S*teel *I*nstitute—10

AIT *a*dvanced *i*ndividual *t*raining—4

AITS *A*merican *I*nternational *T*ravel Service—3

AITU *A*lliance of *I*ndependent *T*elephone *U*nions—21

AIU Amco Industries, Inc.—9B

AJ A. J. Industries—9A

*A*ssociate *J*ustice—7

AJC *A*merican *J*ewish *C*ommittee (or Congress)—16

AJN *A*merican *J*ournal of *N*ursing—17, 22

AJT Aerojet-General Corp.—9B

AJX Ajax Magnethermic—9B

AK *a*n*t*edi*l*uvian *k*night (old actor)—8, 25

*a*ss-*k*isser—8

AKA *a*lso *k*nown *a*s—7, 8

AKC *A*merican *K*ennel *C*lub—2, 11

AKG Arkansas Louisiana Gas Co.—9B

AKI Alaska Interstate Co.—9B

AKN Aiken Industries—9B

AKP Arkansas Power and Light Co.—9B

AL *A*be *L*incoln (refers to $5 bill)—8

Alcan Aluminium—9A

*a*l*u*minum—17A

*A*merican *L*eague—11

*A*merican *L*egion—2

*A*nglo-*L*atin—15

*a*utographed *l*etter—9

ALA Allegheny Airlines, Inc.—9B

*A*lliance for *L*abor *A*ction—21

*A*merican *L*ibrary *A*ssociation—20

*A*ssociate in *L*iberal *A*rts—5

*A*uthors' *L*eague of *A*merica—20

*A*utomobile *L*egal *A*ssociation—10

ALBM *a*ir-*l*aunched *b*allistic *m*issile—4

ALC *A*merican *L*utheran *C*hurch—16

Atlantic Coast Line Co.—9B

*a*utomatic *l*evel *c*ontrol (tape recorders)—25

ALCAN *Al*aska-*Can*ada highway—1, 14

ALCC *a*irborne *l*aunch *c*ontrol center—17

ALCOA *Al*uminum *C*ompany of *A*merica—3, 14

ALCOM *Al*aska *Com*mand—4, 14

ALCS *a*utomatic *l*aunch *c*ontrol *s*ystem—17

ALD *a*t a *l*ater *d*ate—9

ALF Alterman Foods, Inc.—9B

ALFA *A*nonima *L*ombarda *F*ábbrica *A*utomobili (Alfa Romeo) —3, 14

ALG *a*nti*l*ymphocyte *g*lobulin—17

ALGEC *a*l*g*orithmic language for *eco*nomic problems—14, 17

ALGM *a*ir-*l*aunched *g*uided *m*issile—4

ALGOL *a*l*g*orithmic *l*anguage—14, 17

ALI Airlift International—9B

*A*merican *L*aw *I*nstitute—20

ALITALIA *A*ero*l*inee *Italia*ne (Italian Airlines)—1, 14

ALK Alaska Airlines, Inc.—9B

ALL Adams-Millis Corp.—9A

A&LM *A*rkansas and *L*ouisiana *Mi*ssouri Railroad—1

ALM Allied Maintenance Corp.—9A

*A*merican *L*eprosy *M*issions—17

*A*ntilliaanse *L*uchtvaart *M*aatschappij (Dutch Antillean Airline)—1

ALN Allen Electric and Equipment Co.—9B

ALNICO *a*l*u*minum-*n*ickel-*co*balt—9, 14, 17

ALO Alsco, Inc.—9B

ALP Alabama Power Co.—9B

*A*merican *L*abor *P*arty—24

*a*utomated *l*earning *p*rocess—23

ALPA *A*ir *L*ine *P*ilots' *A*ssociation—10

ALR Allright Auto Parks, Inc.—9B

*A*merican *L*aw *R*eports—23

ALRI *a*irborne *l*ong-*r*ange *i*nput—17

ALS Allied Stores Corp.—9A

anti*l*ymphocyte *s*erum—17

*A*ssociate of the *L*innean *S*oci-ety—28

*a*utograph *l*etter, *s*igned—9

ALSEP *A*pollo *l*unar *s*cientific *ex*-periment *p*ackage—14, 17

ALW Altamil Corp.—9B

ALY Aluminum Specialty Co.—9B

A&M *a*gricultural and *m*echanical—23

*a*ncient and *m*odern—16

AM *a*gricultural *m*arketing—7

*am*ericium—17A

*am*pere*m*eter—9

*a*mplitude *m*odulation—17

*a*nno *m*undi (in the year of the world)—19

*a*nte *m*eridiem (before noon)—30

Armour and Co.—9A

*A*rtium *M*agister (Master of Arts)—5

*A*ve Maria (Hail Mary)—16

AMA *A*merican *M*anagement *A*ssoci-ation—20

*A*merican *M*edical *A*ssociation—20

*A*merican *M*issionary *A*ssociation—16

Amfac, Inc.—9A

AMASE *a*dvanced *m*apping *a*nd *s*ur-veying *e*quipment—17

AMB *A*irways *M*odernization *B*oard—6

AMBAC *A*merican-*B*osch-*A*rma Cor-poration—3, 14

AMC *A*berdeen *M*anufacturing Co.—9B

*A*ircraft *M*anufacturers' Coun-cil—10

*A*merican *M*aritime *C*ases—9

*A*merican *M*otors Corp.—3

*a*rmed *m*erchant *c*ruiser—1, 4

*A*rmy *M*ateriel (or *M*issile) Com-mand—4

AMCS *a*irborne *m*issile *c*ontrol sys-tem—4

AMD *a*erospace *m*edical *d*ivision—17

AMDG *a*d *m*ajorem *D*ei gloriam (to the greater glory of God)—16, 19

AME *A*dvanced *M*aster of *E*duca-tion—5

*A*frican *M*ethodist *E*piscopal Church—16

Ametek, Inc.—9A

*a*ngular *m*easurement *e*quipment—17

AMED *A*merican *e*ducation—7, 14, 23

AMEDS *A*rmy *M*edical *S*ervice—4, 14

AMERIND *A*merican *Ind*ian—14

AMEX *A*merican Stock *E*xchange—9, 14

AMEZ *A*frican *M*ethodist *E*piscopal *Z*ion Church—16

AMF *a*ir*m*ail *f*acility—7

*A*merican *M*achine and *F*oundry Corp.—3, 9A

AMG *A*llied *M*ilitary *G*overnment—4

AMGOT *A*llied *M*ilitary *G*overnment of *O*ccupied *T*erritories—4, 14

AMI *a*dvanced *m*anned *i*nterceptor—4

*A*merican *M*anagement *I*nsti-tute—10

*A*merican *M*eat *I*nstitute—10

*A*merican Medical Enterprises, Inc.—9B

AMICE *A*ssociate *M*ember, *I*nstitute of *C*ivil *E*ngineers—28

AMIEE *A*ssociate *M*ember, *I*nstitute of *E*lectrical *E*ngineers—28

AMK *A*merican Seal-*K*ap Corp.—3

AMK Corp.—9A, 9B

AML Ampco Metal, Inc.—9B

AMLS *A*rtium *M*agister (Master of Arts) in *L*ibrary *S*cience—5

AMM *a*nti*m*issile *m*issile—4

AMMLA *A*merican *M*erchant *M*arine *L*ibrary *A*ssociation—2

AMO American Motors Corp.—9A

*a*viation *m*edicine *o*ffice—4, 17

AMOCO *A*merican *O*il *Co.*—3, 14

AMORC *A*ncient *M*ystic Order of the

Rosae Crucis (Rosicrucians)—16

AMOS *a*utomatic *m*eteorological *ob*serving *s*ystem—14, 17

AMP *a*denosine *m*ono*p*hosphate—17

*A*ircraft-*M*arine *P*roducts, Inc.—3

AMP, Inc.—9A

AMPAC *A*merican *M*edical *P*olitical *A*ction Committee—24

AMPAS *A*cademy of *M*otion *P*icture *A*rts and *S*ciences—20, 25

AMPHETAMINE *a*lpha-*m*ethyl-*p*henyl-*e*thyl-*amine*—14, 17

AMPTP *A*ssociation of *M*otion *P*icture and *T*elevision *P*roducers—10

AMR *A*merican *A*irlines, Inc.—9A

*A*tlantic *m*issile *r*ange—4

AMRL *A*erospace *M*edical *R*esearch *L*aboratories—17

AMS *A*gricultural *M*arketing *S*ervice—7

*A*merican *M*anagement *S*ociety—20

*A*merican *M*athematical *S*ociety—20

*A*rmy *m*edical *s*taff—4

AMSA *a*dvanced *m*anned *s*trategic *a*ircraft—4

AMSC *A*rmy *M*edical *S*pecialist *C*orps—4

AMSW *A*rtium *M*agister (Master of Arts) in *S*ocial *W*ork—5

AMT *A*cme-*C*leveland *C*orp.—9A

*A*rtium *M*agister (Master of Arts) in *T*eaching—5

*A*ssociate in *M*echanical *T*echnology—5

*A*ssociate in *M*edical *T*echnology—5

AMTORG *A*merican *T*rade *Org*anization (Soviet Union)—9, 12, 14

AMTRAC *am*phibious *trac*tor—4, 14

AMU *a*stronaut *m*aneuvering *u*nit—17

*a*tomic *m*ass *u*nit—17

AMVETS *A*merican *Ve*terans of World War II and Korea—2, 14

AMX *A*merican *M*etal *C*limax, Inc.—9A

AMY *A*ssociated *M*ortgage *I*nvestors—9B

AMZ *A*merican *S*eating Co.—9A

A&N *A*lbany and *N*orthern *R*ail*road*—1

AN *a*irma*n*—4

*A*ir *R*eduction Co.—9A

*A*nglo-*N*orman—15

*A*palachicola *N*orthern *R*ail*road*—1

*a*rrival *n*otice—9

*A*ssociate in *N*ursing—5

ANA *A*merican *N*umismatic *A*ssociation—2

*A*merican *N*urses *A*ssociation—20

*A*ssociate *N*ational *A*cademician—28

*A*ustralian *N*ational *A*irways—1

ANACDUTRA *an*nual *ac*tive *du*ty for *tra*ining—4, 14

ANC *A*merican *N*ews *C*o.—3, 22

*A*ncorp *N*ational *S*ervices, Inc.—9A

*A*rmy *N*urse *C*orps—4

AND *A*ndrea *R*adio Corp.—9B

ANG *A*ir *N*ational *G*uard—4

*A*merican *N*atural *G*as Co.—9A

*A*merican *N*ewspaper *G*uild—21

ANIP *A*rmy-*N*avy *I*nstrumentation *P*rogram—4, 14

ANK *A*merican *E*nka *C*orp.—9A

ANP *a*ircraft *n*uclear *p*ropulsion—1, 17

*A*ssociated *N*egro *P*ress—22

ANPA *A*merican *N*ewspaper *Pub*lishers' *A*ssociation—10

ANRAC *a*ids to *n*avigation, *r*adio-*c*ontrolled—1, 27

ANS *A*merican *N*umismatic *S*ociety—2

ANT *A*nthony *P*ools, Inc.—9B

ANTA *A*merican *N*ational *T*heatre and *A*cademy—14, 25

ANTU *a*lpha-*n*aphthyl *t*hiourea—17

ANZAC *A*ustralia and *N*ew *Z*ealand *A*rmy *C*orps—4, 14

ANZUS *A*ustralia, *N*ew *Z*ealand, *U*nited *S*tates—7, 14

AO *a*ccount *o*f—9

*A*pril and *O*ctober—9

*A*rmy *o*rder—4

Associated Oil and Gas Co.—9B

*A*utonomous *O*blast (Soviet Union)—27

*a*viation *o*rdnanceman—4

AOA *A*dministration *o*n *A*ging—7

*A*merican *O*ptometric *A*ssociation—20

AOB *a*lcohol *o*n *b*reath—26

AOC *a*viation *o*fficer *c*andidate—4

AOF *A*frique *O*ccidentale *F*rançaise (French West Africa)—27

*A*ncient *O*rder of *F*oresters—2

AOG *a*ll *o*ver *g*ood—8

AOH *A*ncient *O*rder of *H*ibernians—2

AOL Apco Oil Corp.—9A

AOPA *A*irplane *O*wners and *P*ilots *A*ssociation—2

AOR Anchor Post Products, Inc.—9B

AOSO *a*dvanced *o*rbiting *s*olar *o*bservatory—17

AOU *A*merican *O*rnithologists' *U*nion—20

AOX Aerodex, Inc.—9B

A&P *a*irframe and *p*owerplant (of airplane)—1

The Great *A*tlantic and *P*acific Tea Co.—3

AP *a*ccount *p*aid (or *p*ayable)—9

*a*dditional *p*remium—9

*a*ir*p*lane—8

*a*ir *p*olice—4

*A*merican *p*lan (hotel service)—8

*a*nti*p*ersonnel—4

*a*rmor-*p*iercing—4

*a*ssessment *p*aid—9

*a*ssociated *p*arishes (of Episcopal Church)—16

*A*ssociated *P*ress—22

*A*ssociate *P*resbyterian—16

*a*uthority to *p*ay (or *p*urchase)—9

*a*uthor's *p*roof—9

*a*uto*p*ilot—1

APA *A*merican *P*hilological *A*ssociation—20

*A*merican *P*rotective *A*ssociation—10

*A*merican *P*rotestant *A*ssociation—16

*A*merican *P*sychiatric *A*ssociation—20

*A*merican *P*sychoanalytic *A*ssociation—20

*A*merican *P*sychological *A*ssociation—20

Apache Corp.—9A, 9B

*A*ssistance *P*ayments *A*dministration—6

*A*ssociate in *P*ublic *A*dministration—5

*A*ssociation of *P*roducing *A*rtists—25

APB *a*ll *p*oints *b*ulletin—26

*A*merican *P*rogram *B*ureau (lecture bureau)—25

APBA *A*merican *P*ower *B*oat *A*ssociation—11

APC *a*denoidal-*p*haryngeal-*c*onjunctival viruses—17

Alpha Portland Cement Co.—9A

*A*merican *P*ostal *C*orp.—3

*a*rmed *p*ersonnel *c*arrier—4

*a*spirin, *p*henacetin, and *c*affeine—17

APCD *a*ir *p*ollution *c*ontrol *d*istrict—17

APD Air Products and Chemicals—9A

*a*rea *p*ostal *d*irectory—7

APECO *A*merican *P*hotocopy *E*quipment *C*o.—3, 14

APG *A*merican *P*rofessional *G*olfers—11

APH AIC Photo, Inc.—9B

APHA *A*merican *P*ublic *H*ealth *A*ssociation—17

API *A*labama Polytechnic *I*nstitute—23

American Petrofina, Inc.—9B

*A*merican *P*etroleum *I*nstitute—10

APK Ayrshire Collieries Corp.—9B

APL APL Corp.—9B

American President Lines—1

*a*nterior-*p*ituitary-*l*ike substance—17

*a*pplied *p*hysics *l*aboratory—17

APM *a*ir *p*rovost *m*arshal—4

APO *A*ir (or *A*rmy) *p*ost *o*ffice—4

APP *a*dvanced *p*lanetary *p*robe—17

APPR *a*rmy *p*ackage *p*ower *r*eactor—4

APR American Precision Industries, Inc.—9B

APRA *A*lianza *P*opular *R*evolucionaria *A*mericana (Popular American Revolutionary Alliance)—12

APRO *A*erial *P*henomena *R*esearch *O*rganization—2

*A*rmy *P*ersonnel *R*esearch *O*ffice—4

APS *a*ccessory (or *a*uxiliary) *p*ower *s*upply—9

*A*merican *P*eace *S*ociety—2

*A*merican *P*hilatelic *S*ociety—2

*A*merican *P*hilosophical *S*ociety—20

*A*merican *P*hysical *S*ociety—20

*A*merican *P*hysics *S*ociety—20

*A*merican *P*rotestant *S*ociety—16

*a*scent *p*ropulsion *s*ystem—17

APSA *A*erolineas *P*eruanas *S*ociedad *A*nonima (Peruvian Air Lines)—1

*A*merican *P*olitical *S*cience *A*ssociation—20

APSB *A*id to the *P*otentially *S*elf-Supporting *B*lind—7

APT Aberdeen Petroleum—9B

*a*utomatic *p*icture *t*ransmission—9, 17

APU *a*uxiliary *p*ower *u*nit—1

APW API Instruments Co.—9B

APWA *A*merican *P*ublic *W*orks *A*ssociation—10

APX Ampex Corp.—9A

APY American Photocopy Equipment Co.—9A

AQ *a*chievement *q*uotient—23

AQL *a*cceptable (or *a*verage) *q*uality *l*evel—9

AQM Aqua-Chem, Inc.—9A

A&R *A*berdeen and *R*ockfish Railroad—1

*a*rtists and *r*epertoire—25

AR *a*ccount *r*eceivable—9

*A*coustic *R*esearch—3, 25

*a*irman *r*ecruit—4

*a*ll *r*isks—9

American Smelting and Refining Co.—9A

*a*nalytical *r*eagent—17

*a*nnual *r*eturn—9

*a*pplied *r*esearch—17

*a*rmy *r*egulation—4

ARA *A*gricultural *R*esearch *A*dministration—6

*A*merican *R*ailway *A*ssociation—10

ARA Services, Inc.—9A

*A*rea *R*edevelopment *A*ct—7

*A*ssociate of the *R*oyal *A*cademy—28

ARADCOM *A*rmy *A*ir Defense *C*ommand—4, 14

ARAMCO *A*rabian-*A*merican Oil *C*o.—3, 14

ARB *A*udience *R*esearch *B*ureau—3, 25

ARC Atlantic Richfield Co.—9A

*A*merican *R*ed *C*ross—2

ARCA *A*utomobile *R*acing *C*lub of *A*merica—11

ARCO *A*tlantic *R*ichfield *C*o.—3, 14

ARCS *A*chievement *R*ewards for *C*ollege *S*cientists—17, 23

*A*ssociate of the *R*oyal *C*ollege of *S*cience—28

Associate of the Royal College of Surgeons—28

ARD American Research and Development Corp.—9A

ARE Associate in Religious Education—5

AREPG Army Electronic Proving Ground—4, 17

ARES agricultural research—7, 14

ARGMA Army Rocket and Guided Missile Agency—4, 14

ARH Anchor Hocking Corp.—9A

antiradiation homing device—17

ARI audience reaction indicator—25

ARL The Arundel Corp.—9B

ARM antiradar (or radiation) missile—4

The Armstrong Rubber Co.—9A

ARN Aeronca, Inc.—9B

ARO Aro Corp.—9A

ARP air raid precautions—4

Associated Reform Presbyterian—16

ARPA Advanced Research Projects Agency—6

ARQ answer-return query—9

ARRL American Radio Relay League—2

ARRS Aerospace Rescue and Recovery Service—4

ARS advanced record system (of General Services Administration)—7

Agricultural Research Service—6

Air Rescue Service—4

American Rocket Society—2, 17

ARSP Aerospace Research Support Program—17

ART Automatic Radio Manufacturing Co., Inc.—9B

ARU American Railway Union—10

ARV American (Standard) Revised Version (Bible)—16

armored recovery vehicle—4

Arvin Industries, Inc.—9A

ARVN Armed Forces (or Army) of the Republic of Vietnam—12

ARW Arrow Electronics, Inc.—9B

ARX Argus, Inc.—9B

AS academy of science—20

air service—4

Anglo-Saxon—15

apprentice seaman—4

Armco Steel Corp.—9A

arsenic—17A

Associate in Science—5

ASA Acoustical Society of America—20

American Sociological Association—20

American-South African Investment Co., Ltd.—9A

American Standards Association—20

American Statistical Association—20

Army Security Agency—4

Association of Southeast Asia—12

A&SAB Atlanta and St. Andrews Bay Railroad—1

ASAP as soon as possible—8

ASBD advanced sea-based deterrent—4

ASC Acme Markets, Inc.—9A

American Society of Cinematographers—20

ASCAP American Society of Composers, Authors, and Publishers—14, 20

ASCD Association for Supervision and Curriculum Development (of National Education Association)—23

ASCE American Society of Civil Engineers—20

ASCOB any solid color other than black (refers to cocker spaniels)—11, 14

ASD Aeronautical Systems Division—9

ASDA American Stamp Dealers Association—10

ASDC Assistant Secretary of Defense/Comptroller—6

ASDIC Anti-Submarine Detection Investigation Committee—6, 14

ASE Allison Steel Manufacturing Co.—9B

American Stock Exchange—9

ASEAN Association of Southeast Asian Nations—12

ASEE American Society for Engineering Education—23

ASEF Association of Stock Exchange Firms—10

ASF air service force—4

ASGS advanced space guidance system—17

ASH Ashland Oil and Refining Co.—9A

ASHD arteriosclerosis heart disease—17

ASI Astrex, Inc.—9B

ASIS American Society for Industrial Security—10

ASL above sea level—27

ASLA American Society of Landscape Architects—20

ASLBM antisea-launched ballistic missile—4

ASM air-to-surface missile—4

Asamera Oil Corp., Ltd.—9B

ASME American Society of Mechanical Engineers—20

ASMP American Society of Magazine Photographers—20

ASMS advanced surface missile system—4

ASN Army serial (or service) number —4

ASNE American Society of Naval Engineers—20

American Society of Newspaper Editors—20

ASP American selling price—7, 9

Automatic Steel Products, Inc.—9B

ASPAC Asian and Pacific Council—12, 14

ASPCA American Society for the Prevention of Cruelty to Animals—2

ASPR Armed Services procurement regulations—4

ASQ American Safety Equipment Corp.—9B

ASR American Sugar Co.—9A

aviation safety regulations—1

ASROC antisubmarine rocket—4, 14

ASS airborne surveillance system—4

Associate in Secretarial Science (or Studies)—5

ASSR Autonomous Soviet Socialist Republic—12

ASSU American Sunday School Union—16

AST American Standard, Inc.—9A

Atlantic Standard Time—30

ASTA American Society of Travel Agents—10, 14

ASTE American Society of Tool Engineers—20

ASTIA Armed Services Technical Information Agency—4, 14, 17

ASTM American Society for Testing Metals (or Materials)—10

ASTP Army Specialized Training Program—4

ASU Allied Supermarkets, Inc.—9A

American Students' Union—2

Arizona State University—23

ASV American Standard Version (Bible)—16

ASW antisubmarine warfare—4

Association of Scientific Workers—20

ASWR antisubmarine warfare radar—4

ASZ American Sterilizer Co.—9A

AT air temperature—17

airtight—1

American Tobacco Co.—9A

ampere turn—17

antitank—4

assay ton—17

astatine—17A

atomic time—30

automatic transmission—9

ATA *A*ir *T*ransport *A*ssociation—9

*A*merican *T*rucking *A*ssociations—10

*A*ssociate *T*echnical *A*ide—5

ATAE *A*ssociated *T*elephone *A*nswering *E*xchanges—10

ATBM *a*nti*t*actical *b*allistic *m*issile—4

ATC *a*ctive *t*hermal *c*ontrol—17

*A*ir *T*raffic *C*onference of America—10

*a*ir *t*raffic *c*ontrol—1

*A*ir *T*raining (or *T*ransport) *C*ommand—4

*a*rmored *t*roop *c*arrier—4

ATCA *a*ttitude and *t*ranslation *c*ontrol *a*ssembly—17

ATCS *a*ir *t*raffic *c*ontrol *s*atellite—1, 17

ATD *a*id to the *t*otally *d*isabled—7

*A*utomated *B*uilding *C*omponents, Inc.—9B

ATDS *a*ir (or *a*irborne) *t*actical *d*ata *s*ystem—4

ATE Atlantic City Electric Co.—9A

*a*utomatic *t*est *e*quipment—9, 17

ATF Atico Financial Corp.—9B

ATH Athlone Industries, Inc.—9B

ATI *A*ero*t*ransporti *I*taliani (Italian Air Transport)—1

Amtel, Inc.—9A

ATL Atco Chemical-Industrial Products, Inc.—9B

ATLA *A*merican *T*rial *L*awyers' *A*ssociation—20

ATM *a*ir *t*raffic *m*anagement—1, 7

American Technical Industries, Inc.—9B

*a*mpere *t*urns per *m*eter—17

*a*tomic *m*ass—17

AT&N *A*labama, *T*ennessee and *N*orthern Railroad—1

ATO Automatic Sprinkler Corp. of America—9A

ATP *a*denosine *t*ri*p*hosphate—17

*A*ir *T*ravel *P*lan—1

Associated Transport, Inc.—9A

ATR *a*irline *t*ransport *r*ating—1

Alliance Tire and Rubber—9B

ATRA *A*utomatic *T*ransmission *R*ebuilders' *A*ssociation—10

ATS *a*dvanced *t*echnology *s*atellite—17

*A*ir *T*raffic *S*ervice—1, 7

*A*merican *T*emperance *S*ociety—2

*A*merican *T*ract *S*ociety—16

*a*pplications *t*echnology *s*atellite—17

*A*rmy *T*ransport *S*ervice—4

Associates Investment Co.—9A

*A*uxiliary *T*erritorial *S*ervice—4

ATSC *A*ir *T*echnical *S*ervice *C*ommand—4

ATSF *A*tchison, *T*opeka and *S*anta *F*e Railroad—1

AT&T *A*merican *T*elephone and *T*elegraph Co.—3

ATV *a*ll-*t*errain *v*ehicle—1

*A*ssociated *T*elevision (England)—25

ATW *A*merican *T*heatre *W*ing—25

ATWT *a*tomic *w*eigh*t*—17

AU Alloys Unlimited, Inc.—9B

*a*ngstrom *u*nit—17

*a*stronomical *u*nit—17

gold (from *au*rum)—17A

AUA *A*merican *U*nitarian *A*ssociation—16

*A*ustrian *A*irlines—1

AUC *a*nno *u*rbis *c*onditae (from the year the city was founded)—19

AUD Automatic Data Processing, Inc.—9B

AUM *a*ir-to-*u*nderwater *m*issile—4

AUR Aurora Plastics Corp.—9A

AUS *A*rmy of the *U*nited *S*tates—4

AUTODIN *au*to*m*atic *di*gital *n*etwork (Western Union)—14, 22

AV *a*d *v*alorem (in proportion to the value)—19

*a*rterio*v*enous—17

*a*rtillery *v*olunteer—4

*a*trio*v*entricular—17
*a*udio-*v*isual—17
*a*uriculo*v*entricular—17
*A*uthorized *V*ersion (Bible)—16
Avco Corp.—9A, 9B
AVC *A*merican *V*eterans' Committee—2
*A*merican *V*iscose Corporation—3
A. V. C. Corp.—9B
*a*utomatic *v*olume *c*ontrol—17
AVCO *A*viation *C*orp.—3
AVCS *a*dvanced *v*idicon *c*amera *s*ubsystem (or *s*ystem)—17
AVD Avondale Mills—9B
AVE *a*erospace *v*ehicle *e*quipment—1, 17
Avemco Corp.—9B
AVENSA *A*erovías *V*enezolanas *S*ociedad *A*nonima (Venezuelan Airlines)—1
AVIANCA *A*erovias *N*acionales de *C*olombia (Colombian National Airlines)—1, 14
AVM *A*merican *V*oting *M*achine Corp.—3
AVMA *A*merican *V*eterinary *M*edical *A*ssociation—20
AVN Avien, Inc.—9B
AVP Avon Products, Inc.—9A
AVS Avis Industrial Corp.—9B
AVSAT *a*viation *sat*ellite—14, 17
AVT Avnet, Inc.—9A
AVX Aerovox Corp.—9B
AVY Avery Products Corp.—9A
A&W *A*hnapee and *W*estern Railroad—1
*A*tlantic and *W*estern Railroad—1
AW *a*ctual *w*eight—9
Alan Wood Steel Co.—9B
*a*ll *w*ater—1, 9
*A*rkansas *W*estern Railroad—1
*a*rticles of *w*ar—4
*a*tomic *w*eight—17
AWACS *a*irborne *w*arning *a*nd *c*ontrol *s*ystem—4, 14

AWB *a*ir *w*ay*b*ill—9
AWD Arwood Corp.—9B
AWG *A*merican *w*ire *g*auge—9
AWI Airwick Industries, Inc.—9B
*a*ll-*w*eather *i*nterceptor—4
AWK American Water Works Co., Inc.—9A
AWL *a*bsent *w*ith *l*eave—4
AWM *A*merican *W*ar *M*others—2
AWOL *a*bsent *w*ith*o*ut *l*eave—4, 8, 14
A&WP *A*tlanta and *W*est *P*oint Railroad—1
AWT Air West, Inc.—9B
AWU *a*tomic *w*eight *u*nit—17
AWVS *A*merican *W*omen's *V*oluntary *S*ervice—2
AWWA *A*merican *W*ater *W*orks *A*ssociation—10
AXE Airpax Electronics, Inc.—9B
AXR Amrep Corp.—9B
A&Y *A*tlantic and *Y*adkin Railroad—1
AY Allegheny and Western Railway—9A
AYD *A*merican *Y*outh for *D*emocracy—2
AYH *A*merican *Y*outh *H*ostels—2
AYM *A*ncient *Y*ork *M*ason—2
AYP Allegheny Power System—9A
AZ *A*schei*m*-*Z*ondek pregnancy test—17
Atlas Corp.—9A, 9B
AZC *A*merican *Z*ionist *C*ouncil—16
AZP Arizona Public Service Co.—9A

B *b*oron—17A
B&A *B*altimore and *A*nnapolis Railroad—1
*B*angor and *A*roostook Railroad—1
*B*oston and *A*lbany Railroad—1
BA *B*accalaureus *A*rtium (Bachelor of Arts)—5
*b*arium—17A
The Boeing Co.—9A

British *Academy*—20

British *America*—27

British *Association* for the Advancement of Science—20

Buenos Aires—27

BAA Bachelor of *Applied Arts*—5

BAC *Black Affairs Council*—2

British *Aircraft Corp.*—1, 3

BACM British *American Construction* and *Materials*, Limited—3

BAE Bachelor of *Aeronautical Engineering*—5

Bachelor of *Agricultural Economics*—5

Bachelor of *Agricultural Engineering*—5

Bachelor of *Architectural Engineering*—5

Bachelor of *Art Education*—5

Bachelor of *Arts* in *Education*—5

Bureau of *Agricultural Economics*—6

Bureau of *American Ethnology*—6

BAF Banff Oil Ltd.—9B

BAI *Baccalaureus in Arte Ingeniaria* (Bachelor of Arts in Engineering)—5

Basic, Inc.—9A

BAK Baker Industries, Inc.—9B

BAL Baldwin-Securities Corp.—9B

British *anti-Lewisite*—17

BALUN *bal*anced to *un*balanced—14, 17

BAM Bachelor of *Applied Mathematics*—5

Bachelor of *Arts* in *Music*—5

BAN Banister Continental Corp.—9B

BAO Bachelor of *Arts* in *Oratory*—5

BAP Big Apple Supermarkets, Inc.—9B

BAPCT Bachelor of *Arts* in *Practical Christian Training*—5

BAR Barry Wright Corp.—9B

Broadcast *Advertisers Reports*—22

Browning *automatic rifle*—4

BART Bay *Area Rapid Transit* (San Francisco)—6

BAS Bachelor of *Agricultural Science*—5

Bachelor of *Applied Science*—5

Bachelor of *Arts* in *Speech*—5

BASF Badische *Anilin* und *Soda-Fabrik*—3

BAT Bates Manufacturing Co., Inc. —9A

biological *antiseptic tampon*—17

BAU British *Association unit*—17

BAV Butler Aviation International, Inc.—9B

BAW The Babcock and Wilcox Co. —9A

BAX Baxter Laboratories, Inc.—9A

B&B *Benton and Bowles*, Inc.—3

brandy and *benedictine*—8

BB bail bond—8, 26

ball bearing—9

base on balls—11

Big Bear Stores Co.—9B

bluebook—22

B'nai B'rith—2, 16

bottled in bond—8

Brigitte Bardot—29

Bureau of the Budget—6

BBA Bachelor of *Business Administration*—5

born before arrival—17

BBB Barton's Candy Corp.—9B

Better Business Bureau—2

BBC Bergen Brunswig Corp.—9B

British Broadcasting Corp.—12, 25

bromobenzyl cyanide—17

BBDO Batten, Barton, Durstine and Osborn—3

BBI Bloomfield Building Industries, Inc.—9B

BBIA Billiard and Bowling Institute of America—10

BBK Bobbie Brooks, Inc.—9A

BBL Blue Bell, Inc.—9A

BBO Barber Oil Corp.—9A

BBQ barbeq (barbecue)—8

BBR Barton Brands, Inc.—9B

BBS Bachelor of *Business Science*—5

B&C *B*arre and *C*helsea Railroad—1

*B*ennettsville and *C*heraw Railroad—1

BC *B*achelor of *C*hemistry—5

*B*achelor of *C*ommerce—5

*b*ass *c*larinet—8

*b*asso *c*ontinuo (continued or figured bass) (music)—19

*b*attery *c*apacitor (flash photography)—9

*b*attery *c*ommander—4

*b*efore *C*hrist—30

*B*ellefonte *C*entral Railroad—1

*b*ills for *c*ollection—9

*b*oat *c*lub—2

*B*oston *C*ollege—23

*B*ritish *C*olumbia—27

The *B*runswick *C*orp.—9A

BCA *B*illiard *C*ongress of *A*merica—11

BCB *B*ar *C*hris *C*onstruction *C*orp.—9B

BCC *B*oise *C*ascade *C*orp.—9A

BCD *b*ad *c*onduct *d*ischarge—4

*b*inary-*c*oded *d*ecimal—17

*b*usiness *c*ycle *d*evelopment—7, 9

BCE *B*achelor of *C*hemical *E*ngineering—5

*B*achelor of *C*ivil *E*ngineering—5

*B*achelor of *C*hristian *E*ducation—5

*B*achelor of *C*ivil *E*ngineering—5

*b*efore *c*ommon *e*ra—30

*B*ell *E*lectronic *C*orp.—9B

BCG *b*acillus *C*almette-*G*uerin vaccine—17

BCH *B*eech *C*reek R.R. Co., Ltd. —9A

BCI The *B*ali *C*o., *I*nc.—9B

BCL *B*achelor of *C*ivil *L*aw—5

BCM *B*achelor of *C*hurch *M*usic—5

B*A*C*M* Industries, Ltd.—9B

BCP *B*achelor of *C*ity *P*lanning—5

BCPA *B*ritish *C*ommonwealth *P*acific *A*irlines—1

BCPS *b*eam *c*andle*p*ower *s*econds—17

BCR C.R. Bard, Inc.—9A

BCS *B*achelor of *C*hemical *S*cience—5

*B*achelor of *C*ommercial *S*cience—5

BCT *B*ritish *C*aribbean *T*erritories—27

BCU E.L. Bruce Co., Inc.—9B

BCX Beech Aircraft Corp.—9A

BD *B*achelor of *D*ivinity—5

*b*ank *d*ividends—9

*b*ank *d*raft—9

*b*arrels per *d*ay—9

*b*ills *d*iscounted—9

*B*loedel-*D*onovan Railroad—1

*B*onner *D*urchmusterung (catalog of stars)—17

*B*ro-*D*art Industries—9B

*b*rought *d*own—9

BDA William J. Burns International Detective Agency, Inc.—9B

BDC Burndy Corp.—9A

BDF Bradford Speed Packaging and Development Corp.—9B

BDK The Black and Decker Manufacturing Co.—9A

BDM *b*omber *d*efense *m*issile—4

BDP *b*usiness *d*ata *p*rocessing—9

BDS *B*achelor of *D*ental *S*urgery—5

*b*is *d*ie *s*umendum (take twice a day)—18

BDSA *B*usiness and *D*efense *S*ervices *A*dministration—6

BDST *B*ritish *D*ouble *S*ummer *T*ime—30

BDW D. H. Baldwin Co.—9B

BDX Becton, Dickinson and Co.—9A

BDY B. Brody Seating Co.—9B

B&E *B*altimore and *E*astern Railroad —1

*b*reaking and *e*ntering—26

BE *B*achelor of *E*ducation—5

*B*achelor of *E*ngineering—5

*B*ank of *E*ngland—12

*B*aumé scale—17

*B*enguet Consolidated, Inc.—9A

*b*eryllium—17A

bill of entry—9

bill of exchange—9

board of education—6

British Eagle Airlines—1

BEA British European Airways—1

BEC Beckman Instruments, Inc.—9A

Bureau of Employees' Compensation—6

BED Board of Educational Development—23

BEE Bachelor of Electrical Engineering—5

BEF British Expeditionary Force(s)—4

BEI Beco Industries Corp.—9B

BEK Beck Industries, Inc.—9B

BEL Belden Corp.—9A

BELF break-even load factor—1

BEM Bachelor of Engineering of Mines—5

British Empire Medal—28

bug-eyed monster—8

BEMA Business Equipment Manufacturers' Association—10

BEN Benrus Corp.—9B

BENELUX Belgium, the Netherlands, Luxembourg—12, 14

BEP Bachelor of Engineering Physics—5

BER Bearings, Inc.—9A

BES Bachelor of Engineering Science—5

Bureau of Employment Security—6

BET The Bethlehem Corp.—9B

BEV Beverly Enterprises—9B

billion electron volts—17

BEW Board of Economic Warfare—6

BEX Braun Engineering Co.—9B

BF Bachelor of Finance—5

Bachelor of Forestry—5

bloody fool—8

boldface- 22

brought forward—9

The Budd Co.—9A

BFA Bachelor of Fine Arts- 5

BFC Broadcasting and Film Commission (of the National Council of Churches)—16, 25

Buffalo Forge Co.—9A

Bureau of Foreign Commerce—6

BFCU Bureau of Federal Credit Union—6

BFD Brown-Forman Distillers Corp.—9B

BFDC Bureau of Foreign and Domestic Commerce—6

BFE Board for Fundamental Education—23

BFG Brad Foote Gear Works, Inc. —9B

BFO Baruch-Foster Corp.—9B

beat frequency oscillator—17

BFP biologic false-positive reaction—17

BFPV bona fide purchaser for value —9

BFS Bachelor of Foreign Service—5

BFT Bachelor of Foreign Trade—5

BG brigadier general—4

British Guiana—27

BGD billions of gallons per day—9

BGE Bachelor of Geological Engineering—5

Baltimore Gas and Electric Co.—9A

BGG Briggs and Stratton Corp.—9A

BGH Burroughs Corp.—9A

BGO Buttes Gas and Oil Co.—9B

BGT Budget Industries, Inc.—9A

BH Beverly Hills—27

bloody hell—8

British Honduras—27

bulkhead—1

BHC benzene hexachloride—17

BHK H.C. Bohack Co., Inc.—9B

BHL Bachelor of Hebrew Letters (or Literature)—5

BHM BHM Industries—9A

BHN Brinell hardness number—9

BHP brake horsepower —1

B&HS Bonhomie & Hattiesburg Southern Railroad—1

BHT butylated hydroxytoluene—17

BHW Bell and Howell Co.—9A

BHY Belding Heminway Co.—9A

BI bismuth—17A

bodily injury (insurance)—9

Braniff International Airways—1

British India—27

British India Steam Navigation Co., Ltd.—1

National Biscuit Co.—9A

BIA Bureau of Indian Affairs—6

BID Bachelor of Industrial Design—5

bis in die (twice a day)—18

brought in dead—17

BIE Bachelor of Industrial Engineering—5

BIG Big Three Industrial Gas and Equipment Co.—9A

biological insulation garment—17

BII Branch Industries—9B

BIK Bickford's, Inc.—9B

BIN bis in nocte (twice a night)—18

BIOS biological satellite—17

BIOT British Indian Ocean Territory—27

BIR Barnes Engineering Co.—9B

BIS Bank for International Settlements—6

Bishop Industries, Inc.—9B

British Information Service—12

BIT Bachelor of Industrial Technology—5

BIW Bath Industries, Inc.—9A

BJ Bachelor of Journalism—5

BK berkelium—17A

BKO Baker Oil Tools, Inc.—9A

BKY Berkey Photo, Inc.—9A

BL Bachelor of Laws—5

Bachelor of Letters (or Literature)—5

bill of lading—9

Brazilian Light and Power Co., Ltd.—9B

breech-loading—4

BLA Bachelor of Landscape Architecture—5

Bachelor of Liberal Arts—5

B&LE Bessemer and Lake Erie Railroad—1

BLE Brotherhood of Locomotive Engineers—21

BLFE Brotherhood of Locomotive Firemen and Enginemen—21

BLH Baldwin-Lima-Hamilton Corp. —3

BLI Bachelor of Literary Interpretation—5

Bliss and Laughlin Industries, Inc. —9A

BLL Baccalaureus Legum (Bachelor of Laws)—5

Bell Intercontinental Corp.—9A

BLM Bureau of Land Management—6

BLN Barbara Lynn Stores, Inc.—9B

BLS Bachelor of Library Science—5

Bureau of Labor Statistics—6

BLT bacon, lettuce and tomato (sandwich)—8

B&M Boston and Maine Railroad—1

BM Bachelor of Medicine—5

Bachelor of Music—5

bench mark (surveying)—9

bill of material—9

boatswain's mate—4

bowel movement—8

British Museum—12

BMA Bermac Corp.—9A

BMAWS ballistic missile attack warning system—4

BMC Bartell Media Corp.—9B

British Motor Corp.—3, 12

BMD ballistic missile defense—4

BM&E Beaver, Meade and Englewood Railroad—1

BME Bachelor of Mechanical Engineering—5

Bachelor of *Mining Engineering*—5

Bachelor of *Music Education*—5

BMEWS *ballistic missile early warning system*—4

BMI *Broadcast Music, Inc.*—3, 25

BMJ *British Medical Journal*—22

B&ML *Belfast & Moosehead Lake Railroad*—1

BMOC *big man on campus*—8

BMR *basal metabolic rate*—17

BMS *Bachelor of Marine Science*—5

Bemis Co., Inc.—9A

BMT *Bachelor of Medical Technology*—5

Brooklyn-Manhattan Transit (New York City)—1

BMV *Beata Maria Virgo* (Blessed Mary the Virgin)—12, 16

BMW *Bayerische Motoren Werke* (Bavarian Motor Works)—3

BMWE *Brotherhood of Maintenance of Way Employees*—5

BMY Bristol-Myers Co.—9A

BN *Bachelor of Nursing*—5

bank note—9

Borden, Inc.—9A

Burlington Northern Railroad—1

BNA *British North America*—27

Bureau of National Affairs, Inc.—3

BNC The Bank of California National Association—9A

BND Bond Stores, Inc.—9A

BNDD *Bureau of Narcotics and Dangerous Drugs*—6

BNE Bowne and Co., Inc.—9B

BNF Braniff Airways, Inc.—9A, 9B

BNI Burlington Northern, Inc.—9A

BNK Bangor Punta Corp.—9A

BNL Beneficial Finance Co.—9A

BNP *Bureau of Naval Personnel*—4

BNR Banner Industries, Inc.—9B

BNS *Bachelor of Naval Science*—5

Brown and Sharpe Manufacturing Co.—9A

BNY Bundy Corp.—9B

B&O *Baltimore and Ohio Railroad*—1

band and orchestra—25

BO *Bachelor of Oratory*—5

back order—9

bad order—9

Board of Ordnance—4

body odor—8

box office—8, 25

branch office—9

broker's order—9

brought over—9

buyer's option—9

BOAC *British Overseas Airways Corp.*—1

BOD *biochemical oxygen demand*—17

BOK Book-of-the-Month Club, Inc.—9A

BOL Bausch and Lomb, Inc.—9A

BOM Bowman Instrument Corp.—9B

BOMA *Building Owners and Managers Association*—10

BOMARC *Boeing Michigan Aeronautical Research Center*—14, 17

BOMC *Book-of-the-Month Club*—3

BOMEX *Barbados Oceanographic and Meteorological experiment*—14, 17

BOP *balance of payments*—9

BOQ *bachelor officers' quarters*—4

BOR Borg-Warner Corp.—9A

BORAL *borate and aluminum*—14, 17

BORON *borax and carbon*—14, 17

BOT *board of trade*—6

board of trustees—9

Botany Industries, Inc.—9B

BOU Bourns, Inc.—9A

BOW Bowling Corp. of America—9B

BP *Bachelor of Painting*—5

Bachelor of Pharmacy—5

Bachelor of Philosophy—5

beautiful people—8

below proof—9

bills payable—9

birthplace—8

blood pressure—17

blueprint—9

boiling point—17

breach of promise—8

British Petroleum Co., Ltd.—9A, 12

British Pharmacopoeia—18

BPA Bachelor of Professional Arts—5

BPAA Bowling Proprietors' Association of America—10, 11

BPC Belco Petroleum Corp.—9A

BPD barrels per day—9

BPDPA Brotherhood of Painters, Decorators and Paperhangers of America—21

BPE Bachelor of Physical Education—5

BPH Bachelor of Public Health—5

BPI Brooks and Perkins, Inc.—9B

Bureau of Public Inquiries—6

BPOE Benevolent and Protective Order of Elks—2

BPR Bureau of Public Roads—6

BPT British Petroleum Co., Ltd.—9B

BPWC Business and Professional Women's Club—2

BQ British-American Tobacco Ltd.—9B

BR bills receivable—9

Blue Ridge Railroad—1

British Railways—1

bromine—17A

builder's risk—9

Bunker-Ramo Corp.—9A

BRA Brandywine Raceway Association, Inc.—9B

BRC Belt Railway Chicago—1

BRCA Brotherhood of Railway Carmen of America—21

BRCS British Red Cross Society—12

BRD Broadway Hale Stores, Inc. —9A

Bureau of Research and Development—6

BRE Bachelor of Religious Education—5

BREN Brno-Enfield gun—4, 14

BRF Borman Food Stores, Inc.—9A

BRH J.P. Burroughs and Sons, Inc.—9B

BRI Babson's Reports, Incorporated—3, 22

Burlington-Rock Island Railroad—1

BRM British Racing Motors—1

BRN Barnwell Industries, Inc.—9B

BR&T Bowdon Railway and Transportation—1

BRT Brotherhood of Railroad Trainmen—21

BRUNCH breakfast-lunch—14

BRY Beatrice Foods Co.—9A

BRZ Breeze Corporations, Inc.—9B

B&S brandy and soda—8

Brown and Sharpe gauge—9

BS Bachelor of Science—5

Bachelor of Surgery—5

balance sheet—9

Bethlehem Steel Corp.—9A

bill of sale—9

bullshit—8

BSA Bachelor of Science in Agriculture—5

Bachelor of Scientific Agriculture—5

Birmingham Small Arms (motorcycle manufacturer)—1, 3

Boy Scouts of America—2

British South Africa—27

BSAA Bachelor of Science in Applied Arts—5

BSAAC British South American Airways Company—1

BSAE Bachelor of Science in Aeronautical Engineering—5

Bachelor of Science in *A*gricultural *E*ngineering—5

Bachelor of Science in *A*rchitectural *E*ngineering—5

BSBA *B*achelor of *S*cience in *B*usiness *A*dministration—5

BSC *B*achelor of *S*cience in *C*ommerce—5

Butler's Shoe Corp.—9A

BSCE *B*achelor of *S*cience in *C*ivil *E*ngineering—5

BSCP *B*rotherhood of *S*leeping *C*ar *P*orters—21

BSCS *b*iological *s*ciences *c*urriculum *s*tudy—23

BSD *B*achelor of *S*cience in *D*esign—5

BSE *B*achelor of *S*cience in *E*ducation—5

Bachelor of Science in *E*ngineering—5

Boston Edison Co.—9A

Boston Stock Exchange—9

BSEE *B*achelor of *S*cience in *E*lectrical *E*ngineering—5

Bachelor of Science in *E*lementary Education—5

BSEM *B*achelor of *S*cience in *E*ngineering of *M*ines—5

BSEP *B*achelor of *S*cience in *E*ngineering *P*hysics—5

BSES *B*achelor of *S*cience in *E*ngineering *S*ciences—5

BSF *B*achelor of *S*cience in *F*orestry—5

B.S.F. Co.—9B

BSFM *B*achelor of *S*cience in *F*orest *M*anagement—5

BSFS *B*achelor of *S*cience in *F*oreign *S*ervice—5

BSFT *B*achelor of *S*cience in *F*uel *T*echnology—5

BSF&W *B*ureau of *S*port *F*isheries and *W*ildlife—6

BSGE *B*achelor of *S*cience in *G*eneral *E*ngineering—5

BSH *B*ush Universal, Inc.—9A

BSHA *B*achelor of *S*cience in *H*ospital *A*dministration—5

BSHE *B*achelor of *S*cience in *H*ome *E*conomics—5

BSI *B*ritish *S*tandards *I*nstitution—12

BSIE *B*achelor of *S*cience in *I*ndustrial *E*ducation—5

Bachelor of Science in *I*ndustrial *E*ngineering—5

BSIR *B*achelor of *S*cience in *I*ndustrial *R*elations—5

BSIT *B*achelor of *S*cience in *I*ndustrial *T*echnology—5

BSJ *B*achelor of *S*cience in *J*ournalism—5

Bureau of Ships Journal—22

BSL *B*achelor of *S*acred *L*iterature—5

Bachelor of Science in *L*aw—5

Bachelor of Science in *L*inguistics—5

*b*ills of *l*ading—9

BSLM *B*achelor of *S*cience in *L*andscape *M*anagement—5

BSLS *B*achelor of *S*cience in *L*ibrary *S*cience—5

BSM *B*achelor of *S*acred *M*usic—5

Bachelor of Science in *M*edicine—5

Bachelor of Science in *M*usic—5

BSME *B*achelor of *S*cience in *M*echanical *E*ngineering—5

Bachelor of Science in *M*ining *E*ngineering—5

Bachelor of Science in *M*usic *E*ducation—5

BSMT *B*achelor of *S*cience in *M*edical *T*echnology—5

BSN *B*achelor of *S*cience in *N*ursing—5

BSNA *B*achelor of *S*cience in *N*ursing *A*dministration—5

BSOT *B*achelor of *S*cience in *O*ccupational *T*herapy—5

BSP *B*achelor of *S*cience in *P*harmacy—5

BSPA *B*achelor of *S*cience in *P*ublic *A*dministration—5

BSPE *B*achelor of *S*cience in *P*hysical *E*ducation—5

BSPH *B*achelor of *S*cience in *P*ublic *H*ealth—5

BSPHN *B*achelor of *S*cience in *P*ublic *H*ealth *N*ursing—5

BSPT *B*achelor of *S*cience in *P*hysical *T*herapy—5

BSR *B*irmingham *S*ound *R*eproducers, Ltd.—3, 25

BSRT *B*achelor of *S*cience in *R*adiological *T*echnology—5

BSS *B*achelor of *S*ecretarial *S*cience—5

*B*achelor of *S*ocial *S*cience—5

BSSA *B*achelor of *S*cience in *S*ecretarial *A*dministration—5

BSSE *B*achelor of *S*cience in *S*econdary *E*ducation—5

BSSS *B*achelor of *S*cience in *S*ecretarial *S*tudies—5

*B*achelor of *S*cience in *S*ocial *S*cience—5

BS&T *B*lood, *S*weat and *T*ears (musical group)—25

BST *B*ritish *s*ummer *t*ime—30

BST&IE *B*achelor of *S*cience in *T*rade and *I*ndustrial *E*ducation—5

BSU *B*aptist *S*tudent *U*nion—16

*B*lack *S*tudents' *U*nion—23

BSWU *B*oot and *S*hoe *W*orkers' *U*nion—21

BT *B*achelor of *T*heology—5

*b*allistic *t*rajectory—4

*B*ankers *T*rust New York Corp.—9A

BTA Bertea Corp.—9B

BTAM *b*asic *t*elecommunications *a*ccess *m*ethod—17

BTC The Bell Telephone Co. of Canada—9B

BTDC *b*efore *t*op *d*ead *c*enter—1, 17

BTE *B*achelor of *T*extile *E*ngineering—5

*b*attery *t*erminal *e*quipment—9, 17

BTH Barth-Spencer Corp.—9B

BTL *B*ell *T*elephone *L*aboratories—3

BTO *b*ig *t*ime *o*perator—8

BTU *B*ritish *t*hermal *u*nit—17

BTU Engineering Corp.—9B

BU *B*aptist *U*nion—16

*b*ase *u*nit—17

*B*oston *U*niversity—23

*B*rooklyn *U*nion Gas Co.—9A

BUA *B*ritish *U*nited Airline—1

BUC *B*uffalo, *U*nion-*C*arolina Railroad—1

BUE Buell Industries, Inc.—9B

BUFF *b*ig *u*gly *f*at *f*ellow—4, 8, 14

BUG Budget Finance Plan—9A

BUIC *b*ack-*u*p *i*nterceptor *c*ontrol—4

BUMED *Bu*reau of Naval *Med*icine and Surgery—4, 14

BUP *B*ritish *U*nited *P*ress—22

BUPERS *Bu*reau of Naval *Pers*onnel—4, 14

BUR Burlington Industries, Inc.—9A

BUSANDA *Bu*reau of Naval *S*upplies *and* *A*ccounts—4, 14

BV *B*eata *V*irgo (Blessed Virgin)—16, 19

*b*ene *v*ale (farewell)—19

*b*ook *v*alue—9

*b*reakdown *v*oltage—17

BVA *B*achelor of *V*ocational *A*griculture—5

*B*ulova *W*atch Co., Inc.—9A

BVD *B*radley, *V*orhees and *D*ay Co.—3, 8

BVE *B*achelor of *V*ocational *E*ducation—5

BVI Bow Valley Industries, Ltd.—9B

*B*ritish *V*irgin *I*slands—27

BVM *B*eata *V*irgo *M*aria (Blessed Virgin Mary)—16, 19

B&W *b*lack and *w*hite—8

BW *b*acteriological (or *b*iological) *w*arfare—4

*b*eautiful *w*ife—8

*B*org-*W*arner Corp.—3

BWA *B*ritish *W*est *A*frica—27

BWC Board of War Communications—6

BWE Bachelor of Welding Engineering—5

BWG Birmingham wire gauge—9

BWI British West Indies—27

BWIA British West Indies Airways—1

BWN Brown Co.—9A

BWS Brown Shoe Co., Inc.—9A

BWU blue whale units—9

BWV Bach-Werke Verzeichnis (list of Bach's works)—19, 25

BX The Bendix Corp.—9A

BY Bucyrus-Erie Co.—9A

BYK Bayuk Cigars, Inc.—9A

BYOB bring your own bottle—8

BYOG bring your own girl—8

BYS Binney and Smith, Inc.—9B

BYU Brigham Young University—23

C carbon—17A

Chrysler Corp.—9A

CA calcium—17A

Caldor, Inc.—9B

capital account—9

Capitol Airlines—1

cash account—9

Catholic Action—16

Central America—27

chartered accountant—9

chief accountant—9

chronological age—17, 30

coast artillery—4

consular agent—7

county attorney—7

credit account—9

current account—9

CAA Civil Aeronautics Administration—6

Council of African Affairs—6

CAB Civil Aeronautics Board—6

Consumers' Advisory Board—6

CABAL Clifford, Ashley, Buckingham, Arlington, Lauderdale (English courtiers)—14

CAC Coast Artillery Corps—4

continuous air circulation (building)—9

CACM Central American Common Market—12

CADC Continental Air Defense Command—4

CADRE Chicago Area Draft Resisters—2

CAF CNA Financial Corp.—9A

cost and freight—9

cost, assurance, and freight—9

CAGE California Almond Growers Exchange—3, 14

CAI Capitol Industries, Inc.—9B

computer-assisted instruction—23

CAL China Air Lines—1

Continental Air Lines, Inc.—9A

CALEXICO California and Mexico—14, 27

CAM classified advertising manager—22

CAMP companies, agencies, markets, positions—9, 14

CAO chief administrative officer—7

CAP Camas Prairie Railroad—1

Carolina Pipeline Co.—9B

Central Arizona Project—7

Civil Air Patrol—6

combined action platoon—4

community action programs—7

Community Alert Patrol (Los Angeles)—2

Council Against Poverty—6

CAR Carter Wallace, Inc.—9A

Central African Republic—27

civil aeronautical regulations—1, 7

CARE Cooperative for American Remittances to Everywhere (formerly Europe)—2, 14

CARI Civil Aeromedical Research Institute—17

CARIFTA Caribbean Free Trade Association—12, 14

CARIH Children's *A*sthma *R*esearch *I*nstitute and *H*ospital—17

CAS *c*alibrated *a*ir *s*peed—1

A.M. Castle and Co.—9B

Certificate of *A*dvanced *S*tudies—28

collision-*a*voidance *s*ystem—1

CASL *C*ommittee of *A*merican *S*teamship *L*ines—10

CAT *c*ivil *a*ir *t*ransport—1

clear *a*ir *t*urbulence—1

CATV *c*able (or *c*ommunity) *a*ntenna *t*elevision—25

CAV *C*avitron Corp.—9B

CAVU *c*eiling *a*nd *v*isibility *u*nlimited—1, 14

CAX *C*onrac Corp.—9A

CB *C*ape *B*reton—27

*c*ast *b*ronze—9

*C*hildren's *B*ureau—6

*C*hirurgiae *B*accalaureus (Bachelor of Surgery)—5

*c*ircuit *b*reaker—9

*c*itizen's *b*and—22

*c*olum*b*ium—17A

*C*ompanion of the Order of the *B*ath—28

*c*onfined to *b*arracks—4

*C*onstruction *B*attalion ("Seabees")—4

*c*ontra *b*asso (against the bass) (music)—19

*c*urrency *b*ond—9

CBA *c*hemical *b*ond *a*pproach—17

CBC *C*anadian *B*roadcasting *C*orp.—12, 25

CBD *c*ash *b*efore *d*elivery—9

*c*entral *b*usiness *d*istrict—8, 27

CBE *C*ommander of the Most Excellent Order of the *B*ritish *E*mpire—28

*C*ooper Industries, Inc.—9A

CBEL *C*ambridge *B*ibliography of *E*nglish *L*iterature—22

CBI *C*hina, *B*urma, *I*ndia theater of operations—4

computer-*b*ased *i*nstruction—23

CBIT *c*ontract *b*ulk *i*nclusive *t*our—9

CBK *C*B*K Industries, Inc.—9B

CBL *C*orroon and *B*lack Corp.—9B

CBM *C*hese*b*rough-Pond's, Inc.—9A

continental *b*allistic *m*issile—4

CBO The *C*ar*b*orundum Co.—9A

CBQ *C*hicago, *B*urlington & *Q*uincy Railroad—1

CBR *c*hemical, *b*iological, and *r*adiological (weapons)—4

CBS *C*olumbia *B*roadcasting *S*ystem—9A, 25

*C*onfraternity of the *B*lessed *S*acrament—16

CBT *C*abot Corp.—9A

CBU *c*luster *b*omb *u*nit—4

CBW *c*hemical-*b*iological *w*arfare—4, 17

C&C *C*anton & *C*arthage Railroad—1

*c*ash and *c*arry—9

*c*ommand and *c*ontrol—4

CC *C*anadian *C*lub (whiskey)—3, 8

*c*arbon *c*opy—9

*C*arnegie *C*orporation—3

*c*ashier's *c*heck—9

*c*ast *c*opper—9

*c*athartic *c*ompound—17

*C*atholic *c*lergyman—16

*C*ellu-*C*raft, Inc.—9B

*c*hamber of *c*ommerce—10

*c*hief *c*lerk—7, 9

*C*hris-*C*raft—1, 8

*c*hronometer *c*orrection—27

*c*ircuit *c*ourt—6

*c*ity *c*ouncil (or *c*ouncilman or *c*ouncilor)—6, 7

*c*ivil *c*ourt—6

*c*ompany *c*ommander—4

*c*ondemned (prisoners') *c*ells—8, 26

*c*ontinuation *c*lause—9

*c*ounty *c*lerk—7

*c*ounty *c*ommission (or *c*ommissioners)—6, 7

*c*ounty *c*ouncil (or *c*ouncilman or *c*ouncilor)—6, 7

county *c*ourt—6

cream *c*heese—8

cubic *c*entimeter—17

Cumberland Railway and Coal—1

CCA Chief Clerk of the Admiralty—12

Circuit Court of Appeals—6

Commission for Conventional Armaments—6

Container Corporation of America—3

County Court of Appeals—6

Cruising Club of America—11

CCB Capital Cities Broadcasting Corp.—9A

configuration *c*ontrol *b*oard—6

CC&C Cowlitz, Chehalis & Cascade Railroad—1

CCC cathodal closure correction—17

citrated calcium cyanamide (for alcoholism)—17

Civilian Conservation Corps—6

Commodity Credit Corporation—6

Continental Can Co., Inc.—9A

CCD Coburn Corp. of America—9B

CCE Continental Connector Corp.—9B

CCF Cinema Center Films—25

Cook United, Inc.—9A

Cooperative Commonwealth Federation of Canada—12

CCH Campbell Chibougamau Mines, Ltd.—9B

commercial *c*learing *h*ouse—9

CCI CCI-Marquardt Corp.—9A

CCIR Comité Consultatif International des Radiocommunications (International Radio Consultative Committee)—13

CCK Ching Chuan Kang Air Base, Vietnam—4, 27

Crown Cork and Seal Co., Inc.—9A

CCL Carolina, Clinchfield and Ohio Railway—9A

CCM counter-*c*ounter*m*easures—4

CCN Chris-Craft Industries, Inc.—9A

contract *c*hange *n*otice—9

CCNY City College of New York—23

CCP Ceco Corp.—9A

Code of Civil Procedure—7

Court of Common Pleas—6

CCR Commission on Civil Rights—6

CCS Combined Chiefs of Staff—4

CCT The Commodore Corp.—9B

CCTV closed circuit television—9, 25

CCU coronary care unit—17

CCX Continental Copper and Steel Industries, Inc.—9A

CD cadmium—17A

Canada Decoration—28

carried *d*own—9

cash *d*iscount—9

certificate of *d*eposit—9

civil *d*efense—4

Colonial Dames—2

communicable *d*isease(s)—17

companion *d*og (obedience degree)—5

Congressional *d*istrict—7, 24

*c*um (with) *d*ividend—9

curative *d*ose—17

CDA command-and-data acquisition—9

Community Development Agency—6

Control Data Corp.—9A

CDC California Democratic Council—24

Combat Developments Command—4

Communicable Diseases Center—17

Compudyne Corp.—9B

CDD Cunningham Drug Stores, Inc.—9A

CDI Comprehensive Designers, Inc.—9B

CDMB Civil and Defense Mobilization Board—6

CDN *C*hicago *D*aily *N*ews service—22

CDP Cerro Corp.—9A

 *c*ommunications *d*ata *p*rocessor—9

C DS Canadian Superior Oil, Ltd.—9B

CDT *c*entral *d*aylight *t*ime—30

 Certified *D*ental Technician—5

 Condec Corp.—9B

CDU *C*hristian *D*emocratic *U*nion (West Germany)—12

 *c*ommand *d*istribution *u*nit—17

 Conductron Corp.—9B

CDY The Cosmodyne Corp.—9B

CE *c*aveat *e*mptor (let the buyer beware)—19

 *c*entral *e*ngineering—9

 *c*erium—17A

 *c*hemical *e*ngineer—28

 *c*hief *e*ngineer—28

 *c*hloroform and *e*ther—17

 *C*hristian *E*ndeavor—16

 *C*hurch of *E*ngland—16

 *c*ivil *e*ngineer—28

 *c*ommon *e*ra—30

 *C*orps of *E*ngineers (U.S. Army)—4

CEA *c*arcino-*e*mbryonic *a*ntigen—17

 *C*entre *E*st *A*eronautique (French aircraft manufacturer)—1, 3

 The Cessna Aircraft Co.—9A

 *C*ommodity *E*xchange *A*uthority—6

 *C*ouncil of *E*conomic *A*dvisors—6

CEAP *C*ommunity *E*ducational *A*ssistance *P*rogram—23

C EC Center for Educational Change—23

 *C*onsulting *E*ngineers' *C*ouncil—20

CED *C*ouncil for *E*conomic *D*evelopment—2

CEE Cook Electric Co.—9B

CEEB *C*ollege *E*ntrance *E*xamination *B*oard—23

CEEC *C*ouncil for *E*uropean *E*conomic *C*ooperation—12

CEF Canadian *E*xpeditionary *F*orce—4

CEI *C*hicago & *E*astern *I*llinois Railroad—1

CEIR *C*orporation for *E*conomic and *I*ndustrial *R*esearch—3

 *C*ouncil for *E*conomic and *I*ndustry *R*esearch—6

CEL Central Louisiana Electric Co.—9A

CEM Compo Industries, Inc.—9B

CEMA *C*ouncil of *E*conomic *M*utual *A*ssistance—12

CENTO *Cen*tral *T*reaty *O*rganization of the Middle East (Baghdad Pact)—12, 14

CER Central Illinois Light Co.—9A

CET Central Securities Corp.—9B

CEW Central Power and Light Co. (Texas)—9B

CEX Canadian Export Gas and Oil, Ltd.—9B

CEY Century Electric Co.—9B

C&F *c*ost and *f*reight—9

CF *c*ali*f*ornium—17A

 *c*anto *f*ermo (firm song, or chant) (music)—19

 *c*arried *f*orward—9

 *c*enter *f*ield (or *f*ielder)—11

 *c*entrifugal *f*orce—17

 CF&I Steel Corp.—9A

 *c*itrovorum *f*actor—17

 *c*ystic *f*ibrosis—17

CFA *C*ertified *F*inancial *A*nalyst—9

CFC *C*ontrolled *F*oreign *C*orp.—7

CFD Consolidated Foods Corp.—9A

 *c*ubic *f*eet per *d*ay—17

CFG CPC International, Inc.—9A

CFH *C*ouncil on *F*amily *H*ealth—2

 *c*ubic *f*eet per *h*our—17

CFI California Financial Corp.—9A

 *c*ost, *f*reight, and *i*nsurance—9

C FL Continental Football League—11

C FLN Comité Français de Libération Nationale (French National Liberation Committee)—12

CFM *c*ubic *f*eet per *m*inute—17

CFN Carousel Fashions, Inc.—9B
CFO Crest Foam Corp.—9B
CFR Code of Federal Regulations—7
CFS cubic feet per second—17
CFSTI Clearinghouse for Federal Scientific and Technical Information—17
CFY Consolidated Canadian Faraday Ltd.—9B
C&G Columbus & Greenville Railroad—1
CG captain of the guard—4
 center of gravity—17
 centigram—17
 Coast Guard—4
 Columbia Gas System, Inc.—9A
 commanding general—4
 consul general—7
CGA Canoga Industries—9B
 Certified Graphologists of America—10
CGC Colorado Interstate Corp.—9A
CGE Chicago and Eastern Illinois Railroad Co.—9A
CGF City Gas Co. of Florida—9B
CGG Chicago Pneumatic Tool Co.—9A
CGH Clevite Corp.—9A
CGI Chadbourn Gotham, Inc.—9A
CGIL Confederazione Generale Italiana del Lavoro (Italian General Federation of Labor)—21
CGO can go over—22
CGP Coastal States Gas Producing Co.—9A
CGR Carriers and General Corp.—9A
CGS centigram seconds—17
 Coast and Geodetic Survey—6
 Consolidated Oil and Gas, Inc.—9B
CGT Compagnie Générale Transatlantique (General Transatlantic Company, French Steamship Line)—1
 Confédération Générale du Travail (General Confederation of Labor, France)—12, 21
CGTA Compagnie Générale des Transports Aériens (Algerian Air Lines)—1
CGW Chicago Great Western Railroad—1
CGX Canadian Gridoil, Ltd.—9B
CGY Century Geophysical Corp.—9B
CH candle hours—17
 case-hardened—9
 clearing house—9
 Companion of Honor—28
 courthouse—7
 custom house—7
 Cutler-Hammer Inc.—9A
CHA Chattanooga Gas Co.—9B
CHB Champion Home Builders Co.—9B
CHC Checker Motors Corp.—9A
CHD Chelsea Industries, Inc.—9B
 coronary heart disease—17
CHE chemical engineer—17
CHF Chock Full o' Nuts Corp.—9A
CHI Crouse-Hinds Co.—9A
CHJ Cohen-Hatfield Industries, Inc.—9B
CHL Chemical New York Corp.—9A
CHM Champion Spark Plug Co.—9A
CHO Canadian Homestead Oils Ltd.—9B
CHQ corps headquarters—4
CHR Charter Oil Co., Ltd.—9B
 Current Housing Reports—7, 22
CHY Cherry-Burrell Corp.—9B
C&I Cambria & Indiana Railroad—1
CI cast iron—9
 Central Indiana Railroad—1
 certificate of insurance—9
 Channel Islands—27
 color index—9, 17
 cubic inch—17
 curie—17
CIA Central Intelligence Agency—6

CIAA Coordinator of *Inter-A*merican *A*ffairs—6

CIBA *C*hemische *I*ndustrie *B*asel *A*ktiengesellschaft (Chemical Industries of Basel, Switzerland, Company)—3

CIC *c*ombat *i*nformation *c*enter—4

*C*ommander *in* *C*hief—4

The Continental Corp.—9A

*C*ounter*i*ntelligence *C*orps—4

CID *C*oronet *I*ndustries, Inc.—9A

*C*riminal *I*nvestigation *De*partment (Scotland Yard)—12, 26

*c*ubic *i*nch *d*isplacement—9

CIDG *C*ivilian *I*rregular *D*efense Group—4

CIE *C*ommission *I*nternationale de l'*E*clairage (International Lighting Commission)—12, 17

*C*ompanion of the Order of the *I*ndian *E*mpire—28

CIF *c*ost, *i*nsurance, and *f*reight—9

CIG *C*omputer *I*nvestors *G*roup, Inc.—9B

CIGS *C*hief, *I*mperial *G*eneral *S*taff—4

CII *C*astleton *I*ndustries, Inc.—9B

CI&L *C*hicago, *I*ndianapolis & *L*ouisville Railroad—1

C&IM *C*hicago & *I*llinois *M*idland Railroad—1

CIN The Cincinnati Gas and Electric Co.—9A

CINC *C*ommander *in* *C*hief—4

CINCAF *C*ommander *in* *C*hief, *A*siatic *F*leet—4, 14

CINCLANT *C*ommander *in* *C*hief, *At*lantic Fleet—4, 14

CINCUS *C*ommander *in* *C*hief, *U*nited *S*tates Navy—4, 14

CINPAC *C*ommander *in* *C*hief, *Pa*cific Fleet—4, 14

CIO *C*ongress of *I*ndustrial *O*rganizations—21

CIP *C*entral *I*llinois *P*ublic Service Co.—9A

*c*ommercially *i*mportant *p*erson—8

CIPE *C*entre d'*I*nformation et de *P*ublicité des Chemins de Fer *E*uropéens (Publicity and Information Center for European Railroads)—1, 12

CIR Circuit Foil Corp.—9B

CIT *C*alifornia *I*nstitute of *T*echnology—23

*C*arnegie *I*nstitute of *T*echnology—23

C.I.T. Financial Corp.—9A

*C*ounselor *in* *T*raining—23

CIV *C*anadian *I*nternational *P*ower Co., Ltd.—9B

CJ *C*hief *J*ustice—7

*c*orpus *j*uris—7

U.S. Pipe and Foundry Co.—9A

CJT Cooper-Jarrett, Inc.—9B

CJV Canadian Javelin, Ltd.—9B

CK *C*ertified *K*osher—9

Collins and Aikman Corp.—9A

CKC Conchemco, Inc.—9B

CKE Castle and Cooke, Inc.—9A

CKI Cook Industries, Inc.—9B

CKL Clark Equipment Co.—9A

CKO Clark Oil and Refining Corp.—9A

CKP Circle K Corp.—9B

CL *c*ar*l*oad—9

*c*arload *l*ot—9

*c*enter *l*ine—17

*ch*lorine—17A

*c*ivil *l*aw—9

Colgate-Palmolive Co.—9A

CLC *C*anadian *L*abour *C*ongress—21

*C*onsolidated *L*easing *C*orp. of *A*merica—9B

CLE *C*omputer *L*easing Co.—9B

CLF The *C*leveland-*C*liffs Iron Co.—9A

CLGA *C*omposers and *L*yricists *G*uild of *A*merica—20

CLI Cutter Laboratories, Inc.—9B

CLK Clark Cable Corp.—9B

CLL   Continental Oil Co.—9A
CLN   The Coleman Co., Inc.—9B
CLO   Coleco Industries, Inc.—9B
CLR   Clarostat Manufacturing Co., Inc.—9B
CLT   Cominco, Ltd.—9B
CLU   chartered *life* underwriter—9
   Civil Liberties Union—2
   Cluett, Peabody and Co., Inc.—9A
CLW   Colwell Co.—9B
CLX   Clorox Co.—9A
CLY   Clary Corp.—9B
C&M   cocaine and *morphine*—8
CM   call of *more* (stocks)—9
   celestial mechanics—17
   centimeter—17
   church *missionary*—16
   circulation *manager*—22
   command *module*—17
   common *measure* (hymns)—25
   common *meter* (hymns)—25
   Congregation of the Mission (Vincentians)—16
   corresponding *member*—9
   court-*martial*—4
   curium—17A
   Curtis Mathes Manufacturing Co.—9B
CMA   *Creative Management Associates*—25
CMB   Chase Manhattan Corp.—9A
CMC   Commercial Metals Co.—9B
CME   *Christian Methodist Episcopal* Church—16
   Colored Methodist Episcopal Church—16
   courtesy *motorboat examination* (of the U.S. Coast Guard auxiliary)—2, 11
CMEA   *Council of Mutual Economic Aid* (or *Assistance*)—12
CMG   *Companion of the Most Distinguished Order of St. Michael and St. George*—28
CMH   Campbell Machine, Inc.—9B

CMI   Chicago Musical Instrument Co.—9A
CMK   Carnation Co.—9B
CML   *Connecticut Mutual Life* Co.—3
CMM   Community Public Service Co.—9B
CMN   Callahan Mining Corp.—9A
CMO   chief *medical officer*—7
   Continental Mortgage Investors—9A
CMR   communication-by-*moon* relay—17
   Continental Motors Corp.—9A
CMS   *Consumer and Marketing Service*—2
   Consumers Power Co.—9A
CMSP&P   *Chicago, Milwaukee, St. Paul and Pacific* Railroad—1
CMTC   *citizens' military training* camp—4
CMW   Canadian Marconi Co.—9B
CMY   Chemway Corp.—9A
CMZ   The Cincinnati Milling Machine Co.—9A
CN   *Canadian National* Railway—1
   Charter New York Corp.—9A
   chloroacetophenone—17
   circular *note*—9
   compass *north*—27
   credit *note*—9
   cumulonimbus—17
CNA   Cole National Corp.—9B
CNB   Canadian Breweries, Ltd.—9A
CNC   Cenco Instruments Corp.—9A
CND   Consultants and Designers, Inc.—9B
CNF   Consolidated Freightways, Inc.—9A
CNG   Consolidated Natural Gas Co.—9A
CNH   Central Hudson Gas and Electric Corp.—9A
CNI   *communication, navigation, identification*—4
CNJ   *Central of New Jersey* Railroad—1

CNK Crompton and Knowles Corp.—9A

CN&L Columbia, Newberry & Laurens Railroad—1

CNL Consolidated National Shoe Corp.—9A

CNM Cinerama, Inc.—9B

CNO Chief of Naval Operations—4

CNP Crown Central Petroleum Corp.—9B

CNR Comité National de la Résistance (National Resistance Committee)—12

CNS Canadian Southern Railway Co.—9A

central nervous system—17

CNV City Investing Co.—9A

C&NW Carolina & North Western Railroad—1

Chicago & North Western Railroad—1

C&O Chesapeake and Ohio Railroad—1

CO care of—8

carried over—9

cash order—9

castor oil—8, 17

central office—9

certificate of origin—7

Chesapeake and Ohio Railway Co.—9A

cobalt—17A

commanding officer—4

complained of—17

conscientious objector—4, 8

contracting office—9

cost of—9

COBOL common business-oriented language—14, 17

COC Columbus and Southern Ohio Electric Co.—9A

COCU Commission (or Consultation) on Church Unity—14, 16

COD cash on delivery—9

CODSIA Council of Defense and Space Industry Association—17

COE Cone Mills Corp.—9A

COF Catholic Order of Foresters—2

Coffee-Mat Corp.—9B

COG convenience of the government—7

COH Cohu Electronics, Inc.—9B

COIN complete operating information (of Union Pacific Railroad)—1, 14

counterinsurgency—4, 14

COK Cook Paint and Varnish Co.—9B

COLIDAR coherent light detection and ranging—14, 17

COM Crowley, Milner and Co.—9B

COMAC Comité d' Action Militaire (Military Action Committee)—12, 14

COMECON Council for Mutual Economic Assistance—6, 14

COMINCH Commander in Chief—4, 14

COMINFORM Communist Information Bureau—12, 14

COMINTERN Communist International—12, 14

COMSAT Communications Satellite Corp.—3, 14

CON Connelly Containers, Inc.—9B

CONAD Continental Air Defense Command—4, 14

CONAL Companhia Nacional de Avioes Limitada (Brazilian firm)—1, 3, 14

CONELRAD Control of Electromagnetic Radiation—14, 17

CONTRAIL condensation trail—14, 17

CONUS continental United States—4, 14

COP City of Prineville Railroad—1

College of the Pacific—23

constable of police, constable on patrol (possible derivations)—8, 14

COPA Compañia Panameña de Aviación (Panamanian Air Lines)—1, 14

COPE Committee on Political Education (of AFL-CIO)—14, 21, 24

COPEC Conference on Christian Politics, Economics and Citizenship—14, 16

COR Crystal Oil and Land Co.—9B

CORD U.S. Office of Civil Operations and Revolutionary Development Support—6, 14

CORE Congress of Racial Equality—2, 14

COS cash on shipment—9

Copperweld Steel Co.—9A

COSATI Committee (or Council) on Scientific and Technical Information—6, 14

COSPAR Committee (or Cooperative) on Space Research—6, 14, 17

COSPUP Committee on Science and Public Policy (of the National Academy of Sciences)—14, 17

COST Congressional Office of Science and Technology—6, 14, 17

COSVN Central Office of South Vietnam—6

COT Colt Industries, Inc.—9A

COTH cotangent hyperbolic—14, 17

COU Courtaulds, Ltd.—9A

COX Cox Broadcasting Corp.—9A

C&P Cumberland & Pennsylvania Railroad—1

CP Cambridge pulsar—17

Canadian Pacific (airline, railroad, hotels, etc.)—1, 3,

Canadian Pacific Railway Co.—9A

candlepower—17

chemically pure—17

chief patriarch—16

circular pitch—9

command post—4

common pleas—7

common prayer—16

Communist Party—24

construction permit—9

C&PA Coudersport & Port Allegany Railroad—1

CPA Canadian Pacific Airways—1

Certified (or Chartered) Public Accountant—28

chlorophenoxyacetic acid—17

color phase alternation—17

CPAI Canvas Products Association International—10

CPB Campbell Soup Co.—9A

Corporation for Public Broadcasting—25

CPCU Chartered Property and Casualty Underwriter—9

CPD Computer Applications, Inc.—9B

CPFF cost plus fixed fee—9

CPH Certificate of Public Health—5

CPI California Computer Products, Inc.—9B

consumer price index—7

CPIF cost plus incentive fee—9

CPL Carolina Power and Light Co.—9A, 9B

CPM Colonial Police Medal—28

common particular meter (hymns)—25

critical path method—17

cycles per minute—17

CPMW Conference of Personal Managers/West—10, 25

CPO chief petty officer—4

CPR Current Population Reports—7, 22

CPS Columbia Pictures Industries—9A

cycles per second—17

CPSU Communist Party, Soviet Union—12

CPT change, parity, time theorem (physics)—17

colored people's time—8

Computest Corp.—9B

counterpoint—25

CPUSA Communist Party, United States of America—24

CPX command post exercise—4

Copper Range Co.—9A

CPY Clopay Corp.—9B

CQ charge of quarters—4

Communications Satellite Corp.—9A

CQT carburized, quenched, and tempered (steel heat treatment)—9

CR cathode ray—17

chromium—17A

Congregation of the Resurrection—16

control rocket—17

Copper Range Railroad—1

Costa Rica—27

Crane Co.—9A

critical ratio—17

CRA Community Redevelopment Agency—6

CRAF Civil Reserve Air Fleet—4

CRB Corinthian Broadcasting Co.—9A

CRC Civil Rights Commission—6

Coordinating Research Council—6

Crompton Co., Inc.—9B

CRD Crown Drug Co.—9B

CRE Crestmont Oil and Gas Co.—9B

CRF Copeland Refrigeration Corp.—9A

corticotrophin-releasing factor—17

CRG Coro, Inc.—9B

CRH Canal Randolph Corp.—9A

CRI Collins Radio Co.—9A

CRI&P Chicago, Rock Island & Pacific Railroad—1

CRK Campbell Red Lake Mines, Ltd.—9A

CRMD Children with Retarded Mental Development Association—2

CRO Chromalloy American Corp.—9A

CROM Confederación Regional Obrera Mexicana (Mexican Labor Organization)—12, 21

CRP C-reactive protein—17

Creole Petroleum Corp.—9B

CRR Carrier Corp.—9A

CRS Carpenter Technology Corp.—9A

Catholic Relief Services—16

Community Relations Service—7

CRT cathode-ray tube—17

Certain-Teed Products Corp.—9A

CRUS customs regulations of the United States—7

CRW Community Radio Watch—2

Crowell Collier and Macmillan, Inc.—9A

CRX The Connrex Corp.—9B

CRY Conroy, Inc.—9B

C&S clean and sober—26

Colorado & Southern Railroad—1

CS cable ship—1

capital stock—9

Carolina Southern Railroad—1

cesium—17A

Christian Science (or Scientist)—16

cirrostratus—17

Cities Service Co.—9A

civil service—7

corresponding secretary—28

cycles per second—9

CSA Caressa, Inc.—9B

Ceskoslovenski Aerolinia (Czechoslovakian Airlines)—1

Confederate States of America—6

C&SC caps and small caps—22

CSC Civil Service Commission—6

Computer Sciences Corp.—9A

Congregatio Sanctae Crucis (Congregation of the Holy Cross)—16

Conspicuous Service Cross—28

CSEA Civil Service Employees' Association—10

CSF Civil Service Fusion Party—24

CSG Colonial Sand and Stone Co., Inc.—9B

CSI Commission Sportif Internationale (International Sports Commission)—11, 12

CSJ Civil Service Journal—22

CSK The Chesapeake Corp. of Virginia—9A

CSL Carlisle Corp.—9A

CSM cerebrospinal meningitis—17

command space (or command and service) module—17

CSN Cincinnati and Suburban Bell Telephone Co.—9A

CSO chief signal officer—4

commissioners' standard ordinary mortality table—9

CSP Combustion Engineering, Inc.—9A

Congregation of St. Paul the Apostle (Paulist Fathers)—16

CSR Central and South West Corp.—9A

CSS City Stores Co.—9A

Commodity Stabilization Service—6

CSSR Ceskoslovenski Socialisticka Republicka (Czechoslovak Socialist Republic)—27

CST central standard time—30

Christiana Oil Corp.—9B

CSU circuit switching unit—17

CSW Computing and Software, Inc.—9B

CT candidate in theology—16, 23

carbon tetrachloride—17

central time—30

Certron Corp.—9B

Communist terrorist—4, 8

CTA cum testamento annexo (with will attached)—9, 12

CTB Cooper Tire and Rubber Co.—9A

CTC Certified Travel Counselor—28

Citizens' Training Corps—4

Continental Telephone Corp.—9A

CTL Continental Steel Corp.—9A

CTN Chemetron Corp.—9A

CTP Central Maine Power Co.—9A, 9B

CTR Caterpillar Tractor Co.—9A

CTS contractor technical services—9

CTS Corp.—9A

CTU Chicago Title and Trust Co.—9A

Commercial Telegraphers' Union—21

CTV Canadian television—25

CTW can't tell what—8, 9

Children's Television Workshop—25

CTX Central Telephone and Utilities Corp.—9A

CTY Century Industries Co., Inc.—9B

CU close-up—25

Consumers' Union—3

copper (from cuprum)—17A

coronary unit—17

CUB Cubic Corp.—9B

CUC Commonwealth United Corp.—9B

CUD The Cudahy Co.—9A

CUI Computer Instruments Corp.—9B

CUL Culligan, Inc.—9A

CUM Cummins Engine Co., Inc.—9A

CUNY College of the University of New York—23

CUO Continental Materials Corp.—9B

CUSEC one cubic foot per second—14, 17

CV Central Vermont Railroad—1

Commercial Solvents Corp.—9A

CVA cerebrovascular accident (stroke)—17

Columbia Valley Authority—6

CVL Canaveral International Corp.—9B

CVO Commander of the Royal Victorian Order—28

CVP Central Valley Project (California)—6

CVR Chicago Rivet and Machine Co.—9B

continuous video recorder—17

CVWS combat vehicle weapons system—4

CVX The Cleveland Electric Illuminating Co.—9A

C&W Colorado & Wyoming Railroad—1

country and western (music)—25

CW chemical warfare—4

Chesapeake Western Railroad—1

continuous wave—17

Curtiss-Wright Corp.—9A

CWA Civil Works Administration—6

Communication Workers of America—21

C&WC Charleston & Western Carolina Railroad—1

CWD Conwood Co.—9A

CWE Commonwealth Edison Co.—9A

CWEU Council of Western European Union—12

C&WI Chicago & Western Indiana Railroad—1

CWK Chadwick-Miller, Inc.—9B

CWL Cowles Communications, Inc.—9A

CWLA Child Welfare League of America—2

CWO cash with order—9

chief warrant officer—4

Commonwealth Oil Refining Co., Inc.—9A

CWS Chemical Warfare Service—4

CWSP College Work-Study Program—23

CWTS Civil War Token Society—2

CX Colorado and Southern Railway Co.—9A

C&Y children and youth (clinics)—7, 17

CYBORG cybernetic organism—14, 17

CYL Cyclops Corp.—9A

CYM Cypress Mines Corp.—9A

CYO Catholic Youth Organization—16

CZ Canal Zone—27

Celanese Corp.—9A

D Dart Industries, Inc.—9A

DA days after acceptance—9

delayed action—17

Department of the Army—6

deposit account—9

did not answer—9

direct action—9

district attorney—6

documents for (or against) acceptance—9

Dominion Atlantic Railroad—1

DAB Dictionary of American Biography—22

DAC Domestic Affairs Council—6

DAE Dictionary of American English—22

DAF data acquisition facility—9

Department of the Air Force—6

Van Doorne's Automobiel Fabrieken (Van Doorne's Automobile Factory, Netherlands; make of automobile)—1, 3, 14

DAH disordered action of the heart—17

DAI death due to accidental injury(ies)—17

DAL Delta Air Lines, Incorporated—1, 9A

DAMS defense against missile systems—4, 14

DAPCA development and production costs for aircraft—9, 14

DAR Daughters of the American Revolution—2

Defense Aid Reports—7

DASA Defense Atomic Support Agency—6, 14

DASH *d*rone *a*ntisubmarine *h*elicopter—4, 14

DAT Data-Control Systems, Inc. —9B

DATA *D*efense *A*ir *T*ransportation *A*dministration—6, 14

DATO *D*iscover *A*merica *T*ravel *Or*ganizations—3

DAV *D*isabled *A*merican *V*eterans—2

DAY Dayco Corp.—9A

D&B *D*un and *B*radstreet—3

DB *d*ay*b*ook—9

*d*ead *b*ody—26

*d*eci*b*el—17

*D*omes*d*ay (or *D*oom*s*day) *B*ook—22

DBA *D*octor of *B*usiness *A*dministration—5

*d*oing *b*usiness *a*s—9

DBD Diebold, Inc.—9A

DBE *D*ame Commander of the Order of the *B*ritish *E*mpire—28

DBH *d*iameter at *b*reast *h*eight—17

DBO *d*ead *b*lack*o*ut—25

DBR Dominion Bridge Co., Ltd—9B

DBST *d*ouble *B*ritish *s*ummer *t*ime —30

D&C *d*ilation and *c*urettage—17

DC *d*a *c*apo (from the beginning)—19, 25

*d*amage *c*ontrolman—4

*d*ental *c*orps—4

Dictaphone Corp.—9B

*d*irect *c*urrent—17

*D*istrict of *C*olumbia—27

*D*octor of *C*hiropractic—5

*d*ouble *c*olumn—9

*D*ouglas *c*ommercial (airplane, as in DC-8)—1, 3

DCA *D*efense *C*ommunications *A*gency—6

*D*ynamics *C*orp. of *A*merica—9A

DCD *D*aitch *C*rystal *D*airies, Inc.—9B

DCI David Crystal, Inc.—9B

DCL The Diners' Club, Inc.—9A

*D*octor of *C*anon *L*aw—5

*D*octor of *C*ivil *L*aw—5

DCM *D*earborn *C*omputer and *M*arine Corp.—9B

*D*eputy *C*hief of *M*ission—7, 28

*D*istinguished *C*onduct *M*edal—28

DCN Dana Corp.—9A

DCPM *d*i(*c*hloro*p*henoxy)*m*ethane —17

DC&S *D*etroit, *C*aro & *S*andusky Railroad—1

DCS *d*efense *c*ommunications *s*ystem —4

*d*eputy *c*hief of *s*taff—4

*d*eputy *c*lerk of *s*essions—6

*D*istillers *C*orp.-*S*eagrams Ltd.—9A

*D*octor of *C*hristian *S*cience—5

*D*octor of *C*ommercial *S*cience (or *S*tudies)—5

DCSR *d*a *c*apo *s*enza *r*eplica (or *r*ipetizione) (from the beginning without reply, or repetition) (music)—19

DCT D.C. Transit System, Inc.—9B

*d*iversified *c*ooperative *t*raining—23

DD *d*aily *d*ouble—8, 11

*d*ay's (or *d*ays after) *d*ate—9

*d*eaf and *d*umb—8

*d*e *d*ato (of this date)—19, 30

*d*egree *d*ay—17

*d*elayed *d*elivery—9

*d*emand *d*raft—9

*d*ishonorable *d*ischarge—4

*D*octor of *D*ivinity—5

*d*ouble *d*eck—9

*d*ry *d*ock—9

E. I. duPont de Nemours and Co.—9A

DDAS *d*igital *d*ata *a*cquisition *s*ystem—9

DDC *D*efense *D*ocumentation *C*enter—6

*d*igital *d*ata (or *d*isplay) component (or *c*onverter)—17

DDD *d*irect *d*istance *d*ialing—9

DDE Dwight David Eisenhower—29

DDS Doctor of Dental Science (or Surgery)—5

DDT dichlorodiphenyltrichloroethane—17

DDVP dimethyl dichlorovinyl phosphate—17

DE Deere and Co.—9A

destroyer escort—4

development engineering—9

Doctor of Engineering—5

Doctor of Entomology—5

double entry—9

DEC Digital Equipment Corp.—9B

DECA descent engine control assembly—17

DEE digital evaluation equipment—9, 17

DEI Dutch East Indies—27

DEJ DeJur-Amsco Corp.—9B

DEL Del Monte Corp.—9A

DELMARVA Delaware, Maryland, Virginia peninsula—14, 27

DEN Denny's Restaurants, Inc.—9A

DENIM serge de Nîmes (serge from Nîmes) (cloth)—14, 19

DEP Defense Electronic Products—4, 9

Depositors Corp.—9B

DER Dereco, Inc.—9A

DERM delayed echo radar marker—14, 17

DES Detroit Steel Corp.—9A

DET diethyl tryptamine (hallucinatory drug)—17

DETA Direcção de Exploração dos Transportes Aéreos (Mozambique Airline)—1

DEW Delmarva Power and Light Co.—9A

Distant Early Warning—4, 14

DEX The Dexter Corp.—9A

DF damn fool—8

Defensor Fidei (Defender of the Faith)—19

direction finding—27

Distrito Federal (federal district) (Mexico City)—19, 27

Doctor of Forestry—5

Drug Fair-Community Drug Co., Inc.—9B

DFA Doctor of Fine Arts—5

DFC Dial Finance Co.—9A

Distinguished Flying Cross—28

DFG Department of Fish and Game—6

DFI Defiance Industries, Inc.—9B

DFL Democrat-Farmer-Labor Party—24

DFM Distinguished Flying Medal—28

DFP diisopropyl fluorophosphate—17

DG Associated Dry Goods Corp.—9A

decigram—17

degenerate—8

DGA Directors' Guild of America—20

DGG Deutsche Gramophon Gesellschaft (German recording society)—12, 25

DGR Denver and Rio Grande Western Railroad—9A

D&H Delaware and Hudson Railroad—1

DH deadhead—9

Doctor of Humanics (or Humanities)—5

DHE dihydroergotamine methanesulfonate—17

DHIA Dairy Herd Improvement Association—10

DHL Doctor of Hebrew Letters (or Literature)—5

DHM Dillingham Corp.—9A

DHV design hourly volume (highway construction)—1, 9

DI Department of the Interior—6

disability insurance—7, 9

Dresser Industries, Inc.—9A

drill instructor—4

DIA Diamond Shamrock Corp.—9A

Defense Intelligence Agency—6

DIAC Defense Industry Advisory Council—10, 17

DIC dependency and indemnity compensation—7, 9

Diplomate of the Imperial College—5

DICBM defense intercontinental ballistic missile—4

DID dimethylphthalate indalone dimethylcarbonate (insect repellant)—17

DIG DiGiorgio Corp.—9A

DIL Distillers Co., Ltd.—9B

DIN data identification number —9

Deutsche Industrie-Normen (German industrial standard)—9, 19

DINFIA Dirección Nacional de Fabricaciones e Investigaciones Aeronáuticas (National Directorate of Aeronautical Manufacture and Research, Argentina)—1, 3

DINFOS Defense Information School—4, 14

DIO Diodes, Inc.—9B

DIS Walt Disney Productions—9A

DIV The Diversey Corp.—9B

DJ disk jockey—8, 25

district judge—6

Doctor Juris (Doctor of Law)—5

DJI Dow-Jones industrial average—9

DJS Doctor of Juridical Science—5

DJSC Daily Journal of the Supreme Court—22

DJT Doctor of Jewish Theology—5

DK Danish Kingdom—27

DL day letter—22

demand loan—9

difference of latitude—27

DLF Development Loan Fund—7

DLI Del Laboratories, Inc.—9B

DLL Dillon Companies, Inc.—9A

DLN Daylin, Inc.—9B

DLP Dunlop Co., Ltd.—9B

DLS Doctor of Library Science—5

DLT The Deltona Corp.—9B

direct lunar transport—1, 17

DL&W Delaware, Lackawanna & Western Railroad—1

DLY The Duraloy Co.—9B

D&M Detroit and Mackinac Railroad—1

DM Deputy Master—28

deutsche mark—9, 19

diphenylaminechlorarsine—17

Doctor of Mathematics—5

Doctor of Music—5

Domes Mines, Ltd.—9A

DMB Defense Mobilization Board—6

DMC Diversified Metals Corp.—9B

DMD Dentariae Medicinae Doctor (Doctor of Dental Medicine)—5

DME defense microelectronics—4, 17

distance measuring equipment—17

DMEA Defense Minerals Exploration Administration—6

DMF decayed, missing or filled (teeth, dentistry)—17

DMH DMH Corp.—9B

DMI Day Mines, Inc.—9B

DM&IR Duluth, Missabe & Iron Range Railroad—1

DMK Dominick Fund, Inc.—9A

DML Dan River Mills, Inc.—9A

Doctor of Modern Languages—5

DMN Damon Engineering, Inc.—9B

DMO data management officer—9

Dymo Industries, Inc.—9A

DMP Dome Petroleum, Ltd.—9B

DMS Doctor of Medical Science (or Services)—5

DMSO dimethyl sulfoxide—17

DMT dimethyl tryptamine (hallucinatory drug)—17

DMV Department of Motor Vehicles—6

DMZ demilitarized zone (Vietnam) —4

DN *d*ebit *n*ote—9

Department of the *N*avy—6

*d*extrose: *n*itrogen ratio—17

*D*iamond *I*nternational Corp.—9A

DNA *d*eoxyribose *n*ucleic (or *d*e-oxyribo*n*ucleic) *a*cid—17

*d*oes *n*ot *a*pply—9

DNB *D*eutsche *N*achrichten*b*uro (German News Bureau)—22

*D*ictionary of *N*ational *B*iography—22

Dun and Bradstreet, Inc.—9A

DNC *D*rew *N*ational *C*orp.—9B

DNF *d*id *n*ot *f*inish—11

DNP *d*i*n*itro*p*henol—17

DNR *d*o *n*ot *r*educe—9

DNS *D*ispatch *N*ews *S*ervice—22

DNY R.R. Donnelly and Sons Co.—9A

DO *d*efense *o*rder—4

*d*elivery *o*rder—9

*d*istrict *o*ffice—9

*D*octor of *O*ptometry—5

*D*octor of *O*steopathy—5

*d*uty *o*fficer—4

DOA *d*ead *o*n *a*rrival—26

DOBRO *Do*pyera *Bro*thers (type of guitar)—25

DOC *D*epartment *o*f *C*ommerce—6

Dr. Pepper Co.—9A

DOCA *d*eoxy*c*orticosterone *a*cetate—17

DOD *D*epartment *o*f *D*efense—17

*d*erelicti*o*n of *d*uty—4

DOHC *d*ouble (or *d*ual) *o*ver*h*ead *c*amshaft—1, 9

DOI *D*epartment *o*f the *I*nterior—6

*d*escent *o*rbit *i*nsertion—17

DOJ *D*epartment *o*f *J*ustice—6

DOM *D*eo *O*ptimo *M*aximo (to God, the Best and Greatest)—16, 19

DOP *d*eveloping *o*ut *p*aper—9

DOPA *d*ihydr*o*xy*p*henylalanine—14, 17

DOR *d*ischarged *o*n *o*wn *r*ecognizance—26

Dorr-Oliver, Inc.—9A, 9B

DORAN *Do*ppler *ran*ge—14, 17

DOS *d*isk *o*perating *s*ystem (computers)—9

DOT *D*epartment *o*f *T*ransportation—6

DOV Dover Corp.—9A

DOVAP *Do*ppler *v*elocity *a*nd *p*osition—14, 17

DOW The Dow Chemical Co.—9A

DOWB *d*eep *o*cean *w*ork*b*oat—17

DP by *d*irection of the *P*resident—7

*d*egree of *p*olymerization—17

*d*ementia *p*raecox—17

*d*iametrical *p*itch—17

*d*irectione *p*ropria (with proper direction)—18

*d*isplaced *p*erson—8

DPA *D*eutsche *P*ress *A*gentur (German Press Agency)—22

*D*octor of *P*ublic *A*dministration—5

DPC Data Products Corp.—9B

*D*efense *P*lant *C*orp.—7, 9

DPF Data Processing Financial and General Corp.—9B

DPH Deseret Pharmaceutical Co., Inc.—9B

*d*iamond *p*yramid *h*ardness—9

*D*iploma (or *D*iplomate) in *P*ublic *H*ealth—5

*D*octor of *P*ublic *H*ealth—5

DPL The Dayton Power and Light Co.—9A

DPMA *D*ata *P*rocessing *M*anagement *A*ssociation—10

DPN *d*i*p*hos*p*ho*p*yridine *n*ucleotide—17

DPPP *d*eferred *p*remium *p*ayment *p*lan—9

DPS *D*octor of *P*ublic *S*ervice—5

DPW *D*epartment of *P*ublic *W*orks—6

DQ&E *De*Queen & *E*astern Railroad
—1

DQU Duquesne Light Co.—9A

DR *D*aughters of the *R*evolution—2

*d*ead *r*eckoning—27

*d*eposit *r*eceipt—9

*d*ouble *r*eduction gearing (ships)
—1

*D*utch *R*eformed Church—16

National Distillers and Chemical
Corp.—9A

DRC Doric Corp.—9B

DRE *D*octor (or *D*irector) of *R*eligious *E*ducation—5

D&RGW *D*enver & *R*io *G*rande *W*estern Railroad—1

DRH Driver-Harris Co.—9B

DRNA *d*eoxyribose *n*ucleic *a*cid—17

DRPA *D*elaware *R*iver *P*ort *A*uthority—6

DRS *D*ivision of *R*esearch *S*ervice (of
National Institute of
Health)—17

DRT *D*aughters of the *R*epublic of
Texas—2

DRV Dravo Corp.—9A

DRVN *D*emocratic *R*epublic of *V*iet*n*am—12

DRY Dreyfus Corp.—9A

D&S *D*urham & *S*outhern Railroad—1

DS *d*al *s*egno (from the sign) (music)—19

*d*ays after *s*ight—9

*d*extrose in *s*aline—17

*D*octor of *S*cience—5

DSA *D*efense *S*upply *A*gency—6

DSAI *d*igital *s*olar *a*spect *i*ndicator—17

DSB *D*epartment of *S*tate *B*ulletin
—22

DSC *D*efense *S*upplies *C*orporation
—7, 9

*D*istinguished *S*ervice *C*ross—28

*D*octor of *S*urgical *C*hiropody—5

DSE *D*etroit *S*tock *E*xchange—9

DSM *D*istinguished *S*ervice *M*edal
—28

*D*octor of *S*acred *M*usic—5

DSMA *D*efense *S*upply *M*anagement
*A*gency—6

DSN *d*eep *s*pace *n*etwork—17

Dennison Manufacturing Co.—9A,
9B

DSO DeSoto, Inc.—9A

Companion of the *D*istinguished
*S*ervice *O*rder—28

*d*istrict *s*taff *o*fficer—7

DSP *d*eep *s*pace *p*robe—17

Dentsply International, Inc.—9A

DSRV *d*eep *s*ubmergence *r*escue *v*ehicle—4, 17

DSS *D*octor of *S*ocial *S*cience—5

DSS&A *D*uluth, *S*outh *S*hore & *A*tlantic Railroad—1

DSSV *d*eep *s*ubmergence *s*earch *v*ehicle—4, 17

DST *d*aylight *s*aving *t*ime—30

*D*octor of *S*acred *T*heology—5

DSW *D*octor of *S*ocial *W*elfare (or
*W*ork)—5

DSY The Dorsey Corp.—9B

DT *d*elirium *t*remens—8, 17

DTA *D*irecção de *E*xploração dos
*T*ransportes *A*éreos (Angola
Airlines)—1

DTAS *d*ata *t*ransmission *a*nd *s*witching system—9

DTC Domtar, Ltd.—9B

DTD *d*entur *t*ales *d*oses (give such
doses)—18

DTE Detroit Edison Co.—9A

DT&I *D*etroit, *T*oledo & *I*ronton Railroad—1

DTL Deltec International Ltd.—9A

DTM *D*octor of *T*ropical *M*edicine—5

DTN Deltown Foods, Inc.—9B

DTO Detecto Scales, Inc.—9B

D&TSL *D*etroit & *T*oledo *S*hore *L*ine
Railroad—1

DTX Dominion Textile Co., Ltd—9B

DU *d*ucks *u*nlimited—2

DUI *d*riving *u*nder the *in*fluence (of alcohol)—26

DUK Duke Power Co.—9A

DUP The Duplan Corp.—9A

DUR Duro-Test Corp.—9B

DV *D*eo *v*olente (God willing)—16, 19

*d*istinguished *v*isitor—8

*D*ouay *V*ersion (Bible)—16

DVB *D*epartment of *V*eterans' *B*enefits—6

DVL Duval Corp.—9B

DVM *D*octor of *V*eterinary *M*edicine—5

DVS *D*octor of *V*eterinary *S*urgery—5

D&W *D*anville & *W*estern Railroad—1

DW *d*ead *w*eight—17

*d*extrose in *w*ater—17

*d*ock *w*arrant—26

DWI *d*riving *w*hile *in*toxicated—26

DW&P *D*uluth, *W*innipeg & *P*acific Railroad—1

DWP *D*epartment of *W*ater and *P*ower—6

DWT *d*ead*w*eight *t*ons—1

DXC Penn-Dixie Cement Corp.—9A

DXL Dixilyn Corp.—9B

DY *dy*sprosium—17A

DYL Daryl Industries, Inc.—9B

DYN Dynalectron Corp.—9B

DZ *d*rop *z*one—4

EA *E*astern *A*irlines—1

*E*ducational *A*ge—23

Electronic Associates, Inc.—9A

EAA *E*ngineer in *A*eronautics and *A*stronautics—28

EAC Electronic Assistance Corp.—9B

EAD Eastern Air Devices, Inc.—9B

EAF Emery Air Freight Corp.—9A

EAL Eastern Air Lines, Inc.—9A

EAM *E*thniko *A*pelevtherotiko *M*e-topo (National Liberation Front, Greece)—12

EAS Eason Oil Co.—9B

EASE *e*ducational *a*nd *s*cientific establishment—8, 14

EASEP *e*arly *A*pollo *s*cientific *e*xperiments *p*ackage (or *p*ayload)—17

EAT *E*xperiments in *A*rt and *T*echnology (designers)—3

EAZ Eazor Express, Inc.—9B

EB *e*ast*b*ound—1

EBASCO *E*lectric *B*ond *a*nd *S*hare Co.—3, 14

EBF *E*ncyclopaedia *B*ritannica *F*ilms—23

Ennis Business Forms, Inc..—9A

EBS Ebasco Industries, Inc.—9A

*e*mergency *b*roadcast *s*ystem—7

EBU *E*uropean *B*roadcasting *U*nion—12

EC *E*ast *C*arolina Railroad—1

*e*mergency *c*argo vessel—1

*E*ngineering *C*orps—4

*E*stablished *C*hurch—16

*e*xempli *c*ausa (lit. for the sake of example, for example)—19

ECA *E*conomic *C*ommission for *A*frica—13

*E*conomic *C*ooperation *A*dministration—6

Electronics Corp. of America—9B

ECAC *E*astern *C*ollege *A*thletic Conference—11

ECAFE *E*conomic *C*ommission for *A*sia and the *F*ar *E*ast—13

ECCM *e*lectronic *c*ounter-*c*ountermeasures—4

ECE *E*conomic *C*ommission for *E*urope—13

ECG *e*lectro*c*ardio*g*ram—17

ECH The *E*chlin Manufacturing *Co.—9A*

ECIN *e*conomic *in*dicators—7, 9, 14

ECK *E*ckerd Drugs of Florida, Inc.—9A

ECL ECL Industries, Ltd.—9B

ECLA Economic Commission for Latin America—13

ECM electric cipher (or coding) machine—9

electronic countermeasures—4

ECN engineering change notice—9

ECO Ecological Science Corp.—9B

ECOM U.S. Army Electronics Command—4, 14

ECOSOC Economic and Social Council—13, 14

ECP Electronic Computer Programming Institute, Inc.—9B

engineering change (or cost) proposal—9

ECPS effective candlepower seconds—17

ECS environmental control system—17

ECSC European Coal and Steel Community—12

ECT electro-convulsive therapy—17

ECU English Church Union—12, 16

ED Consolidated Edison Co. of New York, Inc.—9A

effective dose—17

election district—7, 24

EDA Economic Development Administration—6

EDB Economic Development Board—6

EDC European Defense Community—12

EDD English Dialect Dictionary—22

EDE The Empire District Electric Co.—9A, 9B

EDIS engineering data information system—17

EDM Edmos Corp.—9B

electrical discharge machining—9

EDO Edo Corp.—9B

EDP electronic data processing—9

EDR equivalent direct radiation (heating measurement)—17

EDS engineering data system—9

EDT eastern daylight time—30

EE Early English—15

electrical engineer (or engineering)—9

errors excepted—9

Esquire Radio and Electronics, Inc.—9B

EEC Electronic Engineering Co. of California—9B

European Economic Community—12

EEE eastern equine encephalitis—17

EEG electroencephalogram—17

Electrographic Corp.—9B

EEI essential elements of information—4, 8

EEM earth entry module—17

EE&MP Envoy Extraordinary and Minister Plenipotentiary—28

EEN Eastern Educational Network—23, 25

EENT eye, ear, nose, and throat—17

EEOC Equal Employment Opportunities Commission—6

EFC Empire Financial Corp.—9B

EFD Eurofund International, Inc.—9A

EFS Erie Forge and Steel Corp.—9B

EFTA European Free Trade Area (or Association) (the Outer Seven)—12

EFTS Electronic Funds Transfer System—9

EFU Eastern Gas and Fuel Associates—9A

EFW Eastern Freight Ways, Inc.—9B

EG exempli gratia (lit. for the sake of example, for example)—19

EGADS electronic ground automatic destruct system—14, 17

EG&G Edgerton, Germeshausen and Grier, Inc.—3

EGG EG and G, Inc.—9A

EGL Eagle Clothes, Inc.—9B

EGO eccentric orbiting geophysical observatory—14, 17

EGR   Esgro, Inc.—9B

EH   Electric Hose and Rubber Co.—9B

EHC   Ets-Hokin Corp.—9B

EHF   *e*xtremely *h*igh *f*requency—17

EHFA   *E*lectric *H*ome and *F*arm *Au*thority—6

EHP   *e*ffective *h*orse*p*ower—9

EHR   Ehrenreich Photo-Optical Industries, Inc.—9B

EI   *E*ast *I*ndies (or *I*ndian)—27
  Emery Industries, Inc.—9B

EIA   *E*lectronic *I*ndustries *A*ssociation—10

EIB   *E*uropean *I*nvestment *B*ank—12
  Export-*I*mport *B*ank—6

EJ&E   *E*lgin, *J*oliet & *E*astern Railway—1

EJN   Endicott Johnson Corp.—9A

EK   Eastman Kodak Co.—9A

EKC   *E*astman *K*odak *C*o.—3

EKG   *e*lektro*k*ardiogramme (electrocardiogram)—17

EKO   Epko Shoes, Inc.—9B

EKR   Eckmar Corp.—9B

ELAS   *E*t h n i k o s *L*a i k o s *A*p- elevtherotikos *S*tratos (National Popular Liberation Army, Greece)—12

ELDO   *E*uropean *L*auncher *D*evelopment *O*rganization—12, 14

ELF   *e*xtremely *l*ow *f*requency—17

ELG   El Paso Natural Gas Co.—9A

ELINT   *e*lectronic (or *e*lectromagnetic) *int*elligence system—14, 17

ELK   Elcor Chemical Corp.—9B

ELM   *e*xtended *l*unar *m*odule—17

ELMA   *E*mpresa *L*ineas *M*aritimas *A*rgentinas (Argentine Ship Lines)—1, 14

ELO   Elco Corp.—9B

E&LS   *E*scanaba & *L*ake *S*uperior Railroad—1

ELS   Electronic Specialty Co.—9A

ELT   El-Tronics, Inc.—9B
  *E*quity *L*ibrary *T*heatre—25

ELX   Electrospace Corp.—9B

EM   *E*arl *M*arshal—28
  *e*ast *m*ark (East German currency)—7
  *e*lectro*m*agnetic—17
  *E*ngineer of *M*ines—28
  *e*nlisted *m*an (or *m*en)—4

EMA   *E*uropean *M*onetary *A*greement—12

EMAD   *e*ngine *m*aintenance, *a*ssembly, and *d*isassembly—9, 17

EME   Emenee Corp.—9B

EMF   *e*lectro*m*otive *f*orce—17
  *e*very *m*inute *f*ix-it—8

EMH   Emhart Corp.—9A

EMI   *E*lectric and *M*usical *I*ndustries, Ltd.—9A, 12, 25

EML   The Eastern Co.—9B

EMP   *e*lectro*m*agnetic *p*ulse—17
  Emporium Capwell Co.—9A
  *e*x *m*odo *p*rescripto (after the manner prescribed, or as directed)—18

EMR   *e*lectro*m*agnetic *r*esistance—17
  The Emerson Electric Co.—9A
  *e*motionally and *m*entally *r*etarded (or *e*ducable *m*entally *r*etarded)—17, 23

EM&S   *e*quipment *m*aintenance and *s*upport—9

EMU   *e*lectro*m*agnetic *u*nit—17

E&N   *E*squimalt & *N*anaimo Railroad—1

ENE   *e*ast *n*orth*e*ast—27

ENDC   *E*ighteen-*N*ation *D*isarmament *C*ommittee—13

ENG   Engelhard Minerals and Chemicals Corp.—9A

ENIAC   *e*lect*r*onic *n*umerical *i*ntegrator *a*nd *c*alculator (or *c*omputer)—9, 14

ENT   *e*ar, *n*ose, and *t*hroat—17

ENW   Elgin National Industries, Inc.—9A, 9B

ENX Eaton Yale and Towne, Inc.—9A

EO engineering order—9

executive order—7

ex officio (by virtue of the office)—19

EOB Educational Opportunity Bank—7, 23

Executive Office Building (Washington, D.C.)—7

E&OE errors and omissions excepted—9

EOM end of the month—9

EOR earth orbit rendezvous—17

EOS Edison Brothers Stores, Inc.—9A

Extraordinary Occasion Service (of the Associated Press)—22

E&P Extraordinary and Plenipotentiary—28

EP estimated position—27

European Plan (hotel service)—8

extended play—25

EPA European Productivity Agency—12

EPBM electroplated britannia metal—9

EPC Educational Policies Commission (of the National Education Association)—23

European Political Community—12

EPDA Education Professions Development Act—7

EPI Eagle-Picher Industries, Inc.—9A

EPNLDB effective perceived noise-level decibels—17

EPO earth parking orbit—17

EPS electronic protection system—3

EPT excess profits tax—7, 9

EPU European Payments Union—12

EQ educational quotient—23

EQF Equity Funding Corp. of America—9B

EQT Equitable Gas Co.—9A

EQU The Equity Corp.—9B

ER Eduardus Rex (King Edward)—19, 28

en route—1, 8

erbium—17A

ERA earned run average—11

Electronic Research Associates, Inc.—9B

Emergency Relief Administration—6

ERBM extended-range ballistic missile—4

ERC Electronics Research Center (NASA)—17

ERE Edison responsive environment—23

ERIC Educational Research Information Center—7, 14

ERMA electronic recording machine accounting—9, 14

ERO Ero Industries, Inc.—9B

EROS earth resources observation satellite—14, 17

ERP European Recovery Program (Marshall Plan)—7

ERS earth resources satellite—17

Economic Research Service—6

environmental research satellite—17

ERTS earth resources technology satellite—14, 17

ERV English Revised Version (Bible)—16

ES Easco Corp.—9A

educational specialist—23

ESB electrical stimulation of the brain—17

electric storage battery—3

ESB, Inc.—9A

ESC Economic and Social Council—6

ESCP Earth Science Curriculum Project—23

ESD Electronic Systems Division (U.S. Air Force)—4

ESE east southeast—27

electrical support equipment—17

ESEA Elementary and Secondary Education Act (1965)—7

ESG electrostatic gyroscope—17
ESH Earl Scheib, Inc.—9B
ESP Espey Manufacturing and Electronics Corp.—9B
    extrasensory perception—8, 17
ESQ Esquire, Inc.—9A
ESR electro-slag remelting process (steel)—9
ESRO European Space Research Organization—12, 17
ESS electronic switching system—3
ESSA Environmental Science Services Administration—6, 14
EST eastern standard time—30
    Eastern States Corp.—9B
    electroshock therapy—17
ESTEC European Space Technical Organization—12, 14, 17
ESU electrostatic unit—17
ESX Essex Chemical Corp.—9B
ET eastern time—30
    elapsed time (auto racing)—11
    electrical transcription—25
    electronics technician—4
    Eltra Corp.—9
ETA estimated time of arrival—1, 8
ETC European Travel Commission—6
ETD estimated time of departure—1
ETO estimated time over—1
    European Theater of Operations—4
ETS Educational Testing Service—23
    electronic test set—17
    engine test stand—9, 17
ETV educational television—23, 25
ET&WNC East Tennessee & Western North Carolina Railroad—1
EU entropy unit—17
    europium—17A
    Evangelical Union—16
EUA Eastern Utilities Associates—9A
EUB Evangelical United Brethren—16
EV electron volt—17
    English Version (Bible)—16

EVA extravehicular activity (or astronaut)—17
EVEA extravehicular engineering activity—17
EVR electronic video recording—25
    Eversharp, Inc.—9A
EVS Evans-Aristocrat Industries, Inc.—9B
EVY Evans Products Co.—9A
EWP emergency war plans—4
EXC Essex International, Inc.—9A
EXQ Exquisite Form Industries, Inc.—9B
EXU Executone, Inc.—9B
EY Ethyl Corp.—9A
EYOA Economic and Youth Opportunity Agency—6

F fluorine—17A
    Ford Motor Co.—9A
FA February and August—9
    field artillery—4
    free alongside—9
    Frontier Airlines, Inc.—9B
FAA Federal Aviation Agency—6
FAAAS Fellow, American Academy of Arts and Sciences—28
    Fellow, American Association for the Advancement of Science—28
FAB Fabien Corp.—9B
FAC Factor and Co.—9A
    Federal Aviation Commission—6
    forward air control—4
FACCA Fellow, Association of Certified Corporate Accountants—28
FACP Fellow, American College of Physicians—28
FACS Fellow, American College of Surgeons—28
FAD flavin-adenine dinucleotide—17
FAGO Fellow, American Guild of Organists—28

FAGS *Fellow, American Geographical Society*—28

FAI *Fédération Aeronautique Internationale* (International Aeronautic Federation)—12

FAIA *Fellow, American Institute of Architects*—28

FAL Falstaff Brewing Corp.—9A
Frontier Air Lines—1

FAM Family Finance Corp.—9A
Free and Accepted Masons—2

FANU *Flota Argentina Navegación Ultramar* (Argentine Ship Line)—1, 14

FAO *Food and Agricultural Organization*—13

FAP *Family Assistance Plan*—7

FAPS *Fellow, American Physical Society*—28

FAQ *free alongside quay*—9

FAS Famous Artists Schools, Inc.—9B
Foreign Agricultural Service—6
free alongside ship—9

FAST *fence against satellite threats*—4, 14

FATE *fuzing, arming, test, and evaluation*—4, 14, 17

FB *Farmers' Bulletin*—22
flanker back—11
freight bill—9
fullback—11

FBA *Fellow, British Academy*—28

FBD Fibreboard Corp.—9A

FBG Fabergé, Inc.—9A

FBI Fab Industries, Inc.—9B
Federal Bureau of Investigation—6

FBM *fleet ballistic missile*—4

FBO Federal Paper Board Co., Inc.—9A

F&C Frankfort & Cincinnati Railroad—1

FC *fire control (or controlman)*—4
follow copy—22
foot candle—17

Ford Motor Co. of Canada, Ltd.—9B

FCA Farm Credit Administration—6
Fellow, Chartered Accountants—28

FCB Foote, Cone and Belding, Inc.—3, 9A

FCC *Federal Communications Commission*—6
First Class Certificate—7
Florida Capital Corp.—9B

FCDA *Federal Civil Defense Administration*—6

FCE Forest City Enterprises, Inc.—9B

FCF First Charter Financial Corp.—9A

FC&G Fernwood, Columbia & Gulf Railroad—1

FCI Fairchild Camera and Instrument Corp.—9A

FCIC *Federal Crop Insurance Co.*—6

FCS *Farmer Cooperative Service*—7
Fellow, Chemical Society—28

FCSC *Foreign Claims Settlement Commission*—6

FD The Central Foundry Co.—9A
fire department—6
fourth day—9

FDA *Food and Drug Administration*—6

FD&C United States Federal Food, Drug and Cosmetic Act—7

FDI Filter Dynamics International, Inc.—9B

FDIC *Federal Deposit Insurance Corp.*—6

FDL *fast deployment logistics*—4
Federal's, Inc.—9A

FDM Federated Mortgage Investors—9A

FDP Florida Power Corp.—9A

FDR Federal Resources Corp.—9B
Franklin Delano Roosevelt—29

FDS Federated Department Stores, Inc.—9A

FE iron (from *ferrum*)—17A
*f*orest *e*ngineer—28

FEC *F*lorida *E*ast *C*oast Railroad—1

FED *F*ederated Purchaser, Inc.—9B

FEI *Fé*dération *É*questre *I*nternationale (International Equestrian Federation)—11

FEL *F*elmont Oil Corp.—9B

FEN *F*airchild-Hiller Corp.—9A

FEPA *F*air *E*mployment *P*ractices *A*ct—7

FEPC *F*air *E*mployment *P*ractices *C*ommittee—6

FERA *F*ederal *E*mergency *R*elief *A*dministration—6

FET *f*ederal *e*xcise *t*ax—7, 9
*f*ield *e*ffect *t*ransistor—17

FF *F*ord *F*oundation—3
*F*riendly *F*rost, Inc.—9B

FFA *f*ree *f*rom *a*longside ship—9
*F*uture *F*armers of *A*merica—2

FFC *F*oreign *F*unds *C*ontrol—9
*f*ree *f*rom *c*hlorine—17

FFI *F*inancial *F*ederation, Inc.—9A
*f*ree *f*rom *in*fection—17
*F*orces *F*rançaises de l'*I*nterior (French Forces of the Interior)—12

FFN *F*airfield-*N*oble Corp.—9B

FFP *f*irm *f*ixed *p*rice—9

FFS *F*ood *F*air *S*tores, Inc.—9A

FFV *f*irst *f*amilies of *V*irginia—8

FFY *F*anny *F*armer Candy Shops, Inc.—9B

FG *f*ield *g*oal—11
*F*isher *G*overnor Co.—9B
U.S. *F*idelity and *G*uaranty Co.—9A

FGA *f*ield *g*oals *a*ttempted—11

FGL *F*inancial *G*eneral Corp.—9B

FGM *f*ield *g*oals *m*ade—11

FGS *F*ellow, *G*eological *S*ociety—28

FGSA *F*ellow, *G*eological *S*ociety of *A*merica—28

FH *f*iat *h*austus (make a draught)—18

FHA *F*armers' *H*ome *A*dministration—6
*F*ederal *H*ousing *A*dministration—6

FHB *f*amily *h*old *b*ack (colloquialism: family members should not eat too much when there are guests)—8

FHLBA *F*ederal *H*ome *L*oan *B*ank *A*dministration—6

FHLBB *F*ederal *H*ome *L*oan *B*ank *B*oard—6

FHS *F*ellow, *H*orticultural *S*ociety—28

FI *F*alkland *I*slands—27

FIA *F*édération *I*nternationale de l'*A*utomobile (International Automobile Federation)—11, 12

FIAT *F*ábbrica *I*taliana di *A*utomobili, *T*orino (Italian Automobile factory at Turin)—1, 3, 14

FIC *I*nstitutum *F*ratrum *I*nstructionis *C*hristianae de *P*loermel (Brothers of Christian Instruction of Ploermel)—16

FICA *F*ederal *I*nsurance *C*ontributions *A*ct—7

FIDO *f*og *in*vestigation *d*ispersal *o*perations—14, 17

FIFO *f*irst *in*, *f*irst *o*ut—1, 9

FIGHT *f*reedom, *in*dependence (or *in*tegration), *G*od, *h*onor, *to*day—2, 14

FII *F*rier *I*ndustries, Inc.—9B

FIM *F*irst *M*ortgage *I*nvestors—9A

FINAST *F*irst *N*ational *S*tores—3, 14

FIO *f*ree *i*n and *o*ut—1, 9

FIR *F*irestone Tire and Rubber Co.—9A

FIS *F*ischbach and Moore, Inc.—9A

FISL *F*ederal *I*nsured *S*tudent *L*oan—7, 23

FJ&G *F*onda, *J*ohnstown & *G*loversville Railroad—1

FJQ *F*edders Corp.—9A

FKM John Fluke Manufacturing Co., Inc.—9B

FKS Frank's Nursery Sales, Inc.—9B

FL Farmer-*L*abor Party—24

*f*ocal *l*ength—17

FLA Florida East Coast Railway Co.—9A

FLAK *Fl*iegerabwehr*k*anone (aircraft defense cannon)—14, 19

FLB Federal *L*and *B*ank—6

FLC Federal *L*ibrary *C*ommission—6

FLD Fieldcrest Mills, Inc.—9A

FLE Fleetwood Enterprises, Inc.—9B

FLES *f*oreign *l*anguage in *e*lementary *s*chools—23

FLG Florida Gas Co.—9A

FLIP *fl*oating *i*nstrument *p*latform —14, 17

FLIR *f*orward-*l*ooking *i*nfra*r*ed—17

FLM Fleming Co., Inc.—9A

FLN *F*ront de *L*ibération *N*ationale (National Liberation Front, Algeria)—12

FLOSY *F*ront for the *L*iberation of *O*ccupied *S*outh *Y*emen--12, 14

FLP Fields Plastics and Chemicals, Inc.—9B

FLQ *F*ront de *L*iberation *Q*uebeçoise (Front for the Liberation of Quebec)—12

FLR The Fluor Corp., Ltd.—9A

FLS *F*ellow, the *L*innean *S*ociety—28

Florida Steel Corp.—9A

FLT Filtrol Corp.—9A

FLW Felsway Shoe Corp.—9B

Frank *L*loyd *W*right—29

FLY Flying Tiger Line, Inc.—9A

F&M *F*ranklin and *M*arshall College—23

FM *f*iat *m*istura (make a mixture)—18

*f*ield *m*agnet—17

*f*ield *m*anual—4

*f*ield *m*arshal—28

*f*requency *m*odulation—17

FMB Federal Maritime Board—6

FMC *F*ederal *M*aritime *C*ommission—6

FMC Corp.—9A

*F*ood *M*achinery and *C*hemical Corp.—3

FMCS *F*ederal *M*ediation and *C*onciliation *S*ervice—6

FMF Fairmount Foods Co.—9A

FMI The Fed-Mart Corp.—9B

FMN *fl*avin *m*ono*n*ucleotide—17

FMO Federal-Mogul Corp.—9A

FMS *f*at-*m*obilizing *s*ubstance—17

FMT Fairmount Chemical Co., Inc. —9B

FMV *f*air *m*arket *v*alue—9

FN St. Louis-San Francisco Railway Co.—9A

FNC First National City Corp.—9A

FNL Fansteel, Inc.—9A

FNMA *F*ederal *N*ational *M*ortgage *A*ssociation ("Fannie Mae")—6

FNR First National Realty and Construction Corp.—9B

FO *f*allout—4, 17

*f*ield *o*fficer—4

The Flintkote Co.—9A

*F*oreign *O*ffice (Great Britain)—7

*f*ouled *o*ut—11

*f*uel *o*il—1

*f*ull *o*rgan—25

FOA *F*oreign *O*perations *A*dministration—6

FOB *f*ree (or *f*reight) *o*n *b*oard—9

FOBS *f*ractional-*o*rbit (or *f*ractional *o*rbital) *b*ombardment *s*ystem—4, 14

FOE Ferro Corp.—9A

*F*raternal *O*rder of *E*agles—2

FOIR *f*ield-*o*f-*i*nterest *r*egister—17

FOR Foremost McKesson, Inc.—9A

*f*ree (or *f*reight) *o*n *r*ails—9

FORTRAN *for*mula *tran*slation (computers)—9, 14

FOS *f*ree (or *f*reight) *o*n *s*hipboard (or steamer)—9

FOT *free on truck*—9
FOUO *for official use only*—7
FOX The Foxboro Co.—9A
FP *fiant pilulae* (let pills be made)—18

Fischer and Porter Co.—9B
fixed price—9
foot-pound—17
former priest—8
freezing point—17
fully paid—9
FPA Franklin Pierce Adams—29
FPC Federal Pacific Electric Co.—9A
Federal Power Commission—6
fish protein concentrate—17
FPHA Federal Public Housing Authority—6
FPI *fixed price incentive*—9
FPIS *forward propagation ionospheric scatter*—17
FPL Florida Power and Light Co.—9A
FPM *feet (or frames) per minute*—17
FPO *field (or fleet) post office*—4
FPR *federal procurement regulations*—7, 9
FPS *feet (or frames) per second*—17
FPSA Fellow of the Photographic Society of America—28
FPV *free piston vessel*—1
FQA Fuqua Industries, Inc.—9A
FR Federal Register—7
Federal Reserve—6
francium—17A
freight release—9
FRA Farah Manufacturing Co., Inc.—9A
Fleet Reserve Association—2, 4
FRAM Fellow, Royal Academy of Music—28
FRAS Fellow, Royal Astronomical Society—28
FRB Federal Reserve Bank (or Board)—6
FRC Federal Radio Commission—6

Flight Research Center (of NASA)—1, 17
FRCP Fellow, Royal College of Physicians—28
FRCS Fellow, Royal College of Surgeons—28
FRE The Fresnillo Co.—9B
FRGS Fellow, Royal Geographical Society—28
FRP Family Record Plan, Inc.—9B
fiberglass-reinforced plastic—9
FRPS Fellow of the Royal Photographic Society—28
FRS Federal Reserve System—6
Fellow, Royal Society—28
FRSL Fellow, Royal Society of Literature—28
FRSS Fellow, Royal Statistical Society—28
FRX Forest Laboratories, Inc.—9B
FS Fisher Scientific Co.—9A
fixed satellite—17
foot-second—17
Forest Service—7
FSA Farm Security Administration—6
Federal Security Agency—6
Fellow, Society of Antiquaries—28
FSB Federal Specifications Board—6
Financial Corp. of Santa Barbara—9B
FSC Franklin Stores Corp.—9A
FSD Falcon Seaboard Drilling Co.—9B
FSG Institutum Fratrum Instructionis Christianae a Sancto Gabriele (Brotherhood of Christian Instruction of St. Gabriel) (Christian Brothers)—16, 23
FSH M. H. Fishman Co., Inc.—9B
follicle-stimulating hormone—17
FSK *frequency-shift keying*—17
FSLIC Federal Savings and Loan Insurance Corp.—6
FSM Foodarama Supermarkets, Inc.—9B

GAP The Great Atlantic and Pacific Tea Co., Inc.—9A

GAR Grand Army of the Republic—4

GARIOA Government and Relief in Occupied Areas—6

GARP global atmosphere research project—17

GAS Northern Illinois Gas Co.—9A

GAS&C Georgia, Ashburn, Sylvester & Camilla Railroad—1

GAT Gateway Industries, Inc.—9B
General American Transportation Co.—3
Greenwich apparent time—30

GATT General Agreement on Tariffs and Trade—13

GAW guaranteed annual wage—7

GAY Gateway Sporting Goods Co.—9B

GB The Granby Mining Co. Ltd.—9A
Great Britain—27

GBD General Builders Corp.—9B

GBE Grand Cross of the British Empire—28

GBI Grand Bahama Island—27

GBR Great Basins Petroleum Co.—9B

GBS General Bancshares Corp.—9A
George Bernard Shaw—29

GBT Gilbert Shoe Stores, Inc.—9B

GB&W Green Bay & Western Railroad—1

GBW Great Lakes Recreation Co.—9B

GBY General Battery and Ceramic Corp.—9B

GC Gaylord Container Railroad—1
George Cross (a decoration)—28
Gold Coast—27
gonococcus—17
Graham County Railroad—1
Knight Grand Commander (or Cross)—28

GCA GCA Corp.—9A
ground-controlled approach—1

GCB Knight Grand Cross of the Order of the Bath—28

GCC Greyhound Computer Corp.—9B

GCD greatest common divisor—17

GCF greatest common factor—17

GCI Gannett Co., Inc.—9A
ground-controlled interception—4

GCIE Grand Commander of the Indian Empire—28

GCLH Grand Cross of the Legion of Honor—28

GCM greatest common measure—17

GCMG Knight Grand Commander (or Cross) of the Most Distinguished Order of St. Michael and St. George—28

GCMI Glass Container Manufacturers' Institute—10

GCMP Greater Cleveland Mathematics Program—23

GCN General Cinema Corp.—9B

GCO Genesco, Inc.—9A

GCR General Cigar Co., Inc.—9A
ground-controlled radar—1, 4

GCSS global communications satellite system—17, 22

GCT Greenwich civil time—30

GCVO Knight Grand Cross of the Royal Victorian Order—28

GD gadolinium—17A
General Dynamics Corp.—3, 9A
God damn—8
Graduate in Divinity—5
grand duchess (or duke)—28

GDB Goldblatt Brothers, Inc.—9B

GDC Gardner, Denver Co.—9A
guidance display computer—9

GDD Gladding Corp.—9B

GDR German Democratic Republic (East Germany)—27

GDS Glenmore Distilleries Co.—9B

GDV General Development Corp.—9A

GE General Electric Co.—3, 9A
germanium—17A

gilt *edges*—22

GEB Gerber Products Co.—9B

GEICO *Government Employes' Insur-ance Co.*—3, 14

GEL Granite Equipment Leasing Corp.—9B

Graphic Editions of Los Angeles (art)—22

GEM *Gas Equipment Manufacturers' Group*—10

Gemini Fund, Inc.—9A

GEN General Telephone and Electronics Corp.—9A

GEOS *geo*detic *satellite*—14, 17

GES Genisco Technology Corp.—9B

GESTAPO *Ge*heime *Sta*ats *Po*lizei (secret state police)—12, 14

GET Getty Oil Co.—9A

ground *elapsed time*—1

G&F *Georgia & Florida* Railroad—1

GF General Foods Corp.—9A

GFC Gibraltar Financial Corp. of California—9A

GFE *government-furnished equip-ment*—7, 9

GFI GF Industries, Inc.—9B

GFO Gulf, Mobile and Ohio Railroad Co.—9A

GFS Giant Food, Inc.—9B

GFTU *General Federation of Trade Unions*—21

GG *gamma globulin*—17

Green Giant Co.—9A

GGB Glen-Gery Corp.—9B

GGM *ground-to-ground missile*—4

GGS *ground guidance system*—1

GH General Host Corp.—9A

GHA *Greenwich hour angle*—27

GHOST *global horizontal sounding technique*—14, 17

GHQ *general headquarters*—4

GI *galvanized iron*—9

gastrointestinal—17

general issue—4, 8

Gimbel Bros., Inc.—9A

government issue (now refers to a soldier)—4, 8

GIA *Gummed Industries Associ-ation*—10

GID Giddings and Lewis, Inc.—9A

GIL Gilbert Flexi-Van Corp.—9B

GIS General Mills, Inc.—9A

GIT *General Information Test*—23

General Interiors Corp.—9B

GK General Cable Corp.—9A

GL *Graduate in Law*—5

Great Lakes—27

GLA Glasrock Products, Inc.—9B

GLB Globe-Union, Inc.—9A

GLE General Electric Co., Ltd. (England)—9B

GLF General Telephone Co. of Florida—9A

GLI General Time Corp.—9A

GLK Great Lakes Chemical Corp.—9B

GLM Global Marine, Inc.—9A

GLMA *Great Lakes Mink Associ-ation*—10

GLO G-L Industries, Inc.—9B

GLP The General Fireproofing Co.—9A

GLR Grolier, Inc.—9A

GLU William Gluckin Co., Ltd.—9B

GLW Corning Glass Works—9A

GM *Gainesville Midland* Railroad—1

general manager—9

general mortgage—9

General Motors Corp.—3, 9A

George Medal—28

grand marshal—28

grand master—28

guided missile—4

gunner's mate—4

GMA *Grocery Manufacturers of America*—10

GMAC *General Motors Acceptance Corp.*—3

GMAT *Greenwich mean astronomical time*—30

GMB   Grand Master of the Bath—28

GMC   General Motors Corp.—3

GML   The Gray Manufacturing Co.—9B

GM&O   Gulf, Mobile & Ohio Railroad—1

GM&S   general medical and surgical—17

GMS   general military science—4, 23

GMT   General American Transportation Corp.—9A

Greenwich mean time—30

GMW   gram-molecular weight—17

G&N   Greenville & Northern Railroad—1

guidance and navigation—27

GN   gaseous nitrogen—17

Georgia Northern Railroad—1

glucose:nitrogen ratio—17

graduate nurse—28

Great Northern Railway Co.—1, 9A

GN&A   Graysonia, Nashville & Ashdown Railroad—1

GNB   Gould National Batteries, Inc.—9A

GNI   Great Northern Iron Ore Properties—9A

GNMA   Government National Mortgage Association ("Ginnie Mae")—6

GNP   gross national product—7, 9

GNY   General Alloys Co.—9B

GO   general office—9

general order—4

general organization—8

great (pipe) organ—25

Gulf Oil Corp.—9A

GOA   gone on arrival—26

GOC   Gulf Oil Canada Ltd.—9B

GOFAR global ocean floor analysis research—14, 17

GOI   Gearhart-Owen Industries, Inc. —9B

Government of Indonesia—27

GOK   God only knows—8, 17

GOM   Grand Old Man (reference to W.E. Gladstone)—8, 29

GOO   get oil out (Santa Barbara, Calif.)—2, 14

GOP   Grand Old Party—8, 24

GOR   Gordon Jewelry Corp.—9A

GOW   Georgia Power Co.—9B

GOX   gaseous oxygen—17

GP   galactic probe—17

general paresis—17

general practitioner—8, 17

general purpose—4, 8

Georgia-Pacific Corp.—9A

Gloria Patri (Glory to the Father)—16, 19

Graduate in Pharmacy—5

grand prix—11

GPA   grade point average—23

GPAC   general purpose airborne computer—1, 9

GPC   Genuine Parts Co.—9A

GPCD   gallons per capita per day—7

GPH   gallons per hour—17

GPI   general paralysis of the insane—17

GPM   gallons per minute—17

GPO   general post office—6

Giant Portland Cement Co.—9A

Government Printing Office—6

GPP   Great Northern Paper Co.—9A

GPS   gallons per second—17

GPT   General Portland Cement Co.—9A

GPU   General Postal Union—12

General Public Utilities Corp.—3, 9A

Gosudarstvennoe Politicheskoe Upravlyenie (Russian Secret Police)—12

GPX   Greyhound Package Express—3

GPY   General Plywood Corp.—9B

GQ   general quarters—4

Grumman Aircraft Engineering Corp.—9A

GR *G*eorgius *R*ex (King George)—19, 29

B.F. Goodrich Co.—9A

*g*overnment *r*ubber—9

GRA W.R. Grace and Co.—9A

GRAS *g*enerally *r*ecognized *a*s *s*afe (Food and Drug Administration)—7, 14

GRB The Gerber Scientific Instrument Co.—9B

GRC Granite City Steel Co.—9A

GRE Gulf Resources and Chemical Corp.—9A

GRG Granger Associates—9B

GRH Greer Hydraulics, Inc.—9B

GRI Great American Industries, Inc.—9B

GRK Garland Corp.—9B

GRL General Instrument Corp.—9A

GRO Grow Chemical Corp.—9B

GRS *g*overnment *r*ubber *s*tyrene—9

GRU Gruen Industries, Inc.—9B

GRV Guardsman Chemical Coatings, Inc.—9B

GRW Greater Washington Investors, Inc.—9A

GRX General Refractories Co.—9A

GRY Gray Drug Stores, Inc.—9A

G&S *G*ilbert and *S*ullivan—29

GS *g*eneral *s*ecretary—9

*g*eneral *s*taff—4

The Gillette Co.—9A

*G*overnment *S*ervice—7

GSA *G*eneral *S*ervices *A*dministration—6

*G*eological *S*ociety of *A*merica—20

*G*irl *S*couts of *A*merica—2

*G*raduate *S*tudents *A*ssociation—23

GSC *g*eneral *s*taff *c*orps—4

GSC Enterprises, Inc.—9B

GSE *g*round *s*upport *e*quipment—4

GSI General Steel Industries, Inc.—9A

GSK Gamble-Skogmo, Inc.—9A

GSL Gulf States Land and Industries, Inc.—9B

GSP Grocery Store Products Co.—9B

GSR *g*alvanic *s*kin *r*eflex (or *r*esponse)—17

The Green Shoe Manufacturing Co.—9A

GSW *g*un*s*hot *w*ound—26

GSX General Signal Corp.—9A

GT *g*as *t*urbine engine—1, 9

Goodyear Tire and Rubber Co.—9A

*G*rand *T*runk Railroad—1

GTC *g*ood *t*ill *c*ancelled (or *c*ountermanded)—9

GTI GTI Corp.—9B

GTO *g*ran *t*urismo *o*mologato (sports car)—1

GTS *g*as *t*urbine *s*hip—1

GTU Gulf States Utilities Co.—9A

GTY W.T. Grant Co.—9A

GU *g*enito*u*rinary—17

GUL Gulton Industries, Inc.—9A

GUR Guerdon Industries, Inc.—9B

GUX The Grand Union Co.—9A

GV The Goldfield Corp.—9B

*g*ravimetric *v*olume—17

GVL Graniteville Co.—9A

GVN *G*overnment of *V*iet*n*am—12

GVT *g*ravity-*v*acuum *t*ransit—1, 17

GVW *g*ross *v*ehicle *w*eight—1, 7

G&W *G*enesee and *W*estern Railroad—1

*G*ulf and *W*estern Industries—3

GW *G*eorge *W*ashington—29

*G*reat *W*estern Railroad—1

*g*ross *w*eight—1, 7

Gulf and Western Industries, Inc.—9A, 9B

GWA *G*olden *W*est *A*irlines—1

GWB The Griesedieck Co.—9B

GWD Gar Wood Industries, Inc.—9A

GWF Great Western Financial Corp.—9A

GWTW *"Gone with the Wind"*—22, 25

GWU Great Western United Corp.—9A

GWY Goodway, Inc.—9B

GY The General Tire and Rubber Co.—9A

GYK Giant Yellowknife Mines, Ltd.—9B

GYL Gaylords National Corp.—9B

GZ ground zero—4

H *h*ydrogen—17A

HA high angle—17
*h*oc *a*nno (in this year)—19, 30
Holophane Co., Inc.—9B
hour angle—27

HABS *H*istoric *A*merican *B*uildings *S*urvey—7

HAL Halliburton Co., Inc.—9B
*H*olland-*A*merica *L*ine—1

HAR Harvey Aluminum, Inc.—9A

HAS *h*eading-*a*ttitude *s*ystem(s)—1

HAT HCA Industries, Inc.—9A

HATS *h*elicopter *a*ttack *s*ystem—4, 14

HAV Harvard Industries, Inc.—9B

HAW *h*eavy *a*ntitank (or *a*ssault) *w*eapon—4

HAWK *h*oming-*a*ll-*t*he-*w*ay *k*iller—4, 14

HAY Hayes Albion Corp.—9A

H&B *H*ampton & *B*ranchville Railroad—1

HB *h*alfback—11

HBA H & B American Corp.—9B

HBB Hoover Ball and Bearing Co.—9A

HBC *H*udson's *B*ay Company—3

HBD *h*ad (or *h*as) *b*een *d*rinking—26

HBL Heublein, Inc.—9A

HBM *H*is (or *H*er) *B*ritannic *M*ajesty—28

HBPA *H*orsemen's *B*enevolent and *P*rotective *A*ssociation—11

HBS *H*arvard *B*usiness *S*chool—23

H&BTM *H*untington & *B*road *T*op *M*ountain Railroad & Coal Co.—1

HBW Harcourt, Brace and World, Inc.—9A

HBX Hoerner-Waldorf Corp.—9A

HC *h*eld *c*overed—9
Helene Curtis Industries, Inc.—9A
*H*oly *C*ommunion—16
*H*ouse of *C*ommons—12

HCA *H*at *C*orp. of *A*merica (now HCA Industries, Inc.)—3
Hotel Corp. of America—9A

HCC Philip A. Hunt Chemical Corp.—9B

HCF *h*ighest *c*ommon *f*actor—17
*h*oney *c*omb *f*oundation (for polishing lenses)—9

HCI *h*orizon-*c*rossing *i*ndicator—17

HCL high cost of living—8

HCM *H*is (or *H*er) *C*atholic *M*ajesty—28

H&D *H*urter and *D*riffield curve—17

HD *H*ansen's *d*isease—17
*H*ilda *D*oolittle (writer)—29
*h*ourly *d*ifference—27
Hudson Bay Mining and Smelting Co., Ltd.—9A

HDC *h*older in *d*ue *c*ourse—9

HDK *h*usband *d*oesn't *k*now—8

HDL Handleman Co.—9A

HE Hawaiian Electric Co., Inc.—9A
*h*eavy (or *h*igh) *e*xplosive—17
*h*elium—17A
*H*is (or *H*er) *E*minence (or *E*xcellency)—28

HEC Hoffman Electronics Corp.—9A

HEI Heinicke Instruments Co.—9B

HEM Hemisphere Fund, Inc.—9A

HEOS *h*ighly *e*ccentric *o*rbit *s*atellite—14, 17

HER *H*arvard *E*ducational *R*eview—22, 23
Helena Rubinstein, Inc.—9B

HES Hess Oil and Chemical Corp.—9A

HETP *h*exa*e*thyl *t*etra*p*hosphate—17

HEW Department of *H*ealth, *E*ducation and *W*elfare—6

HF *h*a*f*nium—17A

*h*igh *f*requency—17

House of Fabrics, Inc.—9B

HFB Hydromatics, Inc.—9B

HFC *H*ousehold *F*inance *C*orp.—3, 9A

HFO Hygrade Food Products Corp. —9B

HG *H*is (or *H*er) *G*race—28

*H*igh *G*erman—15

*H*ome *G*uard—4

Home Oil Co., Ltd.—9B

mercury (from *h*ydrar*g*yrum)—17A

HGH Hughes and Hatcher, Inc.—9A

HGI Hi-G, Inc.—9B

HH *h*eavy *h*ydrogen—17

*H*is (or *H*er) *H*ighness—28

*H*etch *H*etchy Railroad—1

*H*is *H*oliness—28

Houdaille Industries, Inc.—9A

HHD *h*og*sh*ea*d*—9

HHDN *h*exac*h*loro*h*exa*h*ydroendoexo-*d*imethano*n*aphthalene—17

HHF *h*ouse*h*old *f*urniture—9

HHFA *H*ousing and *H*ome *F*inance *A*gency—6

HHH *H*ubert *H*oratio *H*umphrey—29

HHHH *h*ead, *h*eart, *h*and, *h*ealth (4-H Club)—2

HI Harris-Intertype Corp.—9A

*H*awaiian *I*slands—27

*h*eight *o*f *i*nstrument- 17

*h*uman *i*nterest—22, 25

HIA *H*obby *I*ndustry *A*ssociation—10

Holiday Inns, Inc.—9A

HIFI *h*igh *f*idelity – 14

HIG Higbie Manufacturing Co.—9B

HIH *H*is (or *H*er) *I*mperial *H*igh-ness—28

HII Host International, Inc.—9A

HILAC *h*eavy *i*on *l*inear *a*ccelera-tor—14, 17

HIM *H*is (or *H*er) *I*mperial *M*ajesty —28

HIP *h*ealth *i*nsurance *p*lan—3

Hipotronics, Inc.—9B

HIR Hiram Walker-Gooderham and Worts, Ltd.—9A

HIS Henry I. Siegel Co., Inc.—9A

HISC *H*ouse *I*nternal *S*ecurity *C*om-mittee—7

HIT Hitco—9A

HJ *h*ic *j*acet (here lies)—19

Howard Johnson Co.—9A

HJS *h*ic *j*acet *s*epultus (or *s*itus) (here lies buried)—19

HK *H*ong *K*ong—27

HL Hecla Mining Co.—9A

*H*ouse of *L*ords—12

HLBB *H*ome *L*oan *B*ank *B*oard—6

HLI Heli-Coil Corp.—9A

HLL Hudson Leasing Corp.—9B

HLP C. M. Hall Lamp Co.—9B

HLR Walter E. Heller and Co.—9A, 9B

HLT Hilton Hotels Corp.—9A, 9B

HLY Holly Sugar Corp.—9A

HM *H*is (or *H*er) *M*ajesty—28

Homestake Mining Co. —9A

HMAS *H*is (or *H*er) *M*ajesty's *A*us-tralian *s*hip—1, 4

HMD Hammond Corp.—9A

HMF Hastings Manufacturing Co. — 9B

HML Hammermill Paper Co.—9A

HMS *H*is (or *H*er) *M*ajesty's *s*erv-ice—7

*H*is (or *H*er) *M*ajesty's *s*hip—1, 4

HMT Hall's Motor Transit Co.—9B

HMV *H*is *M*aster's *V*oice—3, 25

HMW Hamilton Watch Co.—9A

HN Hebrew National Kosher Foods, Inc.—9B

HNG Houston Natural Gas Corp.—9A

HNH Handy and Harman—9A
HNM Hanna Mining Co.—9A
HNS Hanes Corp.—9A
HNZ H. J. Heinz Co.—9A
HO *head office*—9
   held over—25
   holdout—8
   holmium—17A
   Home Office—9
HOB The Hobart Manufacturing Co.—9A
HOC Holly Corp.—9A
   Hollywood Overseas Committee—2, 25
HOE R. Hoe and Co., Inc.—9B
HOF Hofmann Industries, Inc.—9B
HOLC *Home Owners' Loan Corp.*—6
HOL Hollinger Mines, Ltd.—9B
HON Honeywell, Inc.—9A
HOR Horn and Hardart Co.—9B
HOU Houston Lighting and Power Co.—9A
HOV The House of Vision, Inc.—9B
HP Helmerich and Payne, Inc.—9A
   high power—9
   high pressure—17
   high priest—16
   highway patrol—26
   horizontal parallax—27
   horsepower—1, 8
HPA *high-power amplifier*—17
HPC Hercules, Inc.—9A
HPD *hand-point defense*—4
HPF *highest possible frequency*—17
HPG W. F. Hall Printing Co.—9A
   human pituitary gonodotrophin—17
HPI Helme Products, Inc.—9A
HPM *high-power multiplier*—17
HPT&D *High Point, Thomasville & Denton Railroad*—1
HQ *headquarters*—4
HQC *headquarters command*—4
HR *home rule*—7

   House of Representatives—7
   human relations—17
   International Harvester Co.—9A
HRA Harvey Radio Co., Inc.—9B
HRC Harnischfeger Corp.—9B
HRE *Holy Roman Empire*—27
   Hubbard Real Estate Investments—9A
HRH *His (or Her) Royal Highness*—28
HRIP *here rests in peace*—8
HRIR *high resolution infrared radiation (or radiometer)*—17
HRL George A. Hormel and Co.—9B
HRT Hartfield-Zodys, Inc.—9B
HS *high school*—23
   home secretary—7
   hora somni (at the hour of sleep, or bedtime)—18
HSC Harsco Corp.—9A
HSH *His (or Her) Serene Highness*—28
   Hi-Shear Corp.—9B
HSK The Hoskins Manufacturing Co.—9B
HSL Hercules Galion Products, Inc.—9B
HSM Hart, Schaffner and Marx—9A
   His (or Her) Serene Majesty—28
HSP *Haute Société Protestante (Protestant High Society)*—8, 12
HSS *Historiae Societatis Socius (Fellow, The Historical Society)*—28
HST *Harry S Truman*—29
   hypersonic transport—1
HSY Hershey Foods Corp.—9A
H&T *hospitalization and treatment*—17
HT *hardtop (automobile)*—1, 8
   high tension—9, 17
HTC The Alfred Hart Co.—9B
   head to come—22
HTN Houghton Mifflin Co.—9A

HT&W *H*oosac *T*unnel & *W*ilmington Railroad—1

HUAC *H*ouse *U*n-American *A*ctivities *C*ommittee—6

HUB Harvey Hubbell, Inc.—9B

HUD Department of *H*ousing and *U*rban *D*evelopment—6

HUF The Huffman Manufacturing Co.—9B

HUT *h*omes *u*sing *t*elevision—9, 25

HV *h*igh *v*oltage—17

HVE High Voltage Engineering Corp.—9A

HVN Haven Industries, Inc.—9B

HVP *h*ydrolized *v*egetable *p*rotein—17

HVPS *h*igh-*v*oltage *p*ower *s*upply—17

HVY Harvey's Stores, Inc.—9B

HW *h*igh *w*ater—27

Howmet Corp.—9A

HWA Hackensack Water Co.—9A

HWP Hewlett-Packard Co.—9A

HXR Hudson and Manhattan Corp.—9B

HY Hycon Manufacturing Co.—9B

HYD Hydrometals, Inc.—9B

HYK Huyck Corp.—9B

HYO Husky Oil, Ltd.—9B

HY&T *H*ooppole, *Y*orktown & *T*ampico Railroad—1

HZ Hazeltine Corp.—9A

I *i*odine—17A

IA *i*mmediately *a*vailable—9

*i*n *a*bsentia (in the absence of)—19

IAAF *I*nternational *A*mateur *A*thletic *F*ederation—11

IACP *I*nternational *A*ssociation of *C*hiefs of *P*olice—2, 26

IACS *i*ntegrated *a*rmament *c*ontrol *s*ystem—4

IAD Inland Steel Co.—9A

*I*nternational *A*strophysical *D*ecade—17

IADB *I*nter-*A*merican *D*efense *B*oard—6

*I*nter-*A*merican *D*evelopment *B*ank—6

IADS *I*nternational *A*gricultural *D*evelopment *S*ervice—6

IAEA *I*nternational *A*tomic *E*nergy *A*gency—13

IAFF *I*nternational *A*ssociation of *F*ire *F*ighters—21

IAGLO *I*nternational *A*ssociation of *G*overnment *L*abor *O*fficials—20

IAHA *I*nternational *A*rabian *H*orse *A*ssociation—2, 11

IAM *I*nternational *A*ssociation of *M*achinists—21

IAMAT *I*nternational *A*ssociation for *M*edical *A*ssistance to *T*ravelers—10

IAOD *i*n *a*ddition to *o*ther *d*uties—8

IAPN *I*nternational *A*ssociation of *P*rofessional *N*umismatists—20

IAS *i*ndicated *a*ir *s*peed—1

*I*nstitute for *A*dvanced *S*tudy—23

*I*nstitute of the *A*eronautical *S*ciences—1, 23

*i*nstrument *a*pproach *s*ystem—1

*i*ntegrated *a*vionics *s*ystem—1

IATA *I*nternational *A*ir *T*ransport *A*ssociation—10

IATSE *I*nternational *A*lliance of *Th*eatrical *S*tage *E*mployees and Motion Picture Machine Operators of the United States and Canada—21

IAU *I*nternational *A*stronomical *U*nion—17

IAW *i*n *a*ccordance *w*ith—9

IB *i*ncendiary *b*omb—4

IBA *I*nvestment *B*ankers' *A*ssociation—10

IBB *I*nternational *B*rotherhood of *B*ookbinders—21

IBBY *I*nternational *B*oard on *B*ooks for *Y*oung People—2, 22

IBC   Interstate Bakeries Corp.—9A

IBEW   *International Brotherhood of Electrical Workers*—21

IBFO   *International Brotherhood of Firemen and Oilers*—21

IBM   *International Business Machines*—3, 9A

IBMA   *isobutylene maleic acid*—17

IBP   *International Biological Program*—17

    Iowa Beef Packers, Inc.—9A

IBRD   *International Bank for Reconstruction and Development*—12

IBSA   *International Bible Students' Association* (Jehovah's Witnesses)—16

IBTCWH *International Brotherhood of Teamsters, Chauffeurs, Warehousemen and Helpers of America*—21

I&C   *installation and checkout*—9

IC   *Iesus Christus* (Jesus Christ)—16

    Illinois Central Railroad—1

    immediate constituent—15

    in charge—8

    index correction—27

    information center—7, 9

    inspected and condemned—4

    Inspiration Consolidated Copper Co.—9A

    integrated circuit—17

    inter cibos (between meals)—18

    internal combustion—9

ICA   Imperial Corp. of America—9A

    International Cooperation Administration—6

ICAAAA *Intercollegiate Association of Amateur Athletes of America*—2, 11

ICAF   *Industrial College of the Armed Forces*—4

ICAO   *International Civil Aviation Organization*—13

ICAT   *International Congress of Air Technology*—17

ICBM   *intercontinental ballistic missile*—4

ICBP   *International Council for Bird Preservation*—2, 12

ICC   *Indian Claims Commission*—6

    Inland Credit Corp.—9B

    intensive coronary care—17

    International Control Commission—12

    Interstate Commerce Commission—6

ICCC   *International Council of Christian Churches*—16

ICI   *International Commission on Illumination*—12, 17

ICJ   *International Court of Justice*—12

ICM   *improved capability missile*—4

ICN   *International Council of Nurses*—20

ICO   *Interagency Committee on Oceanography*—6, 17

ICRC   *International Committee of the Red Cross*—12

ICRM   *intercontinental reconnaissance missile*—4

ICRP   *International Commission on Radiological Protection*—17

ICRU   *International Commission on Radiological Units and Measurements*—12, 17

ICS   Income and Capital Shares, Inc.—9A

    Indian Civil Service—6

    International Correspondence School—3, 23

ICSH   *interstitial cell-stimulating hormone*—17

ICSU   *International Council of Scientific Unions*—12, 17

ICTA   *Institute of Certified Travel Agents*—10

ICW   *in compliance with*—8

    interrupted continuous wave—17

ICWNE *International Conference of Weekly Newspaper Editors*—22

ICWU *I*nternational *C*hemical *W*orkers' *U*nion—21

ICX *I*llinois-*C*alifornia *E*xpress—1, 3

ICY *I*nternational *C*ooperation *Y*ear—12

ICYRANA *I*nter-*C*ollegiate *Y*acht *R*acing *A*ssociation of *N*orth *A*merica—11

ID *id*entification—8

*i*nfantry *d*ivision—4

*i*nside *d*iameter—9

*I*ntelligence *D*epartment—6

IDA Idaho Power Co.—9A

*I*nstitute for *D*efense *A*nalyses—17

*I*nternational *D*evelopment *A*ssociation (of the World Bank)—13

IDAC *i*nstant *d*ata *a*ccess and *c*ontrol—9, 14

IDB *i*llicit *d*iamond *b*uyer—9

*I*nter-*A*merican *D*evelopment *B*ank (of the International Monetary Fund)—7

IDCSP *I*nitial *D*efense *C*ommunications *S*atellite *P*roject—17

IDEA *I*nstitute for *D*evelopment of *E*ducational *A*ctivities—14, 23

IDL Ideal Basic Industries, Inc.—9A

IDO *i*nternal *d*istribution *o*nly—9

IDP *i*ntegrated *d*ata *p*rocessing—9

*i*nternational *d*riving *p*ermit—1, 8

IDS Investors Diversified Services, Inc.—9B

I&E *i*nformation and *e*ducation—9

IE *i*d *e*st (that is)—19

*I*ndo-*E*uropean—15

*i*ndustrial *e*ngineer—28

IEEE *I*nstitute of *E*lectrical and *E*lectronics *E*ngineers—20

IEL Iowa Electric Light and Power Co.—9A

IEX Industria Eléctrica de México, S.A.—9A

IF *i*ntermediate *f*requency—17

IFALPA *I*nternational *F*ederation of *A*ir *L*ine *P*ilots *A*ssociations—14, 20

IFAP *I*nternational *F*ederation of *A*gricultural *P*roducers—12

IFB *i*nvitation *f*or *b*id—9

IFC *I*nternational *F*inance *C*orp.—6

*I*nternational *F*isheries *C*ommission—6

*I*nternational *F*reighting *C*orp.—6

*I*nvestors *F*unding *C*orp. of New York—9B

IFCS *I*nternational *F*ederation of *C*omputer *S*ciences—20

IFF *id*entification, *f*riend or *f*oe—4, 8

The *I*nstitute *f*or the *F*uture—17

*I*nternational *F*lavors and *F*ragrances, Inc.—9A

IFIM *I*nternational *F*light *I*nformation *M*anual—1

IFLA *I*nternational *F*ederation of *Li*brary *A*ssociations—2

IFLWU *I*nternational *F*ur and *L*eather *W*orkers' *U*nion—21

IFR *i*nstrument *f*light *r*ules—1

IFS *I*rish *F*ree *S*tate—27

IFTU *I*nternational *F*ederation of *T*rade *U*nions—21

IG Imoco-Gateway Corp.—9B

*I*ndo-*G*ermanic—15

*i*nspector *g*eneral—4

IGA *I*ndependent *G*rocers of *A*merica—3

*I*nternational *G*rains *A*rrangement—12

IGC Indiana General Corp.—9A

IGFA *I*nternational *G*ame *F*ish *A*ssociation—11

IGL *I*nternational *M*inerals and *C*hemical Corp.—9A

IGN *I*nternational *G*reat *N*orthern Railroad—1

IGO *I*ndependent *G*arage *O*wners—10

IGU *I*nternational *G*eophysical *U*nion—17

IGY International Geophysical Year—17

IH International Harvester Corp.—3
International Holdings Corp.—9A

IHB Indiana Harbor Belt Railroad—1

IHC IHC, Inc.—9B

IHD Indian Head, Inc.—9A, 9B
International Hydrologic Decade —17

IHF intermediate high frequency—17

IHM Immaculate Heart of Mary—16
Industrial Electronic Hardware Corp.—9B

IHO in honor of—8

IHP indicated horsepower—1

IHS Iesus Hominum Salvator (Jesus, the Savior of Man)—16
in hoc signo (in this sign)—19
Ipco Hospital Supply Corp.—9A

IIA International Institute of Agriculture—12

IIE Institute of International Education—23

III Illinois, Indiana, Iowa (3-I League)—11

IIT Illinois Institute of Technology—23

IITRI Illinois Institute of Technology Research Institute—17

IK Interlake Steel Corp.—9A

IKN Inmont Corp.—9A

IL Illinois Central Industries, Inc.—9A
inside left—11

ILA instrument landing approach—1
International Law Association—20
International Longshoremen's Association—21

ILGWU International Ladies' Garment Workers' Union—21

ILM independent (or instrument) landing monitor—1

ILO in lieu of—8
International Labor Organization—13

ILP Independent Labour Party—12

ILPA International Labor Press Association—22

ILS instrument landing system—1
International Salt Co.—9A

ILTF International Lawn Tennis Federation—11

ILWU International Longshoremen's and Warehousemen's Union—21

IM index medicus—17, 22
intermodulation—17
International Mining Corp.—9A
intramuscularly—17
Isle of Man—27

IMCO improved combustion—1, 9, 14
Intergovernmental Maritime Consultative Organization—13, 14

IMF International Monetary Fund—12

IMG IMC Magnetics Corp.—9B

IMM impairing the morals of a minor—8, 26

IMO Imperial Oil, Ltd.—9B

IMP Imperial Chemical Industries, Ltd.—9B
international match point (bridge)—11, 14
interplanetary monitoring platform (or probe)—14, 17

IMRO International Macedonian Revolutionary Organization—12

IMT The Imperial Tobacco Group, Ltd.—9B

IMTFE International Military Tribunal, Far East—4, 12

IMU inertial measurement (or measuring) unit—17

IN Illinois Northern Railroad—1
indium—17A

INA INA Corp.—9A
Insurance Company of North America—3

INB Industrial Bancorp, Inc.—9A

INC International Controls Corp.—9B

INCA *In*formation *C*ouncil of the *A*mericas—2

IND *in* *n*omine *D*ei (in the name of God)—16

INF *In*flight Motion Pictures, Inc.—9B

INH *iso*nicotinic acid, *h*ydrazide—17

INI *In*tercontinental Industries, Inc.—9B

INM *in*ternational *n*autical *m*ile—27

INO *i*ssue *n*ecessary *o*rders—9

INP Interpace Corp.—9A

INR Insilco Corp.—9A

INRI *I*esus *N*azarenus *R*ex *I*udaeorum (Jesus of Nazareth, King of the Jews)—16

INS *I*mmigration and *N*aturalization *S*ervice—6

*in*ertial *n*avigational *s*ystem—1

*I*nternational *N*ews *S*ervice—22

INT International Industries, Inc. —9A

INTELSAT *In*ternational *Tele*communications *Sat*ellite Consortium—12, 14

INTERPOL *Intern*ational Criminal *Poli*ce Organization—12

IO *i*nitials *o*nly—22

*i*nput-*o*utput—17

IOC *I*ntergovernmental *O*ceanographic *C*ommission—13

*I*nternational *O*lympic *C*ommittee—11

IOF *I*ndependent *O*rder of *F*oresters—2

IOGT *I*nternational *O*rder of *G*ood *T*emplars—2

IOM *in*ter*o*ffice *m*emorandum—9

IOOF *I*ndependent *O*rder of *O*dd *F*ellows—2

IOP Iowa Power and Light Co.—9A

IOR *in*ternational *o*ffshore *r*ating rule (for yacht racing)—11

IORM *I*mproved *O*rder of *R*ed *M*en—2

IOS *I*nvestors *O*verseas *S*ervices—3

IOU *I* *o*we yo*u*—8

IOW *I*sle *o*f *W*ight—27

IP International Paper Co.—9A

IPA *I*ndependent *P*ress *A*ssociation—22

*I*nternational *P*honetic *A*lphabet (or *A*ssociation)—23

*I*nternational *P*ublishers *A*ssociation—10, 12

IPBM *in*ter*p*lanetary *b*allistic *m*issile—4

IPC Illinois Power Co.—9A

IPH *in*ches *p*er *h*our—17

Interphoto Corp.—9B

IPM *in*ches *p*er *m*inute—17

IPPB *in*termittent *p*ositive *p*ressure *b*reathing—17

IPR *in*ches *p*er *r*evolution—17

Indianapolis Power and Light Co.—9A, 9B

IPS *in*ches *p*er *s*econd—17

*in*tegrated *p*neumatic *s*ystem—1, 17

Iowa Public Service Co.—9A, 9B

IPSA *I*ndependent *P*ostal *S*ystem of *A*merica—3, 14

IPW Interstate Power Co.—9A

IPY *I*nternational *P*olar *Y*ear—17

IQ *i*dem *q*uod (the same as)—19

*i*ntelligence *q*uotient—23

Questor Corp.—9A

IR *i*ndustrial *r*elations—9

*i*nfantry *r*eserve—4

*i*nfra*r*ed—17

Ingersoll-Rand Co.—9A

*i*nside *r*ight—11

*i*ntelligence *r*atio—23

*I*nternal *R*evenue—7

*i*nternational *r*ice—8

*ir*idium—17A

IRA *I*ndependent *R*egulatory *A*gency—6

*I*rish *R*epublican *A*rmy—12

IRAN *i*nspection, *r*eplacement *as* *n*eeded—9, 14

IRB *I*nternal *R*evenue *B*ulletin—7, 22

IRBM *i*ntermediate *r*ange *b*allistic *m*issile—4

IRC *I*nternal *R*evenue *C*ode—7

International *R*ed *C*ross—12

*I*nternation *R*esistance Co.—3

IRD *i*ndependent *r*esearch and *d*evelopment—9, 17

IRE *I*nstitute of *R*adio *E*ngineers—20

International Rectifier Corp.—9A

Iroquois Industries, Inc.—9B

IRIA *i*nfra*r*ed *i*nformation and *a*nalysis—17

IRL Investors Royalty Co., Inc.—9B

IRO *I*nternational *R*efugee *O*rganization—13

IRS *i*nformation *r*etrieval *s*ystem—17, 23

*I*nternal *R*evenue *S*ervice (or *S*ystem)—6

IRT *I*nterborough *R*apid *T*ransit (New York City)—1

IRTS *I*nternational *R*adio and *T*elevision *S*ociety—2

IRV Irvin Industries, Inc.—9B

IS *i*ntegrated *s*atellite—17

*i*ntermediate *s*chool—23

ISC *i*nter*s*tate *c*ommerce—7

ISC Industries, Inc.—9B

ISD Interstate Department Stores, Inc.—9A

ISIS *i*nternational *s*atellite for *i*onospheric *s*tudies—17

ISN Instron Corp.—9B

IS&R *i*nformation *s*torage and *r*etrieval—9

ISS Interco, Inc.—9A

IST International Stretch Products, Inc.—9B

ISU *I*nternational *S*cientific *U*nion—12

*I*owa *S*tate *U*niversity—23

ISY Instrument Systems Corp.—9B

IT *I*llinois *T*erminal Railroad—1

*i*nternational steam *t*able calorie—17

Iti Corp.—9B

ITA *I*nde*p*endent *T*elevision *A*uthority (Great Britain)—12, 25

*i*nitial *t*eaching *a*lphabet—23

ITC Imperial Tobacco Co. of Canada, Ltd.—9B

*i*nter*t*ropical *c*onvergence—17, 27

ITCC *I*nternational *T*ape *C*artridge *C*orp.—3, 25

ITE I-T-E Imperial Corp.—9A

ITF *I*nstitute of *T*ropical *F*orestry—17

ITK Itek Corp.—9A

ITM *i*nterception *t*actical *m*issile—4

ITO *I*nternational *T*rade *O*rganization—6

ITS I T T Consumer Services Corp.—9A

ITT *I*nternational *T*elephone and *T*elegraph Corp.—3, 9A

ITU *I*nternational *T*elecommunication *U*nions—13

*I*nternational *T*ypographical *U*nion—21

ITV *I*ndependent *T*elevision Network (Great Britain)—12, 25

IU *i*mmunizing *u*nit—17

*i*nstrument *u*nit—1

*i*nternational *u*nit—17

International Utilities Corp.—9A

IUC *I*nternational *U*nion of *C*hemistry—12, 17

Interstate United Corp.—9B

IUCD *i*ntra*u*terine *c*ontraceptive *d*evice (also IUD)—17

IUCN *I*nternational *U*nion for the *C*onservation of *N*ature and Natural Resources—2

IUD *i*ntra*u*terine *d*evice—17

IUE *I*nternational *U*nion of *E*lectrical Workers—21

IUOTO *I*nternational *U*nion of *O*fficial *T*ravel *O*rganizations—12

IUTAM *I*nternational *U*nion of *T*heoretical and *A*pplied *M*echanics—17

IV *i*nitial *v*elocity—17

*intra*venous—17

*in*voice *v*alue—9

IVA *in*travehicular *a*ctivity—17

IVS *I*nternational *V*oluntary *S*ervice—2

IW *i*nside *w*idth—9

*I*sle of *W*ight—27

*i*sotopic *w*eight—17

IWA *I*nternational *W*oodworkers of *A*merica—21

IWB *I*ntergalactic *W*orld *B*rain (underground press service)—22

IWC *I*nternational *W*haling Commission—12

IWG Iowa-Illinois Gas and Electric Co.—9A

IWP *i*ndicative *w*orld *p*lan for agricultural development (of FAO)—13

IWR *i*nfrared *w*arning *r*eceiver—17

IWW *I*ndustrial *W*orkers of the *W*orld ("wobblies")—21

J Standard Oil Co. (New Jersey)—9A

JA *j*oint *a*ccount—9

*j*oint *a*gent—9

*j*udge *a*dvocate—4

JAC Jackson Atlantic, Inc.—9A

*J*unior *A*ssociation of Commerce—10

JAE The Jaeger Machine Co.—9A

JAG *J*udge *A*dvocate *G*eneral—4

JAMA *J*ournal of the *A*merican Medical *A*ssociation—17, 22

JANAIR *j*oint *A*rmy-*N*avy *air*craft—4, 14

JAL *J*apan *A*ir *L*ines—1

JAT *J*ugoslovenski *A*ero *T*ransport (Yugoslavian Airlines)—1

JATO *j*et-*a*ssisted *t*akeoff—1, 14

JATP *J*azz *A*t *T*he *P*hilharmonic—25

J&B *J*usterini & *B*rooks (scotch whiskey)—3

JB *J*uris *B*accalaureus (Bachelor of Law)—5

JBS John's Bargain Stores Corp.—9B

JC *J*esus *C*hrist—8, 16

*J*ulius *C*aesar—29

*J*unior *C*hamber of Commerce ("Jaycees")—10

*j*unior *c*ollege—23

JCB *J*uris *C*anonici *B*accalaureus (Bachelor of Canon Law)—5

*J*uris *C*ivilis *B*accalaureus (Bachelor of Civil Law)—5

JCD *J*uris *C*anonici *D*octor (Doctor of Canon Law)—5

*J*uris *C*ivilis *D*octor (Doctor of Civil Law)—5

JCL *J*ohnny-*c*ome-*l*ately—8

*J*uris *C*anonici *L*icentiatus (Licentiate in Canon Law)—5

JCP J.C. Penney Co., Inc.—9A

JCS *J*oint *C*hiefs of *S*taff—4

JD *J*une and *D*ecember—9

*J*uris *D*octor (Doctor of Law, or Doctor of Jurisprudence)—5

*j*uvenile *d*elinquent (or *de*linquency)—8, 26

JEEP (from "*GP*," *G*eneral *P*urpose vehicle)—1, 14

JET Jetronic Industries, Inc.—9B

JFK *J*ohn *F*itzgerald *K*ennedy—29

*J*ohn *F*. *K*ennedy International Airport (formerly Idlewild)—1

JG *j*unior *g*rade—4

JGA The Jeannette Glass Co.—9B

JHS *j*unior *h*igh *s*chool—23

JHU The *J*ohns *H*opkins *U*niversity—23

JI J. I. Case Co.—9A

JJ *J*anuary and *J*uly—9

JJN J.J. Newberry Co.—9A

J&L *J*ones and *L*aughlin Steel Corp.—3

JL Jones and Laughlin Steel Corp.—9A

JLN Jaclyn, Inc.—9B

JLP Jefferson Lake Petrochemicals of Canada, Ltd.—9B

JM *J*ohns-*M*anville Corp.—3, 9A

JMY Jamesway Corp.—9B

JNJ Johnson & Johnson—9A

JNR Japan National Railways—1

JO junior officer (s)—1

JOB General Employment Enterprises, Inc.—9B

JOBS Job Opportunities in the Business Sector—3, 14

JOIDES Joint Oceanographic Institutes deep earth sampling—17

JOL Jonathan Logan, Inc.—9A

JOR Earl M. Jorgensen Co.—9A

JOS Jostens, Inc.—9A

JOY Joy Manufacturing Co.—9A

JP Jefferson-Pilot Co.—9A

jet propulsion—1

justice of the peace—7

JPL Jet Propulsion Laboratories ((of California Institute of Technology)—17

JPM J.P. Morgan and Co.—9A

JPN The Japan Fund, Inc.—9A

JRV Jervis Corp.—9B

JSC Johnson Service Co.—9A

JSD Juris Scientiae Doctor (Doctor of Scientific Law)—5

JSP Jessop Steel Co.—9B

JUD Juris Utriusque Doctor (Doctor of Civil and Canon Law)—5

JUP The Jupiter Corp.—9B

JV junior varsity ("jayvees")—11

JW Jehovah's Witnesses—16

JWB Jewish Welfare Board—16

JWC Jim Walter Corp.—9A

JW&NW Jamestown, Westfield & Northwestern Railroad—1

JWT J. Walter Thompson Co.—3

JWV Jewish War Veterans—2

K potassium (from kalium)—17A

Kellogg Co.—9A

KA kiloampere—17

KAL Kalvex, Inc.—9B

Korean Air Lines—1

KAN The Kansas Power and Light Co.—9A

KANU Kenyan African National Union—12, 14

KAV Kavanau Real Estate Trust—9B

KAY Kay Jewelry Stores, Inc.—9B

KB Kaufman and Broad, Inc.—9A, 9B

King's Bench—12

king's bishop (chess)—11

Knight Bachelor—28

KBC Kilembe Copper Cobalt, Ltd.—9B

KBE Knight Commander of the Most Excellent Order of the British Empire—28

KBI Kawecki Berylco Industries, Inc.—9A

KBP king's bishop's pawn (chess)—11

KBR Keebler Co.—9A

KC Kansas City—27

kennel club—11

kilocycle—17

King's Counsel—12

Knight Commander—28

Knights of Columbus—2, 16

KCB Knight Commander of the Bath—28

KCC kathode (cathode) closure contraction—17

KCCH Knight Commander of the Court of Honor—28

KCG Kaiser Cement and Gypsum Co.—9A

KCH Ketchum and Co., Inc.—9B

KCMG Knight Commander of the Most Distinguished Order of St. Michael and St. George—28

KCS Kansas City Southern Railroad—1

kilocycles per second—17

KCSG Knight Commander of the Ancient Order of St. Gregory the Great (the Vatican)—28

KCSI *K*night *C*ommander of the Order of the *S*tar of *I*ndia—28

KCVO *K*night *C*ommander of the Royal *V*ictorian *O*rder—28

KD Katz Drug Co.—9B

*k*nocked *d*own—9

KDE Walter Kidde and Co.—9A

KDT King's Department Stores, Inc.—9A

K&E *K*enyon and *E*ckhardt Co.—3

KE *k*inetic *e*nergy—17

KEL Keller Industries, Inc.—9A

KEN The Kendall Co.—9A

KES Keystone Consolidated Industries, Inc.—9A

KEV *k*ilo*e*lectron *v*olt—17

KEY Keystone Industries, Inc.—9B

KFC Kentucky Fried Chicken Corp.—9A

KFD Kingsford Co.—9B

KFM Kroehler Manufacturing Co.—9A

KG *k*ilo*g*ram—17

*K*night of the Order of the *G*arter—28

S.S. Kresge Co.—9A

KGB *K*omitet *G*osudarstvennoe *B*ezupasnosti (Russian Secret Police)—12

KGE Kansas Gas and Electric Co.—9A, 9B

KGF *k*ilo*g*ram *f*orce—17

KGM *k*ilo*g*ram *m*eter—17

KGR *k*ilo*g*rain—17

KI Kaiser Industries Corp.—9B

KIA *k*illed *i*n *a*ction—4

KIAS *k*not-*i*ndicated *a*ir *s*peed—1

KIN Kin-Ark Oil Co.—9B

KIP *k*ilo*p*ound (1,000 pounds)—14, 17

KIR Kirsch Co.—9A

KISS *k*eep *i*t *s*imple, *s*tupid—8, 14

KIT Kit Manufacturing Co.—9B

KJV *K*ing *J*ames *V*ersion (Bible)—16

KKK *K*u *K*lux *K*lan—2

KKP *k*ing's *k*night's *p*awn (chess)—11

KKT *k*ing's *k*night (chess)—11

KKTP *k*ing's *k*nigh*t*'s *p*awn (chess)—11

KL *k*ilo*l*iter—17

KLK Kliklok Corp.—9B

KLM KLM Royal Dutch Airlines —9A

*K*oninklijke *L*uchtvaart *M*aatschappij (airline, Netherlands)—1

KLR I.B. Kleinert Rubber Co.—9B

KLT Kansas City Power and Light Co.—9A

KLU Kaiser Aluminum and Chemical Corp.—9A

KM *k*ilo*m*eter—17

KMB Kimberly-Clark Corp.—9A

KMC *k*ilo*m*ega*c*ycle—17

KMG Kerr-McGee Corp.—9A

KML Kane-Miller Corp.—9B

KMT Kennametal, Inc.—9B

*K*uo*m*in*t*ang (Nationalist Party, Republic of China)—8, 12

KN Kennecott Copper Co.—9A

*k*ing's *k*night (chess)—11

KNS Kinney National Service, Inc.—9A

KNSM *K*oninklijke *N*ederlandsche *S*toomboot - *M*aatschappij (Royal Netherlands Steamship Company)—1

KNT Knott Hotels Corp—9B

KNY The Coca-Cola Bottling Co. of New York, Inc.—9A

KO Coca-Cola Co.—9A

*k*nock*o*ut ("kayo")—8, 11

KOA *K*ampgrounds *o*f *A*merica, Inc.—3

KOC Kewanee Oil Co.—9B

KOE Koehring Co.—9A

KO&G *K*ansas, *O*klahoma & *G*ulf Railroad—1

KOL Kollmorgen Corp.—9B

KOP Koppers Co., Inc.—9A

KP *k*ing's *p*awn (chess)—11
    *kit*chen *p*olice—4, 8
    *K*night of the Order of St. *Pa*-trick—28
    *K*nights of *P*ythias—2
KPH *k*ilometers *p*er *h*our—1
KPL Kaneb Pipe Line Co.—9B
KR *k*ing's *r*ook (chess)—11
    The Kroger Co.—9A
    *kr*ypton—17A
KRP *k*ing's *r*ook's *p*awn (chess)—11
KSF Quaker State Oil Refining Corp.—9A
KSL The Kissell Co.—9B
KSU Kansas City Southern Industries, Inc.—9A
    *K*ansas *S*tate *U*niversity—23
KT Katy Industries, Inc.—9A
    *k*ilo*t*on—17
    *K*night of the Order of the *T*histle—28
    *K*nights *T*emplar—2
KTN Kenton Corp.—9B
KU Kentucky Utilities Co.—9A
KV *k*ilo*v*olt—17
    *K*öchel-*V*erzeichnis (list of Mozart's works)—25
KVA *k*ilo*v*olt*a*mpere—17
KVAH *k*ilo*v*olt*a*mpere *h*our—17
KVS Kirby Industries, Inc.—9B
KVU Kleer-Vu Industries, Inc.—9B
KW Kelsey-Hayes Co.—9A
    *k*ilo*w*att—17
KWH *k*ilo*w*att *h*our—17
KYR Kayser-Roth Corp.—9A
KZ Kysor Industrial Corp.—9B

L Sinclair Oil Corp.—9A
L&A *L*ouisiana & *A*rkansas Railroad—1
LA *l*anthanum—17A
    *L*atin *A*merica—27
    *l*aw *a*gent—26

    *l*etter of *a*uthority—9
    *l*ocal *a*gent—9
    *L*os *A*ngeles—27
    *l*ow *a*ltitude—1
LAA *L*os *A*ngeles *A*irways—1
LAB *L*loyd *A*ereo *B*oliviano (Bolivian Airline)—1
LAC *l*eading *a*ir*c*raftsman—4
LACC *L*os *A*ngeles *C*ity *C*ollege—23
LACE *l*ysergic *a*cid *c*rypto*e*thelane—14, 17
LACSA *L*íneas *A*éreas *C*ostarricenses *S*ociedad *A*nonima (Costa Rican Airlines)—1
LACW *l*eading *a*ir*c*rafts*w*oman—4
LAD LaSalle-Deitch Co.—9B
LAF Lafayette Radio Electronics Corp.—9B
    *L*ouisiana *F*rench—15
LAFTA *L*atin-*A*merican *F*ree *T*rade *A*ssociation—12, 14
LAG L'Aiglon Apparel, Inc.—9B
LAI *L*inee *A*eree *I*taliane (Italian Air Lines)—1
LALO *l*ow *a*ltitude *o*bservation—4, 14
LAMP *L*unar *A*nalysis and *M*apping *P*rogram—14, 17
LANICA *L*ineas *A*ereas de *Nica*ragua (Nicaraguan Airlines)—1, 14
LAS *l*arge *a*stronomical *s*atellite—17
LASER *l*ight *a*mplification by *s*timulated *e*mission of *r*adiation—14, 17
LASH *l*ighter *a*broad *sh*ip—1, 14
LASV *l*ow *a*ltitude *s*upersonic *ve*hicle—1
LAT *l*ocal *a*pparent *t*ime—30
LATS *l*ong-*a*cting *t*hyroid-stimulating factor—14, 17
LAU The Lau Blower Co.—9B
LAV *L*inea *A*eropostal *V*enezolana (Venezuelan air line)—1
LAW *l*ight *a*ntitank (or *a*ssault) *w*eapon—4
LB LaBarge, Inc.—9B
    *l*anding *b*arge—4

*li*bra (Latin pound)—8

*li*ght *b*omber—4

*Li*tterarum *B*accalaureus (Bachelor of Letters)—5

LBJ *L*yndon *B*aines *J*ohnson—29

LBL *L*and *Be*tween the *L*akes (of Tennessee Valley Authority)—27

LBP *l*ength *b*etween *p*erpendiculars—17

LBY Liberty Fabrics of New York, Inc.—9B

L&C *L*ancaster & *C*hester Railroad—1

LC *l*anding *c*raft—4

*l*eft *c*enter—11

*l*eft *c*orner—11

*l*etter of *c*redit—9

Library of Congress—6

*l*oco *c*itato (in the place cited)—19

*l*ower *c*ase—22

LCA *L*ake *C*entral *A*irlines—1

*l*anding *c*raft, *a*ssault—4

*l*ower *c*ase *a*lphabet—22

*L*utheran *C*hurch in *A*merica—16

LCC *l*anding *c*ontrol *c*raft—4

*L*aunch *C*ontrol *C*enter (of NASA)—17

LCD *l*ocal *c*limatological *d*ata—27

*l*owest *c*ommon *d*enominator—17

LCE Lone Star Cement Corp.—9A

LCF *L*aunch *C*ontrol *F*acility (of NASA)—17

*l*owest *c*ommon *f*actor—17

LCI *l*anding *c*raft, *i*nfantry—4

LCL *l*ess-than-*c*arload *l*ot—9

LCM *l*anding *c*raft, *m*echanized—4

*l*east (or *l*owest) *c*ommon *mul*tiple—17

LCMS *L*utheran *C*hurch-*M*issouri *S*ynod—16

LCN *L*a *C*osa *N*ostra (lit. "our thing"—the mafia)—8

LCR Lanvin-Charles of the Ritz, Inc.—9A

LCSS *l*and-*c*ombat *s*upport *s*ystem—4

LCT *l*anding *c*raft, *t*ank(s)—4

*l*ocal *c*ivil *t*ime—30

LCU *l*anding *c*raft, *u*tility—4

LCVP *l*anding *c*raft, *v*ehicles and *p*ersonnel—4

LD *l*aus *D*eo (praise to God)—16

*l*eft *d*efense—11

*l*ethal *d*ose—17

*l*ong *d*istance—9

*L*ow *D*utch—15

LDF *L*egal *D*efense and Education Fund, Inc. (of NAACP)—2

LDME *l*aser *d*istance-*m*easuring equipment—17

LDN Leeds and Northrup Co.—9A

LDOPA *l*evo*d*ihydro*x*y*p*henyl*al*anine—17

LDP Leasco Data Processing Equipment Corp.—9A, 9B

LDS *L*atter-*D*ay *S*aints (Mormons)—16

*l*aus *D*eo *s*emper (praise to God always)—16

LDX *l*ong-*d*istance *x*erography—17

LDY Lundy Electronics and Systems, Inc.—9B

LE *l*eft *e*nd—11

*l*ow *e*xplosive—17

LEAA *L*aw *E*nforcement *A*ssistance *A*dministration—6

LEB *l*ower *e*quipment *b*ay—17

LEE Lee Motor Products, Inc.—9B

LEH Lehigh Valley Industries, Inc.—9A

LEM The Lehman Corp.—9A

*l*unar *e*xcursion *m*odule—14, 17

LER Lerner Stores Corp.—9B

LES Leslie Fay, Inc.—9B

LEV Levitz Furniture Corp.—9B

*l*unar *e*xcursion *v*ehicle—14, 17

LF *l*eft *f*ield (or *f*ielder)—11

*l*ow *f*requency—17

LFB Leverage Fund of Boston—9A

LFC LFC Financial Corp.—9A

LFE *L*aboratory *f*or *E*lectronics, Inc.—3

LFE Corp.—9A

LFR Lee Filter Corp.—9B

LG Laclede Gas Co.—9B

*l*eft *g*uard—11

*L*ow *G*erman—15

LGL Lynch Corp.—9B

LGM *l*ittle *g*reen *m*en—8

LGS Louisiana Gas Service Co.—9B

LGW Longines-Wittnauer Watch Co., Inc.—9B

LGY Langley Corp.—9B

LH *l*eft *h*alfback—11

*l*eft *h*and—17, 25

*l*uteinizing *h*ormone—17

LHA *l*ocal *h*our *a*ngle—27

LHB *l*eft *h*alfback—11

LHD *L*itterarum *H*umaniorum *D*octor (Doctor of Human Letters, or Humanities)—5

L&HR *L*ehigh & *H*udson *R*iver Railroad—1

LI *l*ight *i*nfantry—4

*l*ithium—17A

*L*ong *I*sland—27

LIAT *L*eeward *I*slands *A*ir Transport—1, 14

LIE *L*ong *I*sland *E*xpressway—1

LIFO *l*ast *i*n, *f*irst *o*ut—9, 14

LIH Quebec Lithium Corp.—9B

LIL Long Island Lighting Co.—9A

LIM *l*inear-*i*nduction-*m*otion engine—1, 14

LIN Lily Lynn, Inc.—9B

LIO The Lionel Corp.—9A

LIRR *L*ong *I*sland *R*ailroad—1

LIT Litton Industries, Inc.—9A

LIU *L*ong *I*sland *U*niversity—23

LJ Libby-McNeil and Libby—9A

LK Lockheed Aircraft Corp.—9A

LKK Lake Shore Mines, Ltd.—9B

LKS Lucky Stores, Inc.—9A

L&L *l*ove and *l*iquor—8

LL *L*ate (or *L*ow) *L*atin—15

*l*eased *l*ine—9

*l*oco *l*audato (in the place quoted)—19

*l*oose-*l*eaf—9

LLA Lilli Ann Corp.—9B

LLB *l*eft *l*inebacker—11

*L*egum *B*accalaureus (Bachelor of Law)—5

LLC Liberty Loan Corp.—9A

LLD *l*actobacillus *l*actis *d*orner factor—17

*L*egum *D*octor (Doctor of Law)—5

LLI Lithonia Lighting, Inc.—9B

LLM *L*egum *M*agister (Master of Law)—5

LLRV *l*unar *l*anding *r*eserve *v*ehicle—17

LLV *l*unar *l*ogistics *v*ehicle—17

LLX Louisiana Land and Exploration Co.—9A

L&M *L*iggett and *M*yers (cigarettes)—3

LM *L*icentiate in *M*edicine—5

Liggett and Myers, Inc.—9A

*l*ong *m*easure (hymns)—25

*L*ord *M*ayor—28

*L*ouisiana *M*idland Railroad—1

*l*unar *m*odule (pronounced "lem")—17

LME *L*ondon *M*etal *E*xchange—9

LMP *L*iterary *M*arket*p*lace—22

LMR LaMaur, Inc.—9B

LMS Lamson and Sessions Co.—9A

LMT *l*ocal *m*ean *t*ime—30

LMTD *l*og *m*ean *t*emperature *d*ifference—17

L&N *L*ouisville & *N*ashville Railroad—1

LN *l*iquid *n*itrogen—17

Louisville & Nashville Railroad Co.—9A

L&NE *L*ehigh & *N*ew *E*ngland Railroad—1

LNG *l*iquefied *n*atural *g*as—9

LNP&W *L*aramie, *N*orth *P*ark & *W*estern Railroad—1

LNR *L*eonard *R*efineries, *I*nc.—9A

LNS *L*iberation *N*ews *S*ervice (underground press association)—22

LNT Lee Enterprises, Inc.—9B

L&NW *L*ouisiana & *N*orth *W*est Railroad—1

LNX Lenox, Inc.—9B

LNY Lane Bryant, Inc.—9A

LO *l*ubricating *o*il—1
*l*unar *o*rbiter—17

LOA *l*eave *o*f *a*bsence—8, 9
*l*ength *o*ver *a*ll—9

LOB *l*eft *o*n *b*ase—11

LOC Locke Manufacturing Co., Inc.—9B

LOF *L*ibbey-*O*wens-*F*ord Co.—3

LOFT *l*ow *f*requency *t*rans-ionospheric satellite—14, 17

LOG Logistics Industries Corp.—9B

LOH *l*ight *o*bservation *h*elicopter—1, 4
Loehmann's, Inc.—9B

LOI *l*etter *o*f *i*nstruction—9
*l*unar-*o*rbit *i*nsertion—17

LOK Lockwood, Kessler and Bartlett, Inc.—9B

LOLA *l*unar-*o*rbit *l*anding *a*pproach—14, 17

LON Londontown Manufacturing Co.—9A

LOOM *L*oyal *O*rder *o*f *M*oose—2

LOP *l*ine *o*f *p*osition—27

LOP&G *L*ive *O*ak, *P*erry & *G*ulf Railroad—1

LOR Loral Corp.—9A
*l*unar-*o*rbit *r*endezvous—17

LORAN *l*ong-*r*ange *a*id to *n*avigation, or *l*o*n*g-*r*ange *n*avigation—14, 27

LORL *l*arge *o*rbital *r*esearch *l*aboratory—17

LOS *l*ine *o*f *s*ight—17
*l*oss *o*f *s*ight—17

LOSS *l*arge-*o*bject *s*alvage *s*ystem—4, 14

LOT *l*arge *o*ptical *t*elescope—14, 17

LOU Louisville Gas and Electric Co.—9A

LOX *l*iquid *o*xygen—17

LP *l*aunch *p*ad—4, 17
The Lehigh Press, Inc.—9B
*l*ow *p*ressure—17
*l*ong *p*laying—8, 25

LPF *l*eukocytosis-*p*romoting *f*actor—17

LPG *l*iquefied *p*etroleum *g*as—9

LPGA *L*adies *P*rofessional *G*olfers' *A*ssociation—11

LPI LaPointe Industries, Inc.—9B

LPIU *L*ithographers and *P*hotoengravers *I*nternational *U*nion—21

LPN *l*icensed *p*ractical *n*urse—5

LPS Lord Privy Seal—28

LPT Lehigh Portland Cement Co.—9A

LR Lee National Corp.—9B
Lloyd's Register—22

LRBM *l*ong-*r*ange *b*allistic *m*issile—4

LRCP *L*icentiate, *R*oyal *C*ollege of *P*hysicians—28

LRCS *L*icentiate, *R*oyal *C*ollege of *S*urgeons—28

LRF *l*aser *r*ange *f*inder—4, 17

LRI Lea-Ronal, Inc.—9B

LRL *l*unar *r*eceiving *l*aboratory—17

L&S *L*aurinsburg & *S*outhern Railroad—1

LS *l*egal *s*ignature—9
*l*eft *s*afety—11
*l*eukocytic *s*erum—17
*l*ibrary *s*cience—23
*L*icentiate in *S*urgery—5
*l*ocus *s*igilli (the place of the seal)—19
*L*ouisiana *S*outhern Railroad—1
Louis Sherry, Inc.—9B

LSC Latrobe Steel Co.—9A

*l*oco *supra citato* (in the place cited above)—19

LSD *l*anding *s*hip, *d*ock—4

*l*ibrae, *s*olidi, *d*enarii (pounds, shilling, pence)—9, 19

*l*ime *j*uice, *s*cotch, *D*rambuie (cocktail)—8

*l*ysergic acid *d*iethylamide—8, 17

LSE *L*ondon *S*tock *E*xchange—9

LSG Lone Star Gas Co.—9A

LS&I *L*ake *S*uperior & *I*shpeming Railroad—1

LSI *l*anding *s*hip, *i*nfantry—4

*l*arge-*s*cale *i*ntegration—17

Lear-Siegler, Inc.—9A

LSL *l*anding *s*hip, *l*ogistic—4

LSM *l*anding *s*hip, *m*edium—4

LSMFT *L*ucky *S*trikes *M*ean *F*ine *To*bacco—3

LSO Leesona Corp.—9A

LSP Lodge and Shipley Co.—9B

LSS *l*ifesaving *s*ervice—2

*l*ife *s*upport *s*ystem—17

LST *l*anding *s*hip, *t*ank—4

*l*ocal *s*idereal *t*ime—30

*l*ocal *s*tandard *t*ime—30

M. Lowenstein and Sons, Inc.—9A

LSU *L*ouisiana *S*tate *U*niversity—23

LT *l*eft *t*ackle—11

*l*etter *t*elegram—22

*l*ocal *t*ime—30

*l*ong *t*on—9

*l*ow *t*ension—17

National Lead Co.—9A

LTA *l*ighter *t*han *a*ir—1

LTV Aerospace Corp.—9B

LTC Leaseway Transportation Corp.—9A

*L*ieutenant *C*olonel—4

LTE LTV Electrosystems, Inc.—9B

LTH *l*uteo*t*rophic *h*ormone—17

LTL *l*ess-*t*han-carload (or truckload) *l*ots—9

LTV Ling Altec, Inc.—9B

LTR Loew's Theatres, Inc.—9A, 9B

LTV *L*ing-*T*emco-*V*ought, Inc.—3, 9B

LTX *L*evin-*T*ownsend *C*omputer Corp.—9A, 9B

LU *l*utetium—17A

LUB *l*east *u*pper *b*ound (mathematics)—17

LUC Lukens Steel Co.—9A

LUD Ludlow Corp.—9A

LUF *l*east *u*sable *f*requency—17

LULACS *L*eague of *U*nited *L*atin-*A*merican *C*itizens—2, 14

LV *l*aunch *v*ehicle—17

*L*ehigh *V*alley Railroad—1

*l*ow *v*oltage—17

LVN *l*icensed *v*ocational *n*urse—5

LVO Livingston Oil Co.—9A

LVT *l*anding *v*ehicle, *t*racked—4

L&W *L*ouisville & *W*adley Railroad—1

LW *l*eft *w*ing—11

LWF *L*utheran *W*orld *F*ederation—16

LWL *l*ength at *w*ater*l*ine—1, 9

*l*imited *w*ar *l*aboratory—4

LWM *l*ow-*w*ater *m*ark—1

LWOP *l*eave *w*ithout *p*ay—9

LWOS *l*ow-*w*ater *o*rdinary *s*prings—27

LWP *l*eave *w*ith *p*ay—9

LWS *L*ate *W*est *S*axon—15

LWV *L*eague of *W*omen *V*oters—2

LY *l*ast *y*ear (or *y*ear's)—9

Lykes-Youngstown Corp.—9A

LZ *l*anding *z*one—4

The Lubrizol Corp.—9A

M Marcor Co.—9A

M&A *M*ississippi & *A*labama Railroad—1

*M*issouri and *A*rkansas Railroad—1

MA *M*agister *A*rtium (Master of Arts)—5

*M*agna *A*rizona Railroad—1

*M*aritime *A*dministration—6

May Department Stores Co.—9A

mental age—23

Mexican-American—8

military academy—23

military attaché—7

milliampere—17

morning after—8

MAA *master-at-arms*—4

Medical Assistance for the Aged—7

MAAG *Military Assistance Advisory Group* (NATO)—7

MAB Mangood Corp.—9B

Medical Advisory Board—17

MAC The E.F. MacDonald Co.—9A

machine-aided cognition—14, 17

Master of Accountancy—5

midair collision—1

Military Air (or Airlift) Command—4

multiple access (to) *computer(s)*—17

MACV *Military Assistance Command, Vietnam*—4

MAD Madison Fund, Inc.—9A

mind-altering drugs—8, 14

mutual assured destruction—4

MAE Master of Aeronautical Engineering—5

Master of Art Education—5

Master of Arts in Education—5

Monroe Auto Equipment Co.—9A

MAF MacAndrews and Forbes Co.—9A

moisture and ash free—9

MAG The Magnavox Co.—9A

MAI Member, Appraisal Institute—28

Microwave Associates, Inc.—9B

MAK The Macke Co.—9A

MAL Mohawk Airlines, Inc.—9B

MALD Master of Arts in Law and Diplomacy—5

MALS Master of Arts in Liberal Studies—5

Master of Arts in Library Science—5

MAN Manpower, Inc.—9A

MANIAC *mechanical and numerical integrator and computer*—9, 14

MAO *monoamine oxidase* (enzyme)—17

MAP Maine Public Service Co.—9B

marketing assistance program—7, 9

modified American plan (hotel service)—3, 8

MAPCO Mid-America Pipeline Co.—3, 14

MAR Maremont Corp.—9A

Master of Arts in Religion—5

MARC *machine readable catalog*—14, 17

MARS *military affiliate radio system*—2, 4, 14

military airborne radar system—4, 14

MAS Masco Corp.—9A, 9B

MASC *magnetic spin control*—14, 17

MASER *microwave amplification by stimulated emission of radiation*—14, 17

MASH *mobile army surgical hospital*—4, 14

MAT Master of Arts in Teaching—5

Mattel, Inc.—9A

MATC Military Air Transport Command—4

MATS Military Air Transport Service—4

MAU Maule Industries, Inc.—9B

M&B Marianna & Blountstown Railroad—1

May and Baker drugs—17

MB Medicinae Baccalaureus (Bachelor of Medicine)—5

Miami Beach—27

Militia Bureau—4

Milton Bradley Co.—9A

MBA Master of Business Administration—5

MBC *magnetic bias coil* (or *control*)—17

MBE Member of the Most Excellent

Order of the *British Em-
pire*—28
M&BR *Meridian & Bigbee River* Rail-
road—1
MBR MWA Co.—9B
MBRV *maneuverable ballistic reentry
vehicle*—4
MBS Maul Brothers, Inc.—9B
Mutual Broadcasting System—25
MBT *main battle tank*—4
MC *Maine Central Railroad*—1
Marine Corps—4
Master of Ceremonies ("em-
cee")—8, 25
Medical Corps—4
megacycle—17
Member of Congress—7
Member of Council—7
methyl cholenthrene—17
Mid-Con, Inc.—9A
Middle Creek Railroad—1
Military Cross—28
Mississippi Central Railroad—1
multichannel—17
municipal code—7
MCA MCA, Inc.—9A
Music Corporation of America—3,
25
MCC Mesta Machine Co.—9A
MCD McDonald Corp.—9A
MCE *Master of Civil Engineering*—5
MCG Michigan Gas Utilities Co.—9A
MCH *mean corpuscular hemoglo-
bin*—17
Michigan Chemical Corp.—9B
MCHC *mean corpuscular hemoglobin
concentration*—17
MCJ *Master of Comparative Ju-
risprudence*—5
MCL *Master of Comparative (or Civ-
il) Law*—5
Moore and McCormack Co.,
Inc.—9A
MCO McCulloch Oil Corp. of Cali-
fornia—9B
Midland Continental Railroad—1

MCP *Master of City Planning*—5
military construction plan (or *program*)—4
MCPO *master chief petty officer*—4
MCR *Master of Comparative Religion*—5
McCord Corp.—9A
MCS *Master of Commercial Science*—5
megacycles per second—17
Merritt-Chapman and Scott Corp.
—9A
MCT Macrodyne-Chatillon Corp.
—9B
MCU *medium close-up*—25
MCV *mean corpuscular volume*—17
MD *mano destra*, or *main droite* (right
hand) (music)—19
McDonnell Douglas Corp.—9A
medical department—9, 17
Medicinae Doctor (Doctor of Medi-
cine)—5
minute difference—27
months after date—9
MDA Mapco, Inc.—9A
methyline dioxyamphetamine (hal-
lucinogen)—17
*Muscular Dystrophy Associations
of America, Inc.*—2, 17
MDAP *Mutual Defense Assistance
Program*—6
MDC Maryland Cup Co.—9A
MDE J. Ray McDermott and Co.,
Inc.—9A
MDI Medalist Industries—9B
MDK Montana-Dakota Utilities Co.
—9A
MDP Meredith Corp.—9A
MDR *minimum daily require-
ment*—17
MD&S *Macon, Dublin & Savannah
Railroad*—1
MDS *Master of Dental Surgery*—5
Mohawk Data Sciences Corp.—9B
MDT Molybdenite Corp. of Canada
Ltd.—9B
mountain daylight time—30

MDW *M*ilitary *D*istrict of *W*ashington—4

ME *m*anaging *e*ditor—22, 28

*m*arbled *e*dges—22

*M*aster of *E*ducation—5

*M*aster of *E*ngineering—5

*m*echanical *e*ngineer—28

*M*ethodist *E*piscopal—16

*M*iddle *E*nglish—15

*M*ilgo *E*lectronic Corp.—9B

*m*ining *e*ngineer—28

MEA *M*aster of *E*ngineering *A*dministration—5

The *M*ead Corp.—9A

*m*inimum *en* route *a*ltitude—1

MEC *M*errill *I*sland *M*ining Corp., Ltd.—9B

MED *m*edical *e*ngineering *d*evelopment—17

MEF *m*arine *e*xpeditionary *f*orce—4

MEG *M*edia *G*eneral, Inc.—9B

MEI *M*innesota *E*nterprises, Inc.—9A

MEM *M*ars *e*xcursion *m*odule—17

*M*em Co., Inc.—9B

MEN *M*enasco *M*anufacturing Co.—9B

MENA *M*iddle *E*ast *N*ews *A*gency—14, 22

MEO *M*edco, Inc.—9B

MEP *M*aster of *E*ngineering *P*hysics—5

MEPA *M*aster of *E*ngineering and *P*ublic *A*dministration—5

MERC *M*iddle Atlantic *E*ducational and *R*esearch *C*enter—14, 17, 23

MERCAST *M*er*c*hant Marine broad*cast*—1, 14

MES *M*elville *S*hoe Corp.—9B

*m*ore *e*ffective *s*chool (or schools)—23

MESA *M*echanics *E*ducational *S*ociety of *A*merica—14, 21

*m*odularized *e*quipment *s*torage *a*ssembly—17

MET *M*etromedia Corp.—9B

METO *M*iddle *E*ast *T*reaty *O*rganization—12, 14

MEV *m*illion *e*lectron *v*olts—17

MEW *m*icrowave *e*arly *w*arning—4

MEX *M*ississippi *E*xport Railroad—1

MEXICALI *M*e*xi*co and *Cali*fornia—14, 27

MF *m*ale and *f*emale—9

*M*arshall *F*ield and Co.—9A

*M*aster of *F*orestry—5

*m*edium *f*requency—17

*m*ezzo *f*orte (moderately loud) (music)—19

*M*iddle *F*rench—15

MFA *M*aster of *F*ine *A*rts—5

*M*en's *F*ashion *A*ssociation—10

MFC *M*ill *F*actors *C*orp.—9B

MFG *M*c*Q*uay-*N*orris *M*anufacturing Co.—9A

MFH *m*aster of *f*oxhounds—11

MFR *m*ulti*f*unction *r*adar—17

MFS *M*aster of *F*ood *S*cience—5

*M*aster of *F*oreign *S*ervice (or *S*tudy)—5

*M*ountain *F*uel *S*upply Co.—9A

MFT *M*aster of *F*oreign *T*rade—5

MFX *M*idwestern *F*inancial Corp.—9B

MFY *M*obilization *f*or *Y*outh—23

M&G *M*obile & *G*ulf Railroad—1

MG *m*achinegun—4

*m*agnesium—17A

*m*ain *g*auche (left hand) (music)—19

*m*ajor *g*eneral—4

*m*iddle *g*uard—11

*m*ilitary *g*overnment—4

*m*illi*g*ram—17

*M*onogram Industries, Inc.—9A

*M*orris *G*arage (British automobile)—1, 3

*m*yasthenia *g*ravis—17

MGA *M*agna Oil Corp.—9B

MGB *M*inisterstvo *G*osudarstvennoi *B*ezopasnosti (Soviet Ministry of State Security)—12

MGD McGregor-Doniger, Inc.—9A
*m*illions of *g*allons per *d*ay—9

MGE *m*aintenance *g*round *e*quipment—1
Mangel Stores Corp.—9B

MGI MGIC Investment Corp.—9A

MGIC *M*ortgage *G*uaranty *I*nsurance Co.—3

MGM *M*etro *G*oldwyn *M*ayer—9A, 25

MGO *m*achine*g*un *o*fficer—4

MGR McGraw-Edison Co.—9A

MGU Michigan Sugar Co.—9B

MGW G.W. Murphy Industries, Inc.—9A

MH *m*aleic *h*ydrazide—17
*m*an*h*ole—1, 9
*M*edal of *H*onor—28
*M*inneapolis *H*oneywell Corp.—3
Mobile Home Industries, Inc.—9B

MHA *M*aster of *H*ospital *A*dministration—5

MHC Manufacturers Hanover Corp.—9A

MHD *m*agneto*h*ydro*d*ynamics—17

MHE *M*aster of *H*ome *E*conomics—5

MHF *m*edium *h*igh *f*requency—17

MHG *M*iddle *H*igh *G*erman—15
Miehle-Goss-Dexter, Inc.—9A

MHL *M*aster of *H*ebrew *L*iterature—5

MHP McGraw-Hill, Inc.—9A

MHR *M*ember of the *H*ouse of *R*epresentatives—7

MHS Marriott Corp.—9A
*M*usical *H*eritage *S*ociety—22

MHT Manhattan Industries, Inc.—9A

MHW *m*ean *h*igh *w*ater—1

MI Marshall Industries—9B
*m*ilitary *i*ntelligence—4
*M*issouri-*I*llinois Railroad—1
*m*ounted *i*nfantry—4

MIA *M*aster of *I*nternational *A*ffairs—5
*m*issing *i*n *a*ction—4

MIC Microdot, Inc.—9A

MICE *M*ember, *I*nstitute of *C*ivil *E*ngineers—28

MICOM U.S. Army *M*issile *Com*mand—4, 14

MICU *m*edical *i*ntensive *c*are *u*nit—17

MICUM *M*ission *I*nteralliée de *Co*ntrole des *U*sines et des *M*ines (Inter-Allied Mission to Control Manufacturing and Mining)—12, 14

MID *M*aster of *I*ndustrial *D*esign—5
*m*ention (or *m*entioned) *i*n *d*ispatches—7
Mid-Continent Telephone Corp.—9A

MIDAS *m*issile *d*efense *a*larm *s*ystem—4, 14

MIDEM *M*arché *I*nternational du *D*isque et de l'*E*dition *M*usicale (International Record and Musical Edition Market)—12, 14, 25

MIE *M*aster of *I*ndustrial (or *I*rrigation) *E*ngineering—5

MIG *M*ikoyan and *G*urevich (designers of MIG fighter plane)—14

MIL Miles Laboratories, Inc.—9A

MILR *M*aster of *I*ndustrial and *L*abor *R*elations—5

MIM Marconi International Marine Co., Ltd.—9B

MIN Macoid Industries, Inc.—9B

MINCOM *m*in*i*aturized *com*munications—14, 17

MIP *m*onthly *i*nvestment *p*lan—9

MIR Mirro Aluminum Co.—9B

MIRV *m*ultiple *i*ndependent (or *i*ndependently targeted) (or *i*ndividually targeted) *r*eentry *ve*hicle—4, 14, 17

MIS *m*anagement *i*nformation *s*ystem—9
*M*aster of *I*nternational *S*ervice—5
Mississippi River Corp.—9A

MISER *m*icrowave *s*pace *e*lectronic *re*lay—14, 17

MISS *m*obile *i*ntegrated *s*upport *s*ystem—4, 14

MIT *M*assachusetts *I*nstitute of *T*echnology—23

MJ *M*aster of *J*ournalism—5

MJC *m*ilitary *j*unior *c*ollege—23

MJQ *M*odern *J*azz *Q*uartet—25

MJW J.W. Mays, Inc.—9A

MKC Marion Laboratories, Inc.—9A

MKE Arthur G. McKee and Co.—9A

MKS *m*eter-*k*ilogram-*s*econd—17

MKT *M*issouri-*K*ansas-*T*exas Railroad—1

ML Martin-Marietta Corp.—9A

*M*edieval (or *M*iddle) *L*atin—15

MLA *M*aster of *L*andscape *A*rchitecture—5

*M*odern *L*anguage *A*ssociation—2

MLB *M*aritime *L*abor *B*oard—6

*m*iddle *l*inebacker—11

MLD C.H. Masland and Sons—9B

MLE Marlene Industries Corp—9B

MLF *m*ulti*l*ateral nuclear *f*orce—4

MLN McLean Trucking Co.—9A

MLO Milo Electronics Corp.—9B

MLR Midland-Ross Corp.—9A

M&LS *M*anistique & *L*ake *S*uperior Railroad—1

MLS *M*aster of *L*ibrary *S*cience—5

MLW *m*ean *l*ow *w*ater—1

The Miller-Wohl Co., Inc.—9B

MLX McLouth Steel Corp.—9A

MLY Molybdenum Corp. of America—9B

M&M *M*erchants and *M*anufacturers Association—10

MM Compagnie des *M*essageries *M*aritimes (French ship line)—1

*M*aelzel's *M*etronome—25

*M*arilyn *M*onroe—29

Marine Midland Banks, Inc.—9A

*M*aster *M*ason—5

*M*aster *M*echanic—5

*M*aster of *M*usic—5

*m*illi*m*eter—17

*M*inute*m*an (missile)—4

*M*inute*m*en (organization)—2

MMC Marlennan Corp.—9A

MME *M*aster of *M*echanical (or *M*ining) *E*ngineering—5

*M*aster of *M*usic *E*ducation—5

McNeil Corp.—9A

MMF *m*agneto*m*otive *f*orce—17

MMI Mammoth Mart, Inc.—9B

MMM *m*anned *m*aneuvering module—17

*M*innesota *M*ining and *M*anufacturing Co. (3-M Co.)—3, 9A

MMO Monarch Machine Tool Co.—9A

MMRBM *m*obile *m*idrange *b*allistic *m*issile—4

MMT Midland Mortgage Investment Trust—9B

MMU *m*anned *m*aneuvering *u*nit—17

Marinduque Mining and Industrial Corp.—9B

*m*illi*m*ass *u*nit—17

MN *m*anganese—17A

*M*ay and *N*ovember—9

*M*erchant *N*avy—1

*m*oto *n*ave (motor ship)—1

MNA *M*aster of *N*ursing Administration—5

MNAS *M*ember, *N*ational *A*cademy of *S*ciences—28

MNC Masonite Corp.—9A

M&NE *M*anistee & *N*ortheastern Railroad—1

MNE *M*aster of *N*uclear *E*ngineering—5

M&NF *M*orehead and *N*orth *F*ork Railroad—1

MNP Morton-Norwich Products, Inc.—9A

MN&S *M*inneapolis, *N*orthfield and *S*outhern Railroad—1

MNS *M*aster of *N*utritional Science—5

F.W. Means and Co.—9B

MNY Management Data Corp.—9B

MO *m*ail *o*rder—9

*m*anually *o*perated—9

*m*edical *o*fficer—4

*m*odus *o*perandi (method of operation)—8, 19, 26

*m*olybdenum—17A

*m*oney *o*rder—9

Philip Morris, Inc.—9A

MOB Mobil Oil Corp.—9A

MOG Moog, Inc.—9B

MOH Mohasco Industries, Inc.—9A

MOHOLE *Mo*horovicic *hole*—14, 17

MOI *m*inistry *o*f *i*nformation—6

*m*inistry *o*f the *i*nterior—6

MOIG *M*aster of *O*ccupational *I*nformation and *G*uidance—5

MOL *m*anned *o*rbiting *l*aboratory—17

MOLAB *m*obile *lab*oratory—14, 17

MON Monon Railroad—9A

MONY *M*utual Life Insurance Co. of *N*ew *Y*ork—3

MOP *m*anned *o*rbiting *p*latform—14, 17

Missouri Pacific Railroad—9A

MOR *m*iddle *o*f the *r*oad (pop music)—8, 25

Morse Electro Products Corp.—9B

MORC *M*idget *O*cean *R*acing *C*lub yachts—11

MORL *m*anned *o*rbiting *r*esearch *l*aboratory—17

MORS *M*ilitary *O*perations *R*esearch *S*ociety—4

MOS *m*anagement (or *m*anufacturing) *o*perating *s*ystems—9, 17

*m*etal *o*xide *s*emiconductor—17

*m*ilitary *o*ccupational *s*pecialty—4

*m*it *o*ut (without) *s*ound—8, 25

Morton's Shoe Stores, Inc.—9B

MOST *m*anned *o*rbital *s*olar *t*elescope—14, 17

MOT *m*anned *o*rbiting *t*elescope—17

Motorola, Inc.—9A

MOU Mountain States Telephone and Telegraph Co.—9A

MOUSE *m*inimum *o*rbital *u*nmanned *s*atellite of the *e*arth—14, 17

MOV Movielab, Inc.—9B

MOX Millmaster Onyx Corp.—9B

M&P *M*aryland & *P*ennsylvania Railroad—1

MP *m*achine *p*istol—4

*m*agnifying *p*ower—17

*M*cIntyre *P*orcupine *M*ines, Ltd.—9A

*m*elting *p*oint—17

*M*ember of *P*arliament—7

*M*ethodist *P*rotestant—16

*m*etropolitan *p*olice—26

*m*ilitary *p*olice—4

Missouri Pacific Railroad—1

*m*odo *p*raescripto (in the manner prescribed)—18

*m*ounted *p*olice—26

MPA *M*agazine *P*ublishers' *A*ssociation—10

*M*aster of *P*rofessional *A*ccounting—5

*M*aster of *P*ublic *A*dministration (or *A*ffairs)—5

MPAA *M*otion *P*icture *A*ssociation of *A*merica—10

MPB *m*aximum *p*articipation *b*ase—7

MPC *m*aximum *p*ermissible *c*oncentration (of radioactivity)—17

*m*ilitary *p*ayment *c*ertificate—4

MPD *M*edusa *P*ortland *C*ement Co.—9A

MPE *M*aster of *P*hysical *E*ducation—5

MPEA *M*otion *P*icture *E*xport *A*ssociation—10

MPF *m*ulti*p*urpose *f*ood—17

MPG *m*iles *p*er *g*allon—1

MPH *M*aster of *P*ublic *H*ealth—5

*m*iles *p*er *h*our—1

G.L. Murphy Co.—9A

MPHPS *m*iles *p*er *h*our *p*er *s*econd—1

MPI MPI Industries, Inc.—9B

MPL *M*aster of *P*atent *L*aw—5

Minnesota Power and Light Co.—9A, 9B

MPN Monongahela Power Co.—9B

MPO MPO Videotronics, Inc.—9B

MPS *Master of Personnel Service*—5

MPV Missouri Public Service Co.—9A

MPX *multiplex*—17

MQ *Metolquinol*—17

MQC Marquette Cement Manufacturing Co.—9A

MQF *mobile quarantine facility (of NASA)*—17

M&R *maintenance and repair*—1, 9

MR Mallory Randall Corp.—9B

milliroentgen—17

Mineral Range Railroad—1

moral rearmament—16

motivational research—17

MRA *Menswear Retailers of America*—10

moral rearmament—16

MRAS *Member, Royal Academy of Sciences*—28

MRB *Modification Review Board*—4, 6

MRBM *medium-range ballistic missile*—4

MRC *Metals Reserve Co.*—6

Mississippi River Commission—6

MRCP *Member, Royal College of Physicians*—28

MRCS *Member, Royal College of Surgeons*—28

MRE *Master of Religious Education*—5

MRF Merchants Refrigerating Co.—9B

MRK Merck and Co., Inc.—9A

MRM *Mars reconnaissance mission*—17

MRN *meteorological rocket network*—17

MRO Marathon Oil Co.—9A

MRP *Master of Regional Planning*—5

Missouri Portland Cement Co.—9A

Mouvement Républicain Populaire (Popular Republican Movement, France)—12

MRRC *Military Requirements Review Committee*—4

MRS Morse Shoe, Inc.—9A

multipurpose reusable spacecraft—17

MRSH *Member, Royal Society of Health*—28

MRSV *maneuverable recoverable space vehicle*—17

MRV *maneuvering reentry vehicle*—17

MRX Memorex Corp.—9A

MRY P.R. Mallory and Co., Inc.—9A

M&S *medical and surgical*—17

MS *mail steamer*—1

mano sinistra (left hand) (music)—19

manuscript—22

Master of Science—5

Master of Surgery—5

March and September—9

McCrory Corp.—9A, 9B

meters per second—17

military science—4, 23

months after sight—9

most severe—17

motor ship—1

multiple sclerosis—17

MSA *Malaysia-Singapore Airlines*—1

Master of Science in Agriculture—5

Mesa Petroleum Co.—9B

Mutual Security Agency—6

MSAE *Master of Science in Aeronautical Engineering*—5

MSAM *Master of Science in Applied Mechanics*—5

MSB Mesabi Trust—9A

MSBA *Master of Science in Business Administration*—5

MSBC Master of Science in Building Construction—5

MSC Manned Spacecraft Center (of NASA)—17

minesweeper, coastal—4

MSCE Master of Science in Civil Engineering—5

MSCP Master of Science in Community Planning—5

MSD Master of Science in Dentistry—5

most significant digit—17

MSE Massey-Ferguson, Ltd.—9A

Master of Science in Education—5

Master of Science in Engineering—5

Midwest Stock Exchange—9

MSEE Master of Science in Electrical Engineering—5

MSEM Master of Science in Engineering Mechanics—5

Master of Science in Engineering of Mines—5

MSF The Mansfield Tire and Rubber Co.—9B

Master of Science in Forestry—5

minesweeper, fleet—4

MSFM Master of Science in Forest Management—5

MSFN manned space-flight network (of NASA)—17

MSG Madison Square Garden Corp.—9A

monosodium glutamate—17

MSGM Master of Science in Government Management—5

MSH melanocyte-stimulating hormone—17

Mohs' scale hardness—9, 17

MSHA Master of Science in Hospital Administration—5

MSHE Master of Science in Home Economics—5

MSI Movimento Sociale Italiano (Italian Social Movement)—12

MSIE Master of Science in Industrial Engineering—5

MSJ Master of Science in Journalism—5

MSL Master of Science in Linguistics—5

mean sea level—27

Minneapolis & St. Louis Railroad—1

MSL Industries, Inc.—9A

MSM Master of Sacred Music—5

Master of Science in Music—5

Mott's Super Markets, Inc.—9B

MSME Master of Science in Mechanical Engineering—5

MSN Master of Science in Nursing—5

MSPE Master of Science in Physical Education—5

MSPH Master of Science in Public Health—5

MSPHE Master of Science in Public Health Engineering—5

MSP&SSM Minneapolis, St. Paul & Sault Ste. Marie Railroad—1

MSR missile site radar—17

MSS manuscripts—22

mariner scout ship—1

Master of Social Science (or Service)—5

Mission Corp.—9A

MSSE Master of Science in Sanitary Engineering—5

MST Master of Science in Teaching—5

Mercantile Stores Co., Inc.—9A

mountain standard time—30

MSTS Military Sea Transport Service—4

MSU Michigan State University—23

Middle South Utilities, Inc.—9A

M&SV Mississippi & Skuna Valley Railroad—1

MSW *M*aster of *S*ocial *W*elfare (or *W*ork)—5

MT *m*echanical *t*ranslation—17

*mega*t*on*—17

*m*etric *t*on—17

*M*idland *T*erminal Railroad—1

*m*ountain *t*ime—30

MTA *m*edical *t*echnical *a*ssistant—17

*M*etropolitan *T*ransportation *Au*thority (New York City)—1, 6

MTB *M*ichigan *S*eamless *T*ube Co.—9A

MTBF *m*ean *t*ime *b*etween *f*ailures—17

MTC Monsanto Co.—9A

MTD *m*itte *t*ales *d*oses (send such doses)—18

MTDS *m*arine *t*actical *d*ata *s*ystem—1, 9

MTE Mite Corp.—9B

*m*ultisystem *t*est *e*quipment—17

MTF *m*ean *t*ime to *f*ailure—17

MTI *m*oving *t*arget *i*ndicator—4

MTO *M*editerranean *t*heater of *op*erations—4

*m*otor *t*ransport *o*fficer—4

MTP *m*obilization *t*raining *p*rogram—4

The Montana Power Co.—9A

MTR The Muter Co.—9B

MTS *m*otor *t*urbine *s*hip (or *t*win *s*crew)—1

MTT Metropolitan Edison Co.—9A

MTUR *m*ean *t*ime between *u*nscheduled *r*emovals—1

MU *m*ultiple *u*nit (railroads)—1

MUL Multi-Amp Corp.—9B

MUN Munsingwear, Inc.—9A

MUP *M*aster of *U*rban *P*lanning—5

MUR Murphy Oil Corp.—9A

MV *m*arket *v*alue—9

*m*ean *v*ariation—17

*mega*v*olt*—17

mezza *v*oce (with half the voice) (music)—19

*M*idland *V*alley Railroad—1

*m*illi*v*olt—17

*m*otor *v*essel—1

MVA *mega*v*olt* *a*mpere—17

*M*issouri *V*alley *A*uthority—6

MVC *M*issouri *V*alley *C*onference—11

MVD *M*inisterstvo *V*nutrennikh *D*el (Ministry of Internal Affairs, Soviet Union)—12

MVO *M*ember of the Royal *V*ictorian *O*rder—28

MVP *m*ost *v*aluable *p*layer—11

MVS Movie Star, Inc.—9B

MVW Mount Vernon Mills, Inc.—9B

MW *m*edium *w*ave—17

*mega*w*att*—17

*micro*w*ave*—17

Midwest Rubber Reclaiming—9B

*milli*w*att*—17

*M*innesota *W*estern Railroad—1

*M*ontana *W*estern Railroad—1

*M*ost *W*orshipful (or *W*orthy)—28

MWA *M*odern *W*oodmen of *A*merica—2

*M*ystery *W*riters of *A*merica— 2

MWGM *M*ost *W*orthy *G*rand *M*aster—28

MWO Midwest Oil Corp.—9A

MWT *M*aster of *W*ood *T*echnology—5

MX Maxson Electronics Corp.—9B

MY The Marley Co.—9B

*m*otor *y*acht—1

MYF *M*ethodist *Y*outh *F*ellowship—16

MYG The Maytag Co.—9A

MYO Murray Ohio Manufacturing Co.—9B

MYOB *m*ind *y*our *o*wn *b*usiness—8

MZ R.H. Macy and Co., Inc.—9A

N International Nickel Co. of Canada, Ltd.—9A

*n*itrogen—17A

NA National Academician—28
National Academy—23
National Airlines—1
national army—4
National Association—9
sodium (from natrium)—17A
nautical almanac—1, 27
no account—9
North America—27
Northern Alberta Railroad—1
not applicable—9
not available—9
numerical aperture—17

NAA naphthaleneacetic acid—17
National Aeronautic Association—2
National Archery Association—11
National Association of Accountants—20
North American Aviation Corp.—3

NAACP National Association for the Advancement of Colored People—2

NAB National Association of Broadcasters—10
naval air base—4

NABAC National Association of Bank Auditors and Comptrollers—20

NABET National Association of Broadcast Engineers and Technicians—14, 20

NABISCO National Biscuit Co.—3, 14

NABS National Association of Black Students—14, 23

NAC National Can Corp.—9A

NACA National Advisory Committee for Aeronautics—6

NACE National Advisory Committee for Electronics—6

NAD National Academy of Design—20
nicotinamide adenine dinucleotide—17
no appreciable disease—17

NADA National Automobile Dealers' Association—10

NADC Naval Air Development Center—4, 17

NADGE NATO (which see) Air Defense Ground Environment—4, 14

NADP nicotinamide adenine dinucleotide phosphate—17

NAE National Academy of Engineering—20

NAEB National Association of Educational Broadcasters—23, 25

NAEBM National Association of Engine and Boat Manufacturers—10

NAFC National Association of Food Chains—10

NAHB National Association of Home Builders—10

NAHSA National Association of Hearing and Speech Agencies—2

NAIA National Association of Intercollegiate Athletics—11

NAIC National Association of Investment Clubs—2

NAIRE National Association of Internal Revenue Employees—21

NAIRO National Association of Intergroup Relations Officials—23

NAIS National Association of Independent Schools—23

NAL National Airlines, Inc.—9A
National Association of Laymen—16
New American Library—3, 22

NALC National Association of Letter Carriers of the United States of America—21

NAM National Association of Manufacturers—10

NAMA National Automatic Merchandising Association—10

NAMM National Association of Music Merchants—10

NANA North American Newspaper Alliance—14, 22

NAO Narco Scientific Industries, Inc.—9A

NAP Napco Industries, Inc.—9B

NAPALM *n*aphthene *palm*itate—14, 17

NAPAN *N*ational *A*ssociation for the *P*revention of *A*ddiction to *N*arcotics—2, 14

NAPCA *N*ational *A*ir *P*ollution *C*ontrol *A*dministration (of HEW)—6, 14

NAPM *N*ational *A*ssociation of *P*urchasing *M*anagement—20

NAR *N*ew *A*merican *R*eview—22

North American Royalties, Inc.—9B

NARA *N*arcotic *A*ddict *Re*habilitation *A*ct—7

NARAS *N*ational *A*cademy of *R*ecording *A*rts and *S*ciences—10, 14

NARC *N*ational *A*ssociation for *Re*tarded *C*hildren—2

NARDA *N*ational *A*ppliance and *Ra*dio-Television *D*ealers of *A*merica—10, 14

NAREB *N*ational *A*ssociation of *R*eal *E*state *B*oards—10

NARM *N*ational *A*ssociation of *R*ecord *M*erchandisers—10

NAS *N*ational *A*cademy of *S*ciences—17

National Service Industries, Inc.—9A

*n*aval *a*ir *s*tation—4

NASA *N*ational *A*eronautics and *S*pace *A*dministration—6, 14

NASAC *N*ational *A*ssociation of *S*cientific *A*ngling *C*lubs—11, 14

NASAO *N*ational *A*ssociation of *S*tate *A*viation *O*fficials—1, 20

NASCAR *N*ational *A*ssociation of *S*tock *C*ar *A*uto *R*acing—11, 14

NASCOM *N*ational *A*eronautics and *S*pace *A*dministration *com*munications network—6, 14

NASD *N*ational *A*ssociation of *S*ecurities *D*ealers—10

NASDAQ *N*ational *A*ssociation of *Se*curities *D*ealers' *a*utomated *q*uotations—9

NASNRC *N*ational *A*cademy of *S*ciences and *N*ational *R*esearch *C*ouncil—17

NASSP *N*ational *A*ssociation of *S*econdary *S*chool *P*rincipals—20, 23

NATAS *N*ational *A*cademy of *T*elevision *A*rts and *S*ciences—10

NATEC *N*ational *E*nvironment *Corp.*—3, 14

NATO *N*ational *A*ssociation of *T*heater *O*wners—10, 14

*N*ational *A*ssociation of *T*ravel *O*rganizations—10, 14

*N*orth *A*tlantic *T*reaty *O*rganization—12, 14

NATOUSA *N*orthern *A*frican *t*heater of *o*perations, *U*nited *S*tates *A*rmy—4, 14

NATS *N*aval *A*ir *T*ransport *S*ervice—4, 14

NAVSAT *nav*igation *sat*ellite—14, 17

NAYRU *N*orth *A*merican *Y*acht *R*acing *U*nion—11, 14

NAZI *Na*tional *So*zialist (German National Socialist Party)—12, 14

NB *N*ational *B*ellas Hess, Inc.—9B

*N*ew *B*runswick (Canada)—27

*ni*o*b*ium—17A

*n*orth*b*ound—1

*n*ota *b*ene (note well)—19

NBA *N*ational *B*asketball *A*ssociation—11

*N*ational *B*ook *A*ward—22

*N*ational *B*oxing *A*ssociation—11

NBAA *N*ational *B*usiness *A*ircraft *A*ssociation—10

NBC *N*ational *B*iscuit *Co.*—3

*N*ational *B*roadcasting *Co.*—3, 25

NBG *n*o *b*loody *g*ood—8

NBO NBO Industries—9B

NBS *N*ational *B*ureau of *S*tandards—6

NBTA *National Baton Twirling Association*—2

NC *national cemetery*—7

national coarse (screw thread designation)—9

nitrocellulose—17

noncallable—9

North Carolina—27

Nurse Corps—4

NCA *National Council on the Aging*—2

North Central Airlines—1

North Central Association—23

NCAA *National Collegiate Athletic Association*—11

NCAI *National Congress of American Indians*—2

NCAR *National Center for Atmospheric Research*—17

NCC *National Citizens' Committee*—2

NCCB *National Council of Catholic Bishops*—16

NCCD *National Council on Crime and Delinquency*—2

NCCJ *National Conference of Christians and Jews*—16

NCCM *National Council of Catholic Men*—2, 16

NCCW *National Council of Catholic Women*—2, 16

NCD North Canadian Oils, Ltd.—9B

NCDC *National Communicable Disease Center*—17

NCDH *National Committee Against Discrimination in Housing*—2

NCE *Navy civil engineer*—28

NCFA *National Cat Fanciers Association*—2

National Commission of Fine Arts—6

NCFM *National Commission on Food Marketing*—6

NCGE *National Council for Geographic Education*—23

NCH National Chemsearch Corp.—9A

NCI *National Cancer Institute*—17

National Radio Co., Inc.—9B

NCIC *National Crime Information Center* (of FBI)—6

NCK National Casket Co., Inc.—9B

NCM National Acme Co.—9A

NCO *noncommissioned officer*—4

The North American Coal Corp.—9A

NCOA *National Council on Alcoholism*—2, 17

NCOMP *National Catholic Office for Motion Pictures*—16, 25

NCR *National Cash Register* Co.—3, 9A

NCRP *National Committee on Radiation Protection*—17

NCS *Numerical Control Society*—2

NC&SL *Nashville, Chattanooga & St. Louis Railroad*—1

NCSS *National Council for the Social Studies*—20

NCWC *National Catholic Welfare Conference* (or *Council*)—16

ND National Dairy Products Corp. —9A

neodymium—17A

next day—9

no date—9

North Dakota—27

NDA *new drug application*—17

NDAC *National Defense Advisory Commission*—6

NDI Nuclear Data, Inc.—9B

NDL *Norddeutscher Lloyd* (German ship line)—1

NDRC *National Defense Research Committee*—6

NDT *nondestructive training*—9, 17

NE *naval engineer*—28

neon—17A

New England—27

northeast—27

NEA *National Editorial Association*—22

National Education Association—23

Newspaper Enterprise Association—22

Northeast Airlines, Inc.—1, 9B

NEB Neisner Brothers, Inc.—9A, 9B

New English Bible—16

NEC Negro Ensemble Company—25

not elsewhere classified—9

NED New English Dictionary—22

NEED Near East emergency donations—2, 14

NEF national extra fine (screw thread designation)—9

NEFA nonesterified fatty acids—17

NEI Netherlands East Indies—27

NEL Naval Electronics Laboratory—4, 17

Nelly Don, Inc.—9B

NEM Newmont Mining Corp.—9A

NEMA National Electronics (formerly Electrical) Manufacturers' Association—10

NEP Needham Packing Co., Inc.—9B

new economic plan (or policy) (Soviet Union)—7

NEPA nuclear energy propulsion of aircraft—1, 14, 17

NER National Equipment Rental, Ltd.—9B

NERVA nuclear engine for rocket vehicle application—14, 17

NES New England Electric System—9A

not elsewhere specified—9

NESA National Electric Sign Association—10

NESC National Environmental Satellite Center—17

NET National Educational Television—25

not earlier than—9

NEW National Electric Welding Machines Co.—9B

NF national fine (screw thread designation)—9

national forest—7

national formulary—18

Newfoundland—27

no funds—9

noise figure—17

Norman French—15

NFA National Alfalfa Dehydrating and Milling Co.—9B

NFAH National Foundation on the Arts and Humanities—2

NFC not favorably considered—9

NFD Newfoundland—27

NFE nonferrous extract—17

NFFE National Federation of Federal Employees—21

NFG National Fuel Gas Co.—9A

NFK Norfolk and Western Railway Co.—9A

NFL National Football League—11

NFLPN National Federation of Licensed Practical Nurses—20

NFMC National Federation of Music Clubs—2

NFO National Farmers' Organization—2

NFPA National Fire Protection Association—10

NG National Guard—4

National Gypsum Co.—9A

New Guinea—27

nitroglycerin—17

no good—8

NGA National Glider Association—2

NGB National Guard Bureau—4

NGC National General Corp.—3, 9A, 9B

NGE New York State Electric and Gas Corp.—9A

NGS Niagara Share Corp.—9A

NH New Hampshire—27

NHA National Housing Agency—6

NHCA National Hairdressers and Cosmetologists Association—10

NHG New High German—15

NHH neither help nor hinder—8

NHI national health insurance—7

NHIC *N*ational *H*ome *I*mprovement Council—10

NHL *N*ational *H*ockey *L*eague—11

NHRA *N*ational *H*ot *R*od *A*ssociation—2

NHSC *N*ational *H*ome *S*tudy Council—23

NI *ni*ckel—17A

Northern Indiana Public Service Co.—9A, 9B

*N*orthern *I*reland—27

NIA *N*ational *I*ntelligence *A*uthority—6

*N*ewspaper *I*nstitute of *A*merica—22

NIAMD *N*ational *I*nstitute of *A*rthritis and *M*etabolic *D*iseases—17

NIB *N*ational *I*ndustries for the *B*lind—2

NICAP *N*ational *I*nvestigation Committee on *A*erial *P*henomena—2, 14

NICB *N*ational *I*ndustrial *C*onference *B*oard—6

NID *N*ational *I*nstitute of *D*rycleaning—10

New Idria Mining and Chemical Co.—9B

NIDR *N*ational *I*nstitute of *D*ental *R*esearch—17

NIF *n*ot *i*n *f*iles—9

NIGMS *N*ational *I*nstitute of *G*eneral *M*edical *S*ciences—17

NIH *N*ational *I*nstitute of *H*ealth—17

NII National Industries, Inc.—9A, 9B

NIMH *N*ational *I*nstitute of *M*ental *H*ealth—17

NIMS *n*ationwide *i*mproved *m*ail service—7, 14

NINDB *N*ational *I*nstitute of *N*eurological *D*iseases and *B*lindness—17

NIRA *N*ational *I*ndustrial *R*ecovery *A*ct—7

NIRC *N*ational *I*nstitute of *R*ug *C*leaning—10

NIS *N*ational *I*nformation *S*ystem—6

*n*ot *i*n stock—9

NIT *N*ational *I*nvitation *T*ournament (basketball)—11

NJ *N*ew *J*ersey—27

NJ&NY *N*ew *J*ersey & *N*ew *Y*ork *R*ailroad—1

NKM New Park Mining Co.—9B

NKVD *N*arodnyi *K*ommissariat *V*nutrennikh *D*el (People's Commissariat for Internal Affairs, Soviet Union)—12

NL *N*ational *L*eague—11

natural *l*og (or *l*ogarithm)—17

*N*eo- (or *N*ew) *L*atin—15

new *l*ine—22

*n*ight *l*etter—22

non *l*icet (it is not permitted)—19

non *l*iquet (it is not clear)—19

NLC Nalco Chemical Co.—9A

NLCA *N*orwegian *L*utheran *C*hurch of *A*merica—16

NLF *N*ational *L*iberation *F*ront—12

NLGI *N*ational *L*ubricating *G*rease *I*nstitute (and its numbering system for grease)—9, 10

NLM *N*ational *L*ibrary of *M*edicine—17

NLN *N*ational *L*eague for *N*ursing—20

NLRA *N*ational *L*abor *R*elations *A*ct—7

NLRB *N*ational *L*abor *R*elations *B*oard—6

NLT *n*ot *l*ater *t*han—9

NM *n*anometer—17

*n*autical *m*ile—27

*N*ew *M*exico—27

*n*itrogen *m*ustard—17

*n*onmetallic—17

NMAA *N*ational *M*achine *A*ccountants' *A*ssociation—10

NMAC *n*ear *m*idair *c*ollision—1

NMB *N*ational *M*ediation *B*oard—6

NMCS *n*ational *m*ilitary *c*ommand *s*ystem—4

NMFC *n*ational *m*otor *f*reight classification—9

NMI *n*o *m*iddle *i*nitial—7, 8

NMK Niagara Mohawk Power Corp.—9A

NML *N*orthwestern *M*utual *L*ife Insurance Co.—3

NMPA *N*ational *M*usic *P*ublishers *A*ssociation—10

NMR The Nestle-LeMur Co.—9B

NMRA *N*ational *M*odel *R*ailroad *A*ssociation—2

NMS NMS Industries, Inc.—9B

NMSQT *N*ational *M*erit *S*cholarship *Q*ualifying *T*est—23

NMU *N*ational *M*aritime *U*nion of America—21

NN *N*evada *N*orthern Railroad—1

NNC New England Nuclear Corp. —9B

NND *n*ew and *n*onofficial *d*rugs—17

NNE *n*orth-*n*ortheast—27

NNG Northern Natural Gas Co.—9A

NNP *n*ew *n*ational *p*roduct—9

NNR *n*ew and *n*onofficial remedies—17

NNW *n*orth-*n*orth*w*est—27

NNX Northern Central Railway Co. —9A

NO *n*atural *o*rder—17

*N*ew *O*rleans—27

*n*obelium—17A

NOA North American Car Corp.—9A

NOB Northwest Bancorporation—9A

NOC Northrop Corp.—9A

NODC *N*ational *O*ceanographic *D*ata Center—6, 17

NOE *n*et *o*perating *e*arnings—9

NOIBN *n*ot *o*therwise *i*ndexed *by* name—9

NOL *N*aval *O*rdnance *L*aboratory—4, 17

NO&LC *N*ew *O*rleans & *L*ower *C*oast Railroad—1

NOM Natomas Co.—9A

NOP *n*ot *o*therwise *p*rovided for—9

*n*ot *o*ur *p*ublication—22

NORAD *N*orth American *A*ir *D*efense Command—4, 14

NORC *N*ational *O*pinion *R*esearch Center—17

NOS *n*ot *o*therwise *s*pecified—9

NOSC *N*aval *O*rdnance *S*ystems Command—4

NOT *N*ew *O*rleans *T*erminal Railroad—1

NOV Novo Industrial Corp.—9B

NOVS *N*ational *O*ffice of *V*ital *S*tatistics—6

NOW *N*ational *O*rganization for *W*omen—2, 14

NOZ New Process Co.—9B

NP *N*arragansett *P*ier Railroad—1

*n*e*p*tunium—17A

*n*euro*p*sychiatric (or *p*sychological)—17

*n*ew *p*aragraph—22

*n*isi *p*rius (unless before) court—19

*n*o *p*aging—22

*n*o *p*rotest—9

*N*orthern *P*acific Railway Co.—1, 9A

*n*otary *p*ublic—7

NPA *n*aphthyl*p*hthalamic *a*cid—17

*N*ational *P*lanning *A*ssociation—20

NPD *N*ational*d*emokratische *P*artei *D*eutschlands (German National Democratic Party)—12

*n*orth *p*olar *d*istance—27

NPH *n*eutral *p*rotamine *H*agedorn (type of insulin)—17

North American Philips Corp.—9A

NPI *N*egro *P*ress *I*nternational—22

NPK National Presto Industries, Inc.—9A

NPM Neptune Meter Co.—9A

NPN *n*on*p*rotein *n*itrogen—17

NPPA *N*ational *P*ress *P*hotographers *A*ssociation—20

NPT *n*ormal *p*ressure and *t*emperature—17

NPU *N*ational *P*ostal *U*nion—21

NQOS *n*ot *q*uite *o*ur *s*ort—8

NR *n*oise *r*atio—17

*n*on *r*epetatur (do not repeat, or refill)—18

North American Rockwell Corp.—9A

*n*ot *r*esponsible for—9

NRA *N*ational *R*ecovery *A*dministration—6

*N*ational *R*ifle *A*ssociation—2

NRAB *N*ational *R*ailroad *A*djustment *B*oard—6

NRAO *n*ational *r*adio *a*stronomy *ob*servatory—17

NRC *N*ational *R*esearch *C*ouncil—17

NRD The *N*arda Microwave Corp. —9B

NREC *N*ational *R*esource *E*valuation Center—6

NRF *N*ouvelle *R*evue *F*rançaise (New French Review)—22

NRI Norris Industries, Inc.—9A

NRL *N*aval *R*esearch *L*aboratory —4, 17

NRLCA *N*ational *R*ural *L*etter Carriers *A*ssociation—21

NRM *N*ational *R*ailways of *M*exico—1

NRMA *N*ational *R*etail *M*erchants' *A*ssociation—10

NROTC *N*aval *R*eserve *O*fficers' Training Corps—4

NRPB *N*ational *R*esources *P*lanning *B*oard—6

NRT Norton Co.—9A

NRX *N*ERVA (which see) *r*eactor experiment—17

NRY National Realty Investors—9B

NRZ *n*on*r*eturn to *z*ero—17

NS National Steel Corp.—9A

*n*aval *s*tation—4

*n*ew *s*eries—9

*n*ew *s*tyle—30

*n*imbostratus—17

*N*orfolk *S*outhern Railroad—1

*n*ot *s*pecified—9

*n*ot *s*ufficient—9

*N*ova *S*cotia—27

*n*uclear *s*hip—1

NSA *N*ational *S*ecui ity *A*gency—6

*N*ational *S*hipping *A*uthority—6

*N*ational *S*tandards *A*ssociation—20

*N*ational *S*tudent *A*ssociation—2

NSBA *N*ational *S*chool *B*oards *A*ssociation—23

NSC *N*ational *S*afety *C*ouncil—2

*N*ational *S*ecurity *C*ouncil—6

*N*ational *S*tarch and *C*hemical Corp.—9A

NSCS *n*on*s*cheduled *c*argo *s*ervice—1

NSD National-Standard Co.—9A

N&SE *N*acogdoches & *S*outheastern Railroad—1

NSE *N*ational *S*tock *E*xchange—9

NSF *N*ational *S*anitation *F*oundations—17

*N*ational *S*cience *F*oundation—17

*n*ot *s*ufficient *f*unds—9

NSH Nashua Corp.—9A

NSI Norton Simon, Inc.—9A

NSIA *N*ational *S*ecurity *I*ndustrial *A*ssociation—10

NSID *N*ational *S*ociety of *I*nterior *D*ecorators—20

N&SL *N*orwood & *St*. *L*awrence Railroad—1

NSLI *n*ational *s*ervice *l*ife *i*nsurance—7

NSP Northern States Power Co.—9A

NSPCA *N*ational *S*ociety for the *P*revention of *C*ruelty to *A*nimals—2

NSPCC *N*ational *S*ociety for the *P*revention of *C*ruelty to *C*hildren—2

NSPF *n*ot *s*pecifically *p*rovided *f*or—9

NSPS *n*on*s*cheduled *p*assenger *s*ervice—1

NSR Norfolk Southern Railway Co.—9B

NSRB *N*ational *S*ecurity *R*esources *B*oard—6

NSRP *National States Rights Party*—24

NSSA *National Skeet Shooting Association*—11

NSSC *Navy Ship Systems Command*—4

NSTA *National Student Travel Association*—2, 23

NSU *Neckarsum* (city in Germany, site of NSU engine and automobile factory)—3

NSW *New South Wales*—27

Northwestern Steel and Wire Co.—9A

NSY *National Systems Corp.*—9B

N&T *nose and throat*—17

NT *New Testament*—16

nontight—1

Northern Territory (Australia)—27

NTA *National Aviation Corp.*—9A

NTC *National Teacher Corps*—23

NTDS *naval tactical data system*—4

NTID *National Technical Institute for the Deaf*—17

NTL *National City Lines, Inc.*—9A

National Training Laboratories—17, 23

NTS *North American Sugar Industries, Inc.*—9A

NTO *no try-on(s)* (retail trade)—9

NT&SA *National Trust and Savings Association*—9

NTSB *National Transportation Safety Board*—6

NTSC *National Television Systems Committee*—17

NTT *New England Telephone and Telegraph Co.*—9A

NTY *National Tea Co.*—9A

NU *Northeast Utilities*—9A

nothing unsatisfactory—9

NUC *New University Conference*—23

NUE *Nuclear Corp. of America*—9B

NUEA *National University Extension Association*—23

NUL *National Urban League*—2

NUM *National Union Electric Co.*—9A

NUT *National Union of Teachers*—21, 23

NUWW *National Union of Women Workers*—21

NV *Naamloze Vernootschaap* (Dutch corporation)—12

nonvoting—9

NVA *North Vietnamese Army*—12

NVD *National Video Corp.*—9B

NVF *NVF Co.*—9A

NVP *Nevada Power Co.*—9A

N&W *Norfolk & Western Railway Co.*—1

NW *northwest*—27

NWA *Northwest Airlines, Inc.*—1, 9A

NWC *National War College*—4

NWH *New Hampshire Ball Bearings, Inc.*—9B

NWL *Naval Weapons Laboratory*—4, 17

NWLB *National War Labor Board*—6

NWP *Northwestern Pacific Railroad*—1

NWRC *National Weather Records Center*—6

NWRO *National Welfare Rights Organization*—2

NWT *Northwest Industries, Inc.*—9A

Northwest Territories—27

NY *New York*—27

NYA *National Youth Administration*—6

NYC *Neighborhood Youth Corps*—2

New York Central Railroad—1

New York City—27

NYCO *New York City Opera*—25

NYC&SL *New York, Chicago and St. Louis Railroad*—1

NYD *not yet diagnosed*—17

NYH *New York and Honduras Rosario Mining Co.*—9A

NYK The New York Times Co.—9B

Nippon Yusen Kaisha (Japanese shipping line)—1

NY&LB *N*ew *Y*ork and *L*ong *B*ranch Railroad—1

NYNH&H *N*ew *Y*ork, *N*ew *H*aven & *H*artford Railroad—1

NYO&W *N*ew *Y*ork, *O*ntario and *W*estern Railroad—1

NYP *n*ot *y*et *p*ublished—22

NYSE *N*ew *Y*ork *S*tock *E*xchange—9

NYS&W *N*ew *Y*ork, *S*usquehanna & *W*estern Railroad—1

NYT the *N*ew *Y*ork *T*imes—22

Nytronics, Inc.—9B

NYU *N*ew *Y*ork *U*niversity—23

NZ New Mexico and Arizona Land Co.—9B

*N*ew *Z*ealand—27

NZS *N*ew *Z*ealand *S*hipping Co.—1

O *o*xygen—17A

OA *o*n *a*ccount of—9

OAA *o*ld-*a*ge *a*ssistance—7

OAC *o*riginal *a*ir *c*onditioning—9

OAE *o*rbiting *a*stronomical *e*xplorer—17

OAM *O*ffice of *A*viation *M*edicine—6, 17

OAO *o*rbiting *a*stronomical *o*bservatory—17

OAP *O*ffice of *A*ntarctic *P*rogram—6

OAPC *O*ffice of *A*lien *P*roperty *C*ustodian—6

OAR *O*ffice of *A*erospace *R*esearch—6, 17

OART *O*ffice of *A*dvanced *R*esearch and *T*echnology (of NASA) —17

OAS *O*ld-*A*ge *A*ssistance (or *S*ecurity)—7

*O*rganization of *A*merican *S*tates—12

OASDHI *O*ld-*A*ge, *S*urvivors, *D*isability and *H*ealth *I*nsurance—7

OASDI *O*ld-*A*ge, *S*urvivors and *D*isability *I*nsurance—7

OASI *o*ld-*a*ge and *s*urvivors *i*nsurance—7

OAT The Quaker Oats Co.—9A

OAU *O*rganization of *A*frican *U*nity—12

OAWR *O*ffice for *A*gricultural *W*ar *R*elations—6

OB *o*bstetrics—17

*o*pening of *b*ooks—9

*o*rdered *b*ack—9

OBE *O*fficer of the Most Excellent *O*rder of the *B*ritish *E*mpire—28

OBO *o*re-*b*ulk-*o*il tanker—1

OBSS *o*cean-*b*ottom *s*canning *s*onar—17

OC *o*fficer *c*ommanding—4

*o*n *c*enter—22

*o*pere *c*itato (in the work cited)—19

*o*riginal *c*over (philately)—8

*o*ver*c*harge—9

*o*ver-the-*c*ounter—9

OCAA *O*klahoma *C*ity-*A*da-*A*toka Railroad—1

OCCE *O*ffice of *C*hief, *C*ommunication *E*lectronics—4

OCD *O*ffice of *C*hild *D*evelopment—6

*O*ffice of *C*ivil *D*efense—6

OCDM *O*ffice of *C*ivil and *D*efense *M*obilization—6

OC&E *O*regon, *C*alifornia & *E*astern Railroad—1

OCF *O*wens-*C*orning *F*iberglas Corp.—9A

OCIAA *O*ffice of *C*oordinator of *I*nter-*A*merican *A*ffairs—6

OCMH *O*ffice of *C*hief of *M*ilitary *H*istory—4

OCQ Oneida, Ltd.—9A

OCR *o*ptical *c*haracter *r*eading (or *r*ec*o*gnition)—9, 23

*O*rder of *C*istercian *R*eform (Trappists)—16

OCRD *O*ffice of *C*hief, *R*esearch and *D*evelopment—4

OCS *O*ffice of *C*ontract *S*ettlement—6

officer *c*andidate *s*chool—4

Old Church Slavonic—15

OD *o*culus *d*exter (right eye)—17

*o*fficer of the *d*ay—4

*o*live *d*rab—4, 8

*o*mni *d*ie (every day)—18

*o*n *d*emand—9

*ordi*nary seaman—1, 8

*O*rdnance *D*epartment—4

*o*utside *d*iameter (or *d*imensions)—17

*o*ver*d*ose (of drugs)—8

*o*ver*d*raft (or *d*rawn)—9

ODAR *o*ptical *d*etection *a*nd ranging—14, 17

ODGSO *O*ffice of *D*omestic *G*old and *S*ilver *O*perations (of the Treasury Department)—6

ODR *o*mni*d*irectional radio *r*ange—17

ODT *O*ffice of *D*efense *T*ransportation—6

OE *O*ffice of *E*ducation—6

*O*ld *E*nglish—15

*o*missions *e*xcepted—9

*O*regon *E*lectric Railroad—1

OEC Ohio Edison Co.—9A

OECD *O*rganization for *E*conomic Cooperation and Development—6

OED *O*xford *E*nglish *D*ictionary—22

OEEC *O*rganization for *E*uropean *E*conomic *C*ooperation—12

OEM *O*ffice for *E*mergency *M*anagement—6

*o*riginal *e*quipment *m*anufacturer—9

OEN Oak Electronetics Corp.—9A

OEO *O*ffice of *E*conomic *O*pportunity—6

OEP *O*ffice of *E*mergency *P*lanning—6

OER *o*riginal *e*quipment *r*eplacement—9

OES *O*rder of the *E*astern *S*tar—2

OF *O*ld *F*rench—15

OFC *o*ldest *f*inest *c*anadian (whiskey)—3

The *O*xford *F*inance *C*ompanies, Inc.—9B

OFDI *O*ffice of *F*oreign *D*irect *I*nvestment—6

OFHC *o*xygen-*f*ree *h*igh-*c*onductivity (grade of copper)—9

OFM *O*rder of *F*riars *M*inor (Franciscans)—16

OFPA *O*cean *F*ish *P*rotective *A*ssociation—2, 11

OFS The Offshore Co.—9B

OG *o*fficer of the *g*uard—4

Ogden Corp.—9A

*O*ld *G*erman—15

*o*ld *g*irl—8

*o*riginal *g*um (philately)—8

OGE Oklahoma Gas and Electric Co.—9A

*o*perational *g*round *e*quipment—4

OGO *o*rbiting *g*eophysical *o*bservatory—14, 17

OGPU *O*bedinennoe *G*osudarstvennoe *P*oliticheskoe *U*pravlyenie (United State Political Administration, Soviet Union)—12, 14

OH *o*mni *h*ora (every hour)—18

OHD Overhead Door Corp.—9B

OHG *O*ld *H*igh *G*erman—15

OHMS *O*n *H*er (or *H*is) *M*ajesty's Service—7

OHP Ohio Power Co.—9B

OHS The Ohio Brass Co.—9B

OHV *o*ver*h*ead *v*alve (engine)—1

OI Owens-Illinois, Inc.—9A

OIC *o*fficer *i*n *c*harge—4

OIT *O*ffice of *I*nternational *T*rade—6

OJ *o*range *j*uice—8

OJT *o*n-the-*j*ob *t*raining—9

OK [perhaps] *O*ll *K*orrect; *O*ld *K*inderhook—8

OKC OKC Corp.—9B

OKO The Okonite Co.—9B

OKP O'Okiep Copper Co., Ltd.—9B

OKT Oakite Products, Inc.—9A

OKW *Oberkommando der Wehrmacht* (Army High Command, Germany)—12

OL *oculus laevus* (left eye)—17

Old Latin—15

outside left—11

OLA Olla Industries, Inc.—9B

OLAS Office of Latin-American Solidarity—12

OLD Old Town Corp.—9B

OLG Old Low German—15

OLLA Office of Lend-Lease Administration—6

OLM Olin Mathieson Chemical Corp.—9A

O&M Ohio & Morenci Railroad—1

OM old man—8

omni mane (every morning)—18

Order of Merit—28

Outboard Marine Corp.—9A

OMB Office of Management and Budget—6

OMD Ormand Industries, Inc.—9B

OMK Omork Industries, Inc.—9A

OMPA octomethylpyrophosphoramide—17

OMSF Office of Manned Space Flight—17

O&N Oregon & Northwestern Railroad—1

ON Old Norse—15

omni nocte (every night)—18

Ontario Northern Railroad—1

ONA Overseas National Airways—1

ONC Oregon-Nevada-California (truck line)—1

ONF Old North French—15

ONG Oklahoma Natural Gas Co. —9A

ONI Office of Naval Intelligence—4

ONR Office of Naval Research—4, 17

O&O one and only—8

owned and operated (or owner and operator)—9

OO once-over—8

OOB out of bounds—8

OOC Office of Censorship—6

OP observation post—4

opposite the prompter—25

Order of Preachers (Dominicans) —16

out of print—22

overprint (philately)—8

OPA Office of Price Administration—6

OPCW Office of Petroleum Coordinator for War—6

OPEU International Office and Professional Employees' Union —21

OPK Opelika Manufacturing Corp. —9A

OPM other people's money—8, 9

OPO orbiting planetary observatory—17

OPS Office of Price Stabilization—6

OQMG Office of the Quartermaster General—4

OR operating room—17

operations research—9

outside right—11

owner's risk—9

released on own recognizance—26

ORC Officers' (or Organized) Reserve Corps—4

ORDIR omnirange digital radar—14, 17

ORG Originals, Inc.—9B

ORT Organization for Rehabilitation through Training—2

ORU Orange and Rockland Utilities, Inc.—9A

OS oculus sinister (left eye)—17

Old Saxon—15

old school—8

old series—9

old style—30

ordinary seaman—1

osmium—17A

out of stock—9

outstanding—9

OSA Optical Society of America—20

Order of St. Augustine (Augustinians)—16

OSB Order of St. Benedict (Benedictines)—16

OSCA Officine Specializzato di Construzione Automobili (Special Automobile Construction Factory, OSCA cars)—3, 14

OSD Office of the Secretary of Defense—6

Order of St. Dominic (Dominicans)—16

OSF Order of St. Francis (Franciscans)—16

overgrowth-stimulating factor—17

OSFC Ordo Sancti Francisci Capuccinorum (Order of the Capuchin Franciscans)—16

OSFCW Office of Solid Fuels Coordinator for War—6

OSL Oregon Short Line Railroad—1

O'Sullivan Rubber Co.—9B

OSO orbiting solar observatory—17

OSP obiit sine prole (he died without issue)—19

OSRD Office of Scientific (or Strategic) Research and Development—6

OSS Office of Strategic Services—6

OSSA Office of Space Sciences and Applications (of NASA)—17

OSSR Office of Selective Service Records—6

OST Office of Science and Technology—6

OSU Ohio State University—23

Oklahoma State University—23

Order of St. Ursula (Ursuline)—16

OT occupational therapy—17

oiltight—1

Old Testament—16

old tuberculin—17

Oregon Trunk Railroad—1

orthotolidine—17

Otis Elevator Co.—9A

overtime—9

OTA orthotolidine arsenite—17

OTC officer in tactical command—4

officers' training camp (or corps)—4

Organization for Trade Cooperation—6

over-the-calf (women's fashions)—8, 9

over-the-counter—9

OTH over-the-horizon radar—17

OTR Office of Technical Resources—6

OTS Office of Technical Services (of the Commerce Department)—6

optical technology satellite—17

OTU Office for Technology Utilization—6

The Outlet Co.—9A

OU oculo utro (in each eye)—18

OUAM Order of United American Mechanics—21

OV orbiting vehicle—17

OVT Overnite Transportation Co.—9A

OVU Overseas Securities Co., Inc.—9B

O&W Oneida & Western Railroad—1

OWI Office of War Information—6

OWM Office of War Mobilization—6

OWRR Office of Water Resources Research—6

OX Oxford Electric Corp.—9B

OXM Oxford Industries Co., Inc.—9A

OXY Occidental Petroleum Corp.—9A

OZA Ozark Airlines, Inc.—9B

P Phillips Petroleum Co.—9A

phosphorus—17A

P&A Pennsylvania & Atlantic Railroad—1

price and availability—9

PA partes aequales (in equal parts)—18

participial adjective—15
passenger agent— 1
per annum (by the year)—9, 19
personal appearance—25
post adjutant—4
power amplifier—17
power of attorney—9
press (or publicity) agent—22
private account—9
procurement authorization—9
project analysis—9
prosecuting attorney—7
protactinium—17A
public address (or announcement) system—8
public assistance—7
purchasing agent—9

PAA Pan American World Airways—1

PABA para-aminobenzoic acid— 17

PAC Pacific Telephone and Telegraph Co.—9A
Political Action Committee—24

PACE Project to Advance Creativity in Education—14, 23

PAE Pioneer Systems, Inc.—9B

PAG Pargas, Inc.—9A

PAGEOS passive geodetic satellite—14, 17

PAIFORCE Persia and Iraq Force—12, 14

PAINT postattack intelligence—4, 14

PAIS Public Affairs Information Service—22

PAK Park Chemical Co.—9B

PAKISTAN Punjab, Afghan frontier, Kashmir, Iran, Sind, and Baluchistan—14, 27

PAL Pacific Airlift (of U.S. Post Office)—7
Philippines Air Lines—1
Police Athletic League—26

PAM pulse amplitude modulation—17

PANAGRA Pan-American Grace Airways—1, 14

PAO public affairs officer—4

PAP poco a poco (little by little, or by degrees) (music)—19

PAPA Philippines Alien Property Administration—6

PAR perimeter acquisition radar—17
precision approach radar—17

PARC Predator and Rodent Control (of U.S. Fish and Wildlife Service)—6, 14

PARSEC parallax second—14, 17

PAS Pan American Sulphur Co.—9A
para-aminosalicylic acid—17

PASO Political Association of Spanish-Speaking Organizations—14, 24

PAT picric acid turbidity test—17
point after touchdown—11

PATA Pacific Area Travel Association—10, 14

PATCO Professional Air Traffic Controllers' Organization—14, 20

PATH pituitary adrenotrophic hormone—14, 17

PAU Pan American Union—12

PAW Port Angeles Western Railroad—1

PAX private automatic exchange—9

PAYE pay as you enter—8

PB passed ball (baseball)—11
Pharmacopoeia Britannica—18
piperonyl butoxide—17
lead (from plumbum)—17A
Plymouth Brethren—16
power brakes—9
prayer book—16
Primitive Brethren—16

PBA Patrolmen's (or Policemen's) Benevolent Association—26
Professional Bowler's Association—11
Public Buildings Administration—6

PBC Pubco Petroleum Corp.—9B

PBI Pitney-Bowes, Inc.—9A
protein-bound iodine (in blood)—17

PBL Public Broadcast Laboratory—25

PBM Prudential Building Maintenance Corp.—9B

PBS Public Buildings Service—6

PBX private branch exchange—9

PBY The Pep Boys—Manny, Moe and Jack—9B

PBZ pyribenzamine—17

PC participation certificate—9

past commander—28

Penn-Central Co.—9A

percent—9

petty cash—9

phenol coefficient—17

police constable—26

postal card—7, 8

post cibos (after meals) or post cibum (after food)—18

post commander—28

Preparatory Commission—13

price current—9

prime contractor—9

Prince Consort—28

Privy Council—7

PCA Progressive Citizens of America—2

PCF pounds per cubic foot—17

PCG Pacific Gas and Electric Co.—9A, 9B

PCH patrol craft, hydrofoil—1, 4

PCI Pep Com Industries, Inc.—9B

pounds per cubic inch—17

PCK Pittsburgh Coke and Chemical Co.—9A

PCM pulse code modulation—17

PCO The Pittston Co.—9A

procuring contract (or contracting) office—9

PCP Pacific Clay Products—9B

pentachlorophenol—17

phenylcyclohexylpiperidine (a hallucinogen)—17

platoon command post—4

program change proposal—9

PCR Perini Corp.—9B

PCS-CSS Parents' Confidential Statement of the College Scholarship Service—23

PCSE Pacific Coast Stock Exchange—9

PCT Papercraft Corp.—9A

percent—9

PCV positive crankcase ventilation—1, 9

PD palladium—17A

per diem (by the day)—9, 19

Phelps, Dodge Corp.—9A

polar distance—27

police department—6, 26

potential difference—23

program director—25

public domain—9

PDB paradichlorobenzene—17

PDC Parke, Davis and Co.—9A

PDG People's Drug Stores, Inc.—9A

PDH packaged disaster hospital—17

PDI powered descent initiative—17

PDL Presidential Realty Corp.—9B

PDM Pittsburgh-Des Moines Steel Co.—9B

pulse duration modulation—17

PDP program development plan—9

PD&PL property damage and public liability (insurance)—9

PDQ pretty damn quick—8

PDR preliminary design review—9

PDT pacific daylight time—30

PE petroleum engineer—28

Philadelphia Electric Co.—9A

photoelectric—17

physical education (or exercise)—8, 23

Presiding Elder—16, 28

price-earnings ratio—9

printer's error—22

probable error—9

professional engineer—28

Protestant Episcopal—16

PEG Public Service Electric and Gas Co.—9A

PEI Prince Edward Island—27

PEL Panhandle Eastern Pipe Line Co.—9A

PEMA procurement, equipment and missiles, Army—4, 14

PEN International Association of Poets, Playwrights, Editors, Essayists and Novelists—2, 14

Pentron Electronics Corp.—9B

PEO Petroleum Corp. of America—9A

PEP Pepsico, Inc.—9A

PEPSU Patiala and East Punjab States Union—14, 27

PERT program education (or evaluation) and review technique—14, 17

PET Pet, Inc.—9A

Preliminary Examination Team (of NASA)—17

PETN pentaerythritol tetranitrate (explosive)—17

PF P and F Industries, Inc.—9B

personal foul—11

piu forte (louder) (music)—19

popular force militiaman—4

PFC private first class—4

Puritan Fashions Corp.—9B

PFE Charles Pfizer and Co., Inc.—9A

PFG Pittsburgh Forgings Co.—9A

PFLP Popular Front for the Liberation of Palestine (Arabic)—12

PFM Prudential Foods, Inc.—9B

pulse frequency modulation—17

PFO Perfect Film and Chemical Corp.—9A

PFP Pacific Coast Properties, Inc.—9B

PFR Penn Fruit Co., Inc.—9A

PFT Pittsburgh, Fort Wayne and Chicago Railway Co.—9A

P&G Procter and Gamble Co.—3

PG Past Grand—28

paying guest—9

postgraduate—23

Procter and Gamble Co.—9A

PGA Professional Golfers' Association—11

pteroylglutamic acid—17

PGB Pepsi-Cola General Bottlers, Inc.—9A

PGI Ply-Gem Industries, Inc.—9B

PGL Peoples Gas Co.—9A

PGN Portland General Electric Co.—9A

PGS predicted ground speed—1

PGV The Pierce Governor Co., Inc.—9B

PH Parker-Hannifin Corp.—9A

public health—17

Purple Heart—28

PHA Public Housing Administration—6

PHB Philosophiae Baccalaureus (Bachelor of Philosophy)—5

PHD Philosophiae Doctor (Doctor of Philosophy)—5

PHE Pepi, Inc.—9B

public health engineer—28

PHI Philippine Long Distance Telephone Co.—9B

PHK H.K. Porter Co., Inc.—9A

PHL Philips Industries, Inc.—9A

PHM Philosophiae Magister (Master of Philosophy)—5

PHQ personnel history questionnaire—9

PHR public health reports—17, 22

PHS Public Health Service—6, 17

P&I Paducah and Illinois Railroad—1

principal and interest—9

PI Pacific Industries, Inc.—9B

Philippine Islands—27

private investigator—26

PIA Pakistan International Airlines—1

Piasecki Aircraft Corp.—9B

PIC Potter Instrument Co., Inc.—9B

PICAO Provisional International Civil Aviation Organization—12

PIE Pacific Intermountain Express Co.—1, 9A

PIK Pickwick International, Inc.—9B

PIM *Pro I*ndependence *M*ovement (Puerto Rico)—12

PIN Public Service Co. of Indiana—9A

PIO *p*ublic *i*nformation *o*ffice (or officer)—4

PIPE *Pl*umbing *I*ndustry *P*rogress and *E*ducation Fund—10

PJ *paj*ama—8
*p*residing *j*udge—7

PJM Pennsylvania-New Jersey-Maryland (electric power area)—9

PK *p*rincipal *k*eeper—8, 26
*p*sycho*k*inesis—17

PKE Park Electrochemical Corp.—9B

PKL Papert, Koenig, Lois, Inc.—9B

PKN The Perkin-Elmer Corp.—9A

PKR Parker Pen Co.—9A

PKU *p*henyl*k*eton*u*ria test—17

PKY Parkway Distributors, Inc.—9B

P&L *p*rofit and *l*oss—9

PL Peel-Elder, Ltd.—9B
*p*oet *l*aureate—28
*p*rivate *l*ine—9, 25
*p*ublic *l*aw—7
*p*ublic *l*ibrary—7

PLA People's Liberation Army (China, 1948)—12

PLATS *p*ilot *l*anding *a*nd *t*akeoff system—1, 14

PLC Placer Development Ltd.—9B

PLD Plant Industries, Inc.—9B

P&LE *P*ittsburgh & *L*ake *E*rie Railroad—1

PLF *p*ounds per *l*inear *f*oot—17

PLI pounds per linear inch—17

PLL Pall Corp.—9B

PLM The Polymer Corp.—9B

PLN Planning Research Corp.—9A

PLO Palestine Liberation Organization (Arabic)—12
Plough, Inc.—9A

PL&PD *p*ublic *l*iability and *p*roperty *d*amage (insurance)—9

PLR Plymouth Rubber Co., Inc.—9B

PLSS *p*ortable *l*ife-*s*upport *s*ystem—17

PLT Pacific Lighting Corp.—9A, 9B

PLU *p*eople *l*ike *u*s—8

PLUTO *p*ipe*l*ine *u*nder *t*he *o*cean—14, 17

PLW Plume and Atwood Industries, Inc.—9B

PM *p*ast *m*aster—28
*p*ay*m*aster—9
*P*ere *M*arquette Railroad—1
*p*hase (or *p*ulse) *m*odulation—17
*p*olice *m*agistrate—7
*p*ost*m*aster—7
*p*ost *m*eridiem (after noon)—30
*p*ost *m*ortem (after death)—17
Pratt and Lambert, Inc.—9B
*p*rime *m*inister—28
*p*ro*m*ethium—17A
*p*rovost *m*arshal—4

PMA *P*harmaceutical *M*anufacturers' *A*ssociation—10
*p*henyl*m*ercuric *a*cetate (weed killer)—17
*P*roduction and *M*arketing *A*dministration—6

PMB Palm Beach Co.—9A

PMC *P*ennsylvania *M*ilitary College—23

PMG *p*ay*m*aster *g*eneral—4
*p*ost*m*aster general—7
*p*rovost *m*arshal general—4

PMLA *P*ublications of the *M*odern *L*anguages *A*ssociation—22

PMO *p*rogram *m*anagement *o*ffice (or organization)—9

P&MP *P*aris & *M*ount *P*leasant Railroad—1

PMR *P*acific *m*issile *r*ange—4

PMT *p*ure *m*ilk *t*ablets—17

PMWA *P*rogressive *M*ine *W*orkers of *A*merica—21

P&N *p*sychiatry and *n*eurology—17

PN Pan American World Airways, Inc.—9A
*p*lease *n*ote—9

promissory *note*—9
*psychoneuro*tic—17
PNA *pentose nucleic acid*—17
Pioneer Natural Gas Co.—9A
PNB Pacific Northwest Bell Telephone Co.—9B
PND Pneumo Dynamics Corp.—9B
PNE Penrose Industries Corp.—9B
PNF Penn Traffic Co.—9B
PNN Penn Engineering and Manufacturing Corp.—9B
PNT The Pantasote Co.—9B
PNU Pneumatic Scale Corp.—9B
PNV Pennsylvania Co.—9A
P&NW *Prescott & Northwestern Railroad*—1
P&O *Peninsular and Oriental Steam Navigation Co.*—1
PO Pato Consolidated Gold Dredging Ltd.—9B
per os (by mouth)—18
petty officer—4
pissed off (polite: *put out*)—8
polonium—17A
postal order—7
post office—7
postoperative—17
probation officer—26
put out—11
POA *primary optical area*—17
POAU *Protestants and Other Americans United*—16
POB *post office box*—7
POD *pay on death*—9
pay on delivery—9
Polarad Electronics Corp.—9B
port of debarkation—1
Post Office Department—6
POE *port of embarkation*—1
port of entry—1
POF *Pillar of Fire Church*—16
POGO *polar orbiting geophysical observatory*—14, 17
POL Poloron Products, Inc.—9B
POM *personal opinion message* (Western Union)—9, 22

Potomac Electric Power Co.—9A
PONY *Pennsylvania, Ohio, New York Baseball League*—11, 14
POP *Pacific Ocean Park*—8
point of purchase—9
print-out paper—22
POR *pay on receipt* (or *return*)—9
Portec, Inc.—9A
POSH *port outward, starboard homeward*—14
POV *point of view*—25
POW Power Corp. of Canada, Ltd.—9B
prisoner of war—4
POY Prairie Oil Royalties Co., Ltd.—9B
PP Pacific Petroleums, Ltd.—9A
parcel post—7
parish priest—16
past participle—15
pellagra-preventive factor—17
per procurationem (by proxy)—19
postpaid—9
prepaid—9
private party—8
privately printed—22
pulse pressure—17
PPA Piper Aircraft Corp.—9A
Professional Photographers of America—10
PPC *pour prendre congé* (to take leave)—19
PPD *postpaid*—9
Purolator, Inc.—9A
PPG *Pittsburgh Plate Glass Co.*—3
PPG Industries, Inc.—9A
PPI Peter Paul, Inc.—9A
plan position indicator—17
policy sufficient proof of interest—9
PPK Pioneer Plastics Corp.—9B
PPL Pennsylvania Power and Light Co.—9A
PPLO *pleuropneumonia-like organism*—17
PPM *parts per million*—17
pulse per minute—17

PPP Paterson Parchment Paper Co.—9B

People's Progressive Party (British Guiana)—12

PPPI precision plan position indicator (p3i)—17

PPPPI photographic projection plan position indicator (p4i)—17

PPR present participle—15

PPS post-postscript—8

pulse per second—17

PPW Pacific Power and Light Co.—9A, 9B

PQ previous question—8

Province of Quebec—27

P&R parallax and refraction—27

PR parliamentary report—7

payroll—9

per rectum—17

praseodymium—17A

press release—22

proportional representation—7

public relations—22

Puerto Rico—27

purchase request—9

PRA Public Roads Administration—6

PRB Pre-Raphaelite Brotherhood—2

PRC Products Research and Chemical Corp.—9A

PRD Pesticide Regulation Division (of U.S. Department of Agriculture)—6

Polaroid Corp.—9A

PRE petroleum refining engineer—28

Premier Industrial Corp.—9A

PRG Provisional Revolutionary Government (Vietnam)—12

PRI Price Capital Corp.—9B

PRN pro re nata (as needed)—18

Puerto Rican Cement Co., Inc.—9A

PRO public relations officer—4

PRS Pennsylvania Reading Seashore Railroad—1

Preston Mines, Ltd.—9B

PRSA Public Relations Society of America—20

PRSL Pennsylvania Reading Shore Line—1

PRT Puerto Rico Telephone Co.—9B

PRU Prudent Resources Trust—9B

PRV Parvin-Dohrmann Co.—9B

PRX Purex Corp., Ltd.—9A

PRY Pittway Corp.—9B

P&S Pittsburgh & Shawmut Railroad—1

PS passenger steamer—1

permanent secretary—28

postscript—8

power steering—9

privy seal—28

Proler Steel Corp.—9B

public sale—9

public school—23

PSA Pacific Southwest Airlines—1, 9A, 9B

Photographic Society of America—20

pleasant Sunday afternoon—8

Poultry Science Association—20

PSAC the President's Science Advisory Committee—6, 17

PSAT Preliminary Scholastic (or School) Aptitude Test—23

PS&B power steering and brakes—9

PSC per standard compass—27

Public Service Commission—6

PSD Puget Sound Power and Light Co.—9A

PSEG Public Service Electric and Gas Co.—3

PSF pounds per square foot—17

PSI pounds per square inch—17

Pueblo Supermarkets, Inc.—9A

PSIA pounds per square inch absolute—17

PSID pounds per square inch differential—17

PSIG pounds per square inch gauge—17

PSL Pacific Savings and Loan Association—9B

PSM Pennwalt Corp.—9A

PSO Penobscot Shoe Co.—9B

PSR Public Service Co. of Colorado—9A, 9B

PSSC Physical Science Study Committee—17

PST Pacific standard time—30

PSW Phillips Screw Co.—9B

PSY The Pillsbury Co.—9A

P&T plans and training—4

PT Pacific time—30

past tense—15

patrol (or propeller) torpedo boat—4

physical therapy—17

physical training—23

platinum—17A

postal telegraph—22

pro tempore (for the time being)—19

pupil teacher—23

PTA Parent-Teacher Association—23

PTC Pacific Tin Consolidated Corp.—9A

plasma thromboplastic component—17

PTH parathyroid hormone—17

PTM pulse time modulation—17

PTN Prentice-Hall, Inc.—9B

PTO Pacific theater of operations—4

Petrolane, Inc.—9A

please turn over—22

PTT Cleveland and Pittsburgh Railroad Co.—9A

PU pickup (truck)—8

plutonium—17A

Pullman, Inc.—9A

PUL Publicker Industries, Inc.—9A

PUP People's United Party (British Honduras)—12

P&V piss and vinegar—8

PVC polyvinyl chloride—17

PVH Phillips-Van Heusen Corp.—9A

PVI passenger vehicle inspection—26

PVP polyvinylpyrrolidone—17

PVS Pecos Valley Southern Railroad—1

PVY Providence Gas Co.—9B

PW Pittsburgh and West Virginia Railroad—9B

power windows—9

pressurized water—17

prisoner of war—4

public works—7

Publishers' Weekly—22

P&WA Pratt and Whitney Aircraft—3

PWA Public Works Administration—6

PWBA Professional Woman Bowler's Association—11

PWD Public Works Department—6

PWM pulse width modulation—17

PWOC Protestant Women of the Chapel—16

P&WV Pittsburgh & West Virginia Railroad—1

PX Phoenix Steel Corp.—9B

please exchange—9

post exchange—4

PY prior year—9

PYA Pittsburgh, Youngstown & Ashland Railway Co.—1, 9A

PYC Polychrome Corp.—9B

PYI Pyroil Co., Inc.—9B

PYL The Pyle National Co.—9B

PZG Plaza Group, Inc.—9B

PZL Pennzoil United, Inc.—9A

PZPR Polska Zjednoczona Partia Robotnicza (Polish United Workers' Party)—12

PZT photographic zenith tube—17

Q&A questions and answers—8

QA quality assurance—9

QAM quaque mane ante jentaculum

(every morning before breakfast)—18

QANTAS *Q*ueensland *a*nd *N*orthern Territories *A*ir Service—1, 14

QA&P *Q*uanah, *A*cme & *P*acific Railroad—1

QB *q*uarter*b*ack—11
*Q*ueen's *B*ench—7
*q*ueen's *b*ishop (chess)—11

QBP *q*ueen's *b*ishop's *p*awn (chess)—11

QC *q*uality *c*ontrol—9
*Q*uartermaster *C*orps—4
*Q*uebec *C*entral Railroad—1
*Q*ueen's *C*ounsel—7
*q*uick *c*harge (airplane)—1

QD *q*uaque *d*ie (every day)—18

QE *q*uod *e*st (which is)—19

QE2 *Q*ueen *E*lizabeth *II* (ship)—1

QED *q*uod *e*rat *d*emonstrandum (which was to be proven)—19

QEF *q*uod *e*rat *f*aciendum (which was to be done)—19

QEI *q*uod *e*rat *i*nveniendum (which was to be found)—19

QF *q*uick *f*iring—4

QH *q*uaque *h*ora (every hour)—18

QID *q*uater *i*n *d*ie (four times a day)—18

QJLC *Q*uarterly *J*ournal of the *L*ibrary of *C*ongress—22

QKT *q*ueen's *k*nigh*t* (chess)—11

QKTP *q*ueen's *k*nigh*t*'s *p*awn (chess)—11

QL *q*uantum *l*ibet (as much as desired)—18

QM *q*uaque *m*ane (every morning)—18
*q*uarter*m*aster—4
*Q*uinn *M*artin Productions—25

QMC *Q*uartermaster *C*orps—4

QMG *Q*uartermaster *G*eneral—4

QMORC *Q*uartermaster *O*fficers' *R*eserve *C*orps—4

QMR *q*ualitative *m*ateriel *r*equirement—4

QN *q*uaque *n*octe (every night)—18
*q*ueen's *k*night (chess)—11

QNP *q*ueen's *k*night's *p*awn (chess)—11

QOMAC *q*uarter *o*rbit *m*agnetic *a*ttitude *c*ontrol—17

QP *q*uantum *p*lacet (as much as you please)—18
*q*ueen's *p*awn (chess)—11

QQH *q*uaque *q*uarta *h*ora (every four hours)—18

QQV *q*uae *v*ide (which see, plural)—19

QR *q*uantum *r*ectum (the quantity is correct)—18
*q*ueen's *r*ook (chess)—11
*q*uotation *r*equest—9

QRA *q*uick *r*eaction *a*lert—4

QRP *q*ueen's *r*ook's *p*awn (chess)—11

QS *q*uantum *s*atis (or *s*ufficit) (as much as is sufficient)—18

QSG *q*uasi-*s*tellar *g*allaxy (ies)—17

QT *q*uenched and *t*empered (steel heat treatment)—9
*q*uie*t* (on the "qt")—8

QUASAR *q*ua*s*i-stell*ar* radio sources—14, 17

QV *q*uantum *v*is (as much as you wish)—18
*q*uod *v*ide (which see, singular)—19

R Uniroyal, Inc.—9A

RA *r*adium—17A
*r*ate of *a*pproach—27'
*r*ear *a*dmiral—4
*r*egistered *a*rchitect—28
*r*egular *a*rmy—4
*R*epublica *A*rgentina (Argentine Republic)—27
*r*esearch *a*ssistant—23
*R*estaurant *A*ssociates Industries, Inc.—9B
*r*ight *a*scension—17
*R*oyal *A*cademy (or *A*cademician)—28

RAAF Royal Australian Air Force—4
RAB Radio Advertising Bureau—10
RAC random access computer—9
RACES Radio Amateur Civil Emergency Service—7
RACON radiation (or radio or radar) beacon—14, 17
RAD Rite Aid Corp.—9B
  Rural Areas Development—7
RADA Royal Academy of Dramatic Art—14, 23, 25
RADAR radio detecting (or detection) and ranging—14, 17
RADIAC radiation detection, identification and computation —14, 17
RAE radio astronomy explorer— 17
  Raymond Engineering, Inc.—9B
  Royal Aircraft Establishment—6
RAF Royal Air Force—4
RAH A.H. Robins Co., Inc.—9A
RAI Ramer Industries, Inc.—9B
RAL Ralston Purina Co.—9A
RAM Ramada Inns, Inc.—9B
  reentry antimissile—4, 14
  Revolutionary Action Movement —2, 14
  Royal Academy of Music—23, 25
  Royal Arch Mason—28
RAMS right ascension of mean sun —17
RAND research and development —14, 17
RAOB radiosonde observation—17
RAT ram air turbine—1
RATAN radio and television aid to navigation—14, 17
RATIO radio telescope in orbit—14, 17
RATO rocket-assisted takeoff—1, 14
RAY Raybestos-Manhattan, Inc. —9A
R&B rhythm and blues—25
RB Reading and Bates Off-Shore Drilling Co.—9A
  Renegotiation Board—6

rubidium—17A
RBC red bloodcell count—17
RBD Rubbermaid, Inc.—9A
RBF Royal Business Funds Corp. —9B
RBI runs batted in—11
RBL Roblin Industries, Inc.—9B
RBT Reeves Broadcasting Corp.—9B
RC Red Cross—2
  remote control—9, 17
  Research-Cottrell, Inc.—9B
  Reserve Corps—4
  resistor-capacitor—17
  right center—11
  right corner—11
  roll call—4, 8
  Roman Catholic—16
  Royal Crown (cola)—3
RCA Radio Corporation of America—3
  RCA Corp.—9A
RCAF Royal Canadian Air Force—4
RCB Rex Chain Belt, Inc.—9A
RCC Royal Crown Cola Co.—9A
RCCH Roman Catholic Church—16
RCI Reichhold Chemicals, Inc.—9A
RCIA Retail Clerks International Association—21
RCM radar countermeasures—4
RCMP Royal Canadian Mounted Police—26
RCN Royal Canadian Navy—4
RCO Rico Argentine Mining Co.—9B
RCP Royal College of Physicians—20
RCR Randolph Computer Corp.—9B
RCS reaction (or reentry) control system—17
  The Richardson Co.—9A
  Royal College of Surgeons—20
RCT regimental combat team—4
R&D research and development—17
RD rate of departure—27
  refer to drawer—9
  Reserve Decoration—28

revolutionary development—17

right defense—11

Royal Dutch Petroleum Co.—9A

rural delivery—7

RDA recommended dietary allowances (of the National Academy of Sciences-National Research Council)—17

RDB Research and Development Board (of Department of Defense)—6

RDC rail diesel car—1

Rowan Drilling Co., Inc.—9B

RD&E research, development, and engineering (or evaluation)—9

RDF radio direction finder (or finding)—17

RDG Reading Co.—9A

RDR Ryder Systems, Inc.—9A

RDS Revco D.S., Inc.—9A

RDT&E research, development, testing, and engineering (or evaluation)—9

RE rate of exchange—9

real estate—8

Reformed Episcopal—16

rhenium—17A

right end—11

Right Excellent—28

Royal Engineers—4

REA Railway Express Agency—1, 3

Reading Industries, Inc.—9B

Rural Electrification Administration—6

REACT Radio Emergency Associated Citizens' Team—2, 14

REC Realty Equities Corp. of New York—9B

RED R.E.D.M. Corp.—9B

REE Reliance Electric and Engineering Co.—9A

REI Real Estate Investment Trust of America—9B

REIT Real Estate Investment Trust—9

REM rapid eye movements—17

Remington Arms Co., Inc.—9B

Roentgen equivalent, mammal (or man)—17

REO Remco Industries, Inc.—9B

REP Republic Corp.—9A

Roentgen equivalent, physical—17

RES Reliable Stores Corp.—9A

RETMA Radio-Electronics-Television Manufacturers' Association—10, 14

REV Revlon, Inc.—9A

RF radio frequency—17

range finder—4

rapid fire—4

reducing flame—17

regional force militiamen—4

representative fraction—27

reserve force—4

right field (or fielder)—11

Rockefeller Foundation—3

RFA radio frequency amplifier—17

Royal Field Artillery—4

RFC Reconstruction Finance Corp.—6

Ritter Finance Co., Inc—9B

Royal Flying Cross—28

RFD rural free delivery—7

RFE Radio Free Europe—12

RFF Resources for the Future—2

RFI radio frequency interference—17

Richford Industries, Inc.—9B

RFO radio frequency oscillator—17

RF&P Richmond, Fredericksburg & Potomac Railroad—1

RFP request for proposal—9

RG Rheingold Corp.—9A

right guard—11

RGB R.G. Barry Corp.—9B

RGI Rio Grande Industries—9A

RGP Reigel Paper Corp.—9A

RGS Rio Grande Southern Railroad—1

Rochester Gas and Electric Corp.—9A, 9B

R&H radio and heater—1, 8

RH relative *h*umidity—17

*rh*esus factor (rh factor)—17

*rh*odium—17A

*r*ight *h*alfback—11

*r*ight *h*and—17, 25

*R*oyal *H*ighness—28

RHB *r*ight *h*alfback—11

RHD *R*andom *H*ouse *D*ictionary—22

RHE Rheem Manufacturing Co.—9A

RHH H.H. Robertson Co.—9A

RHIP *r*ank *h*as *i*ts *p*rivileges—8

RHM one *R*oentgen per *h*our at a distance of one *m*eter—17

RHP Rath Packing Co.—9B

RHR Rohr Corp.—9A

R&I *R*egina et *I*mperatrix (queen and empress)—19, 28

*r*ex et *i*mperator (king and emperor)—19, 28

RI Chicago, Rock Island and Pacific Railroad Co.—9A

*R*hode *I*sland—27

RIA *R*esearch *I*nstitute of *A*merica, Inc.—3

RIAA Record Industry Association of America—10

RIAS *R*adio *i*n *A*merican *S*ector—12, 14

RIBA *R*oyal *I*nstitute of *B*ritish *A*rchitects—20

RIE research *i*n *e*ducation—23

RIF *r*eduction *i*n *f*orce—17

RII Raymond International, Inc.—9A

RIIA *R*oyal *I*nstitute of *I*nternational *A*ffairs—20

RIM Riker-Maxson Corp.—9B

RIP *r*equiescat *i*n *p*ace (may he [she] rest in peace)—19

*r*esin-*i*n-*p*ulp process (for uranium ore treatment)—19

RIS *R*ock *I*sland *S*outhern Railroad—1

RIV Ric Group, Inc.—9B

RIX Rixon Electronics, Inc.—9B

RJ *r*oad *j*unction—8

RJR R.J. Reynolds Tobacco Co.—9A

RK Rucker Co.—9A

RKO *R*adio *K*eith *O*rpheum—25

RLB *r*ight *l*inebacker—11

RLC Rollins Leasing Corp.—9B

RLD *r*et*a*il *l*iquor *d*ealer—9

RLDS *R*eorganized Church of Jesus Christ of *L*atter *D*ay *S*aints —16

RLF *r*etro*l*ental *f*ibroplasia—17

RLI Reliance Insurance Co.—9B

RLM Reynolds Metals Co.—9A

RLS *R*obert *L*ouis *S*tevenson—29

RM *r*eichs*m*ark—7

RMA *R*adio *M*anufacturers' *A*ssociation—10

*R*oyal *M*ilitary *A*cademy (Woolwich)—4

RMC *R*oyal *M*ilitary *C*ollege (Sandhurst)—4

RMD *r*eady *m*oney *d*own—8, 9

RMI *R*epublic *M*ortgage *I*nvestors—9B

RML Russell Mills, Inc.—9B

RMN *R*ichard *M*ilhous *N*ixon—29

RMP *r*eentry *m*easurements *p*rogram—17

RMS *r*ailway *m*ail *s*ervice—1, 7

*r*eusable *m*ultipurpose *s*pacecraft—17

*r*oot *m*ean *s*quare—17

*R*oyal *M*ail *S*ervice—7

*R*oyal *M*ail *S*hip—1

RMU *r*emote *m*aneuvering *u*nit—17

RMV *r*eentry *m*easurement *v*ehicle—17

RN *r*ado*n*—17A

*r*egistered *n*urse—28

*R*oyal *N*avy—4

RNA *r*ibo*n*ucleic (or *r*ibose*n*ucleic) *a*cid—17

RNAS *R*oyal *N*aval *A*ir *S*ervice—4

RNI Ranco, Inc.—9A

RNR *R*oyal *N*aval *R*eserve—4

RNVR *R*oyal *N*aval *V*olunteer *R*eserve—4

RNWMP *Royal Northwest Mounted Police*—26

RNZAF *Royal New Zealand Air Force*—4

RO *radio operator*—4
receiving office (or *officer*)—9
regimental order—4
regional office—9
Royal Observatory—17
rule out—17

ROA *Retired Officers' Association*—2

ROB Robintech, Inc.—9B

ROC Rockower Brothers, Inc.—9B

ROCOCO [perhaps] *ro*cailles (rocks) *co*quilles (shells) et *co*rdeau (string)—14

ROF Robertshaw Controls Co.—9A

ROG *receipt of goods*—9
Rogers Corp.—9B

ROH Rohm and Haas Co.—9A

ROI Royal Industries, Inc.—9A

ROK *Republic of Korea*—27
Rockwell Manufacturing Co.—9A

ROL Rollins, Inc.—9A

ROM Rio Algom Mines, Ltd.—9B

RON Ronson Corp.—9A

ROP Roper Corp.—9A
run of paper (or *press*)—22

ROR Rorer-Amchem, Inc.—9A

ROSC *Reserve Officers' Sanitary Corps*—4

ROT *rule of thumb*—8, 17

ROTC *Reserve Officers' Training Corps*—4

ROV *risk, originality, virtuosity* (gymnastics)—11

ROY *rest of you*—8, 14
Royal American Industries, Inc.—9B

RP *real property*—9
rear projection—25
Reformed Presbyterian—16
Regius Professor—28
Republic of Panama—27
rocket projectile—4

Rowland Products, Inc.—9B

RPC Revenue Properties Co., Ltd.—9B

RPD Rapid-American Corp.—9A, 9B

RPF *Rassemblement du Peuple Français* (Reassembly of the French People)—12, 24

RPI *Rensselaer Polytechnic Institute*—23

RPM *revolutions per minute*—17

RPO *railway post office*—1, 7

RPP *Republican Peoples' Party* (Turkey)—12

RPQ *request for price quotations*—9

RPS *revolutions per second*—17

RQ *respiratory quotient*—17

R&R *rest and recuperation* (or *rehabilitation*)—17
rock-and-roll—25

RR *railroad*—1
Raritan River Railroad—1
Right Reverend—28
Roosevelt Raceway, Inc.—9B

RRB *Railroad Retirement Board*—6

RRC *Rubber Reserve Co.*—6

RRM Royal Aluminum Corp.—9B

RRO Rolls-Royce Ltd.—9B

RRR Career Academy, Inc.—9B

RS *recording secretary*—28
reformed spelling—15
Republic Steel Corp.—3, 9A
revised statutes—7
right safety—11
right side—8

RSA *radar signature analysis*—17
Republic of South Africa—27

RSC Reeves Industries, Inc.—9B

RSE *Richmond Stock Exchange*—9

RSFSR *Russian Soviet Federated Socialist Republic*—12

RSK Russeks, Inc.—9B

RSM *regimental sergeant major*—4

RSN Rosenau Brothers, Inc.—9B

RSO Rusco Industries, Inc.—9B

RSP *right sacro posterior*—17

RST Roan Selection Trust, Ltd.—9A

RSV *Revised Standard Version* (Bible)—16

Rous sarcoma virus—17

RSVP *répondez s'il vous plaît* (please reply)—19

RT *radio telephone*—9

Resorts International, Inc.—9B

right tackle—11

RTC Rochester Telephone Corp.—9A

RTD *rapid transit district*—7

research and technology division—9

RTN Raytheon Co.—9A

RTNDA *Radio-Television News Directors' Association*—20

RTS Russ Togs, Inc.—9A

RTW *ready-to-wear*—9

RTX Riegel Textile Corp.—9A

RU *ruthenium*—17A

RUR "*Rossum's Universal Robots*" (theatrical play)—25

RUS Rust Craft Greeting Cards, Inc. —9B

RV *recreational vehicle*—8

Revised Version (Bible)—16

RVB Revere Copper and Brass, Inc. —9A

RVI *Recreational Vehicle Institute*—10

RVO Reserve Oil and Gas Co.—9B

RVR Riviana Foods, Inc.—9A

RVS Reeves Brothers, Inc.—9A

RVSVP *répondez vite s'il vous plaît* (please reply quickly)—19

RW *right of way*—8

right wing—11

Right Worthy (or *Worshipful*)—28

RWDSU *Retail, Wholesale and Department Store Union*—21

RX *Rank Xerox*—3

Resistoflex Corp.—9B

RXM Richardson-Merrell, Inc.—9A

RYH Ryerson and Haynes, Inc.—9B

RYM *Revolutionary Youth Movement*—2

RYT Rayette Fabergé, Inc.—9A

RZ *return-to-zero*—17

S Sears, Roebuck and Co.—9A

sulfur—17A

S&A *Savannah & Atlanta Railroad*—1

SA Safeway Stores, Inc.—9A

Salvation Army—16

seaman apprentice—4

secundum artem (according to art)—18

semiannual—9

semiautomatic—4, 9

sex appeal—8

shipped assembled—9

sine anno (without year)—19

sinoatrial—17

small arms—4

Sociedad Anonima (Spanish) or *Société Anonyme* (French) (anonymous society, or limited liability company)—9

South Africa—27

South America—27

South Australia—27

state's attorney—7

Sturmabteilung (storm trooper division)—12

subject to approval—9

SAA Sanders Associates, Inc.—9A

South African Airways—1

Speech Association of America—20

SAAB *Svenska Aeroplan Aktiebolaget* (Swedish airplane and automobile)—1, 14

SAB *Scientific Advisory Board*—6

SABENA *Société Anonyme Belge d'Expoitation de la Navigation Aerienne* (Belgian Air Lines)—1, 14

SABMIS *sea-based antiballistic missile*—4, 14

SAC Stanley Aviation Corp.—9B

119

Strategic Air Command—4

SACB Subversive Activities Control Board—6

SACEUR Supreme Allied Commander, Europe—4, 14

SACEM Société des Auteurs, Compositeurs et Editeurs de Musique (Society of Authors, Composers, and Editors of Music)—12, 14

SACLANT Supreme Allied Commander, Atlantic—4, 14

SAE Society of Automotive Engineers—20

SAESA Servicios Aeros Especiales Sociedad Anonima (Mexican airline)—1

SAF Santa Fe International Corp.—9A

SAG Screen Actors' Guild—21

semiactive guidance—17

SAGE semiautomatic ground environment (or equipment) rocket system—4, 14

SAI Season-All Industries, Inc.—9B

SAINT satellite interception—4, 14

SAJ St. Joseph Light and Power Co.—9A

SAL Seaboard Air Line Railroad—1

Seligman and Latz, Inc.—9B

SALT Strategic Arms Limitation Talks—7, 14

SAM School of Aerospace Medicine—17, 23

Seaboard Allied Milling Corp.—9B

Society of American Magicians—20

space available mail—7

surface-to-air missile—4, 14

SAMOS satellite and (or anti-) missile observation system—4, 14

SAN San Carlos Milling Co., Ltd.—9B

SAP sintered aluminum powder alloy—9

soon as possible—8

SAR Sons of the American Revolution—2

Stellar Industries, Inc.—9B

SAS Scandinavian Airlines System—1

secure (or status) authentication system—17

SAT Saturn Industries, Inc.—9A

Scholastic Aptitude Test—23

Stanford Achievement Test—23

SATA Sociedade Acoriana de Transportes Aéreas (Portuguese airline)—1, 14

SATC Students' Army Training Corps—4

SATCOM Satellite Communication Agency—4, 14

SAV Savannah Electric and Power Co.—9A

SAX Southwest Airmotive Co.—9A

SAY Sayre and Fisher Co.—9B

SB Scientiae Baccalaureus (Bachelor of Science)—5

Senate bill—7

simultaneous broadcast—25

smoothbore gun—4

southbound—1

South Britain—27

Standard Brands, Inc.—9A

antimony (from stibium)—17A

stolen base—11

SBA Small Business Administration—6

SBC Schmidt-Baker camera—17

Southern Baptist Convention—16

Stokely-Van Camp, Inc.—9A

SBD Seaboard Coast Line Railroad Co.—9A

SBI Sterchi Brothers Stores, Inc.—9A

SBIC Small Business Investment Corp.—6

SBK Storer Broadcasting Co.—9A

SBLI savings bank life insurance—9

SBM Speed-O-Print Business Machines Corp.—9B

SBN Siboney Corp.—9B

Standard Book Number—22

SBO Simmons-Boardman Publishing Corp.—9B

SBP Standard Brands Paint Co.—9A

SBS Salem-Brosius, Inc.—9B

S&C *Sumter & Choctaw Railroad*—1

SC *Sanitary Corps*—4

scandium—17A

Schmidt camera—17

Security Council—13

Shell Transport and Trading Co., Ltd., New York—9A

Signal Corps—4

single column—9

small capitals—22

South Carolina—27

staff corps—4

Supreme Court—6

Sylvania Central Railroad—1

SCA Servo Corp. of America—9B

Shipbuilders Council of America—10

SCAP *Supreme Commander for the Allied Powers in Japan*—4, 14

SCCA *Sports Car Club of America*—2, 11

SCE Southern California Edison Co.—9A, 9B

SCF *standard cubic foot*—17

SCFH *standard cubic foot per hour*—17

SCFM *standard cubic foot per minute*—17

SCG South Carolina Electric and Gas Co.—9A

SCH Schenuit Industries, Inc.—9B

SCI Seaboard Coastline Industries, Inc.—9A

SCL *Seaboard Coast Line Railroad*—1

Stepan Chemical Co.—9B

SCLC *Southern Christian Leadership Conference (or Council)*—2, '6

SCM SCM Corp.—9A

Smith-Corona-Marchant Corp.—3

SCN *specification change notice*—9

SCO Scovill Manufacturing Co.—9A

subcarrier oscillator—17

SCORE *Service Corps of Retired Executives (of Small Business Administration)*—6, 9, 14

SCP Scope Industries—9B

SCPO *senior chief petty officer*—4

SCR Spedcor Electronics, Inc.—9B

SCS *scheduled cargo service*—1

Soil Conservation Service—6

SCT Supercrete, Ltd.—9B

SCUA *Suez Canal Users' Association*—12

SCUBA *self-contained underwater breathing apparatus*—11, 14

SCV *Sons of Confederate Veterans*—2

SCW Screw and Bolt Corp. of America—9A

SCX The L.S. Starrett Co.—9A

S&D *song and dance*—25

SD *Scientiae Doctor (Doctor of Science)*—5

semidiameter—9, 27

senior deacon—16

sight draft—9

sine die (without a date)—19

small date (coins)—8

South Dakota—27

square dance—8

stage door—25

standard deviation—17

Standard Oil Co. of California—9A

supply department—9

SDA *Seventh Day Adventists*—16

SD&AE *San Diego & Arizona Eastern Railroad*—1

SDB Sonderling Broadcasting Co.—9B

SDC *System Development Corp.*—3

SDE Shattuck Denn Mining Corp.—9B

SDG Self-Development Group—2

SDI SMD Industries, Inc.—9B

SDO San Diego Gas and Electric Co.—9A, 9B

SDP Standard Pressed Steel Co.—9A

SDR special drawing rights—9

Standard Dredging Co.—9B

SDS Students for a Democratic Society—2

SDV Scudder Duo-Vest, Inc.—9A

SE selenium—17A

single entry—9

southeast—27

split end—11

SEA Seatrain Lines, Inc.—9A

sound effects amplifier—25

SEAC Southeast Asia Command—4, 14

SEATAC Seattle-Tacoma—8, 14, 27

SEATO Southeast Asia Treaty Organization—12, 14

SEB Seaboard Plywood and Lumber Corp.—9B

SEC Securities and Exchange Commission—6

Southeastern Conference—11

Sterling Electronics Corp.—9B

SED Sozialistische Einheitspartei Deutschlands (German Socialist Unity Party)—12

SEE Seeman Brothers, Inc.—9B

SEEK search for educational elevation and knowledge—14, 23

SEER systems engineering, evaluation, and research—9, 17

SEG Screen Extras Guild—21

SEL Seton Co.—9B

SELC Synod of Evangelical Lutheran Churches—16

SEM Stelma, Inc.—9B

SEND Securities and Exchange Commission News Digest—6, 14, 22

SEP The Saturday Evening Post—22

SEPA Southeastern Power Administration—6

SER The Sierracin Corp.—9B

SERT Space Electric Rocket Test—14, 17

SES Shahmoon Industries, Inc.—9B

SESAC Society of European Stage Authors and Composers—14, 25

SESCO Speed Engineering Service Co. (engines)—3, 14

SETAF U.S. Army Southern European Task Force—4, 14

S&EV Saratoga & Encampment Valley Railroad—1

SEV surface effect vessel—1

SF sacrifice fly—11

San Francisco—27

science fiction—22

sinking fund—9

special forces—4

SFA Scientific-Atlanta, Inc.—9B

SFBF standard forms bureau form (insurance)—9

SFC sergeant first class—4

SFE Safeguard Industries, Inc.—9B

SFF Santa Fe Industries, Inc.—9A

SFI Surveyor Fund, Inc.—9A

SFM surface feet per minute—17

SFN Scott Foresman and Co.—9A

SFR F. and M. Schaefer Corp.—9A

SFSR Soviet Federated Socialist Republic—12

SFW Sheffield Watch Corp.—9B

SFZ Scott and Fetzer Co.—9A

SG Screen Gems—25

Sealectro Corp.—9A

senior grade—4

South Georgia Railroad—1

specific gravity—17

SGA Southern Natural Gas Co.—9A

SGC Superior Surgical Manufacturing Co., Inc.—9B

SGI Sigma Instruments, Inc.—9B

SGL Supermarkets General Corp.—9A

SGM Sangamo Electric Co.—9A

SGN Signal Companies, Inc.—9A

SGS Signode Corp.—9A

SGT Sargeant Industries, Inc.—9B

S&H *S*perry and *H*utchinson Co. (green stamps)—3

SH Schenley Industries, Inc.—9A

SHA *si*dereal *h*our *a*ngle—17

SHAEF *S*upreme *H*eadquarters, *A*llied *E*xpeditionary *F*orces—4, 14

SHAPE *S*upreme *H*eadquarters, *A*llied *P*owers, *E*urope—4, 14

SHC Stein, Hall and Co., Inc.—9B

SHF *s*uper *h*igh *f*requency—17

SHG Sheller-Globe Corp.—9A

SHK Schick Electric, Inc.—9A

SHL Shelter Resources Corp.—9B

SHM *s*imple *h*armonic *m*otion—17

SHO *S*tudent *H*ealth *O*rganizations—17, 23

SHORAN *sho*rt *ra*nge *n*avigation—14, 17

SHP *s*haft *h*orse*p*ower—1

Stop and Shop, Inc.—9B

SHS Shaer Shoe Corp.—9B

*S*ocietatis *H*istoricae *S*ocius (Fellow, The Historical Society)—28

SHU Shulton, Inc.—9A

SHW Sherwin-Williams Co.—9A

SI *S*andwich *I*slands—27

*s*aturation *i*ndex—17

*si*licon—17A

*S*mithsonian *I*nstitution—6, 17, 23

*S*pokane *I*nternational Railroad—1

*S*ports *I*llustrated—22

*S*taten *I*sland—27

SIAL *si*lica and *al*uminum—14, 17

SIAP *s*tandard *i*nstrument *ap*proach—1, 14

SIC *S*atellite *I*nformation *C*enter—17

Silicon Transistor Corp.—9B

SICU *s*urgical *i*ntensive *c*are *u*nit—17

SID *s*emel *in* *d*ie (once a day)—18

*s*tandard *i*nstrument *d*eparture—1

*s*ynchronous *id*entification system—4, 14

SIECUS *S*ex *I*nformation and *E*ducation *C*ouncil of the *U*nited States—14, 23

SIG Southern Indiana Gas and Electric Co.—9A

SII Smith International, Inc.—9A

SIL Singer Manufacturing Co., Ltd.—9B

SIM Simmons Co.—9A

SIMA *si*lica and *m*agnesium—14, 17

SIMCA *S*océété *I*ndustrielle *M*écanique *C*arrosserie *A*utomobile (French automobile)—1, 14

SIMS *S*tudents' *I*nternational *M*editation *S*ociety—2, 14

SINS *s*hip's *i*nertial *n*avigation system—1, 14

SIR Schiller Corp.—9B

*S*ociety of *I*ndustrial *R*ealtors—10

SIRT *S*taten *I*sland *R*apid *T*ransit—1, 14

SIT *s*ilicon-*in*tensifier *t*ube—17

*S*itkin *S*melting and *R*efining, Inc.—9B

SIU *S*eafarers *I*nternational *U*nion of North America—21

*S*ears Industries, Inc.—9B

SIX Spector Industries, Inc.—9B

SJ *S*ocietas *J*esu (Society of Jesus) (Jesuits)—16

SJD *S*cientiae *J*uridicae *D*octor (Doctor of Juridical Science)—5

SJG South Jersey Gas Co.—9A

SJ&LC *S*t. *J*ohnsbury & *L*ake *C*hamplain Railroad—1

SJM J.M. Smucker Co.—9A

SJO St. Joseph Lead Co.—9A

SJR San Juan Racing Association, Inc.—9B

SKA Skaggs Drug Centers, Inc.—9B

SKC Skil Corp.—9A

SKI Head Ski Co., Inc.—9B

*S*loan-*K*ettering *I*nstitute (cancer research, N.Y.)—17

SKL Smith, Kline and French Laboratories—9A

SKO Standard Kollsman Industries, Inc.—9A

SKU Stanrock Uranium Mines, Ltd.—9B

SKW Studebaker-Worthington, Inc. —9A

SKY Skyline Corp.—9A

S&L savings and loan—9

Sydney and Louisburg Railroad—1

SL Sierra Leone—27

Simpsons, Ltd.—9B

sine loco (without place)—19

SLA state liquor authority—6

SLAM supersonic low altitude missile—4, 14

SLBM sea- (or submarine-) launched ballistic missile—4

SLC San Luis Central Railroad—1

SLF Scot Lad Foods, Inc.—9A

SLI The Slick Corp.—9B

SLIC Savings and Loan Insurance Corp.—9

SLP Socialist Labor Party—24

SLR single-lens reflex (camera)—8

SLS Selas Corp. of America—9B

SLSF St. Louis-San Francisco Railroad—1

SLSW St. Louis Southwestern Railroad—1

SLV standard launch vehicle—17

SLVS San Luis Valley Southern Railroad—1

SLX Sterling Extruder Corp.—9B

SLZ Joseph Schlitz Brewing Co.—9A

S&M sadism and masochism—8

supply and maintenance—9

SM samarium—17A

Scientiae Magister (Master of Science)—5

sergeant major—4

short measure (hymns)—25

Smoky Mountain Railroad—1

Soldier's Medal—28

state militia—4

statute mile—27

St. Marys Railroad—1

strategic missile—4

SMA Surplus Marketing Administration—6

SMAZE smoke and haze—8, 14

SMB Sacrae Musicae Baccalaureus (Bachelor of Sacred Music)—5

Sunbeam Corp.—9A

SMC A.O. Smith Corp.—9A

Supply and Maintenance Command—4

SMCC Santa Monica City College—23

SMD Sacrae Musicae Doctor (Doctor of Sacred Music)—5

SME Sherwood Medical Industries, Inc.—9B

SMF The Singer Co.—9A

SMI Spring Mills, Inc.—9A

Super Market Institute—10

SMK Simkins Industries, Inc.—9B

SML Steelmet, Inc.—9B

SMM Sacrae Musicae Magister (Master of Sacred Music)—5

Standard Metals Corp.—9B

SMOG smoke and fog—8, 14

SMOM Sovereign and Military Order of Malta—2

SMP Standard Motor Products, Inc.—9B

SMPTE Society of Motion Picture and Television Engineers—20

SMS Stapling Machines Co.—9B

synchronous meteorological satellite—17

SMSG school mathematics study group—23

SMU self- (or space-) maneuvering unit—17

Southern Methodist University—23

SMWIA Sheet Metal Workers' International Association—21

SMX Simplex Wire and Cable Co.—9B

SN secundum *n*aturam (according to nature)—18

shipping *n*ote—9

Standard Oil Co. (Indiana)—9A

tin (from sta*n*num)—17A

SNA sodium *n*aphthalene *a*cetate—17

SNAFU situation *n*ormal *a*ll *f*ouled up—8, 14

SNAP systems for *n*uclear *a*uxiliary *p*ower—14, 17

SNCC Student *N*onviolent Coordinating Committee ("Snick")—2

SNH The Sperry and Hutchinson Co.—9A

SNK Swank, Inc.—9A

SNL Sun Chemical Corp.—9A

SNPO Space *N*uclear Propulsion Office—17

SNR SunAir Electronics, Inc.—9B

SNS Sundstrand Corp.—9A

SNSE Society of *N*uclear Scientists and Engineers—20

SO sales office—9

seller's option—9

shipping order—9

signal officer—4

The Southern Co.—9A

special order—9

standing order—9

SOA SCOA Industries, Inc.—9A

SOB son of a bitch—8

SOC Superior Oil Co. (Nevada)—9A

SOCMAC socially oriented comprehensive memory assist computer—14, 17

SOCONY Standard Oil Company of New York—3, 14

SOD Solitron Devices, Inc.—9B

SODAR sound detecting and ranging—14, 17

SOFAR sound fixing and ranging—14, 17

SOG Study and Observations Group (of MACV [which see])—4

SOH The Standard Oil Co. (Ohio)—9A

SOHIO Standard Oil Co. (Ohio)—3, 14

SOI space object identification—17

SOL Sola Basic Industries, Inc.—9A

strictly out of luck—8

SOLE Society of Logistics Engineers—20

SOLION solution of ions—14, 17

SOMS synchronous operational meteorological satellite—14, 17

SON Soundesign Corp.—9B

SONAR sound navigation and ranging—14, 17

SOO Soo Line Railroad Co.—9A

SOP standard operating procedure—8, 9

SOR specific operational requirement—9

SOS save our ship—8

services of supply—4

"shit on a shingle" (chipped beef on toast)—4, 8

si opus sit (if necessary)—18

SOS Consolidated, Inc.—9A, 9B

SOTA state of the art—17

SOY Savoy Industries, Inc.—9B

S&P Standard and Poor's Corp.—3

SP self-propelled—1

shore patrol (or police)—4

Simmonds Precision Products, Inc.—9A

sine prole (without issue)—9

Socialist party—24

Southern Pacific Railroad—1

submarine patrol—4

systolic pressure—17

SPA Society of Philatelic Americans—2

Songwriters' Protective Association—10

Southwestern Power Administration—6

Spartan Corp.—9A

Stores' Protective Association, Inc.—10

SPAM spiced ham—3, 14

SPAR seagoing platform for acoustic research—14, 17

semper Paratus (always ready; U.S. Coast Guard Women's Reserve)—4, 14, 19

SPAS Societatis Philosophicae Americanae Socius (Member, American Philosophical Society)—28

SPC Suicide Prevention Center—2

Superior Coach Corp.—9B

SPCA Society for the Prevention of Cruelty to Animals—2

SPCC Society for the Prevention of Cruelty to Children—2

SPCK Society for the Promotion of Christian Knowledge—16

SPD The Standard Products Co.—9B

system program director—9, 17

SPE special purpose equipment—17

Sprague Electric Co.—9A

SPEBSQSA Society for the Preservation and Encouragement of Barber Shop Quartet Singing in America—2

SPF specific pathogen-free (meat-packing)—9

SPG Screen Producers' Guild—20

Society for the Propagation of the Gospel—16

Suburban Propane Gas Corp.—9A

SPIE Society of Photographic Instrumentation Engineers—20

SPK Standard Packaging Corp.—9A

SPM solar-proton monitor—17

SPN Spencer Shoe Corp.—9B

SPO Spectro Industries, Inc.—9B

SPOT speed, position, track (navigation system)—14, 27

SPP Scott Paper Co.—9A

SPQR senatus populusque Romanus (the Senate and people of Rome)—19

SPR Society for Psychical (or Psychophysiological) Research—20

SP&S Spokane, Portland & Seattle Railroad—1

SPS scheduled passenger service—1

service propulsion system—17

Southwestern Public Service Co.—9A

SPSSI Society for the Psychological Study of Social Issues—20

SPT Spartan Industries, Inc.—9A

SPV Southeastern Public Service Co.—9A

SPX Simplex Industries, Inc.—9B

SQB Squibb-Beech Nut, Inc.—9A

SQD Square D Co.—9A

SQN Susquehanna Corp.—9B

SR Saturday Review—22

scanning radiometer—17

seaman recruit—4

sedimentation rate—17

senza ripetizione (without repetition) (music)—19

Sierra Railroad—1

single reduction gearing (ships)—1

Skagit River Railroad—1

solar radiation—17

Sons of the Revolution—2

Southern Railway Co.—9A

strontium—17A

SRAM short-range attack missile—4

SRB Scurry-Rainbow Oil, Ltd.—9B

SRBM short-range ballistic missile—4

SRC Southern Realty and Utilities Corp.—9B

SRE Scientific Resources Corp.—9A

SREB Southern Regional Education Board—23

SRF Self-Realization Fellowship—16

SRG Schering Corp.—9A

SRH Stardust, Inc.—9B

SRI Stanford Research Institute—17, 23

Sternco Industries, Inc.—9B

SRL G.D. Searle and Co.—9A

SRM Spiritual Regeneration Movement—16

SRO Southland Royalty Co.—9B

standing room only—25

SRP Sierra Pacific Power Co.—9A

SRS Social and Rehabilitation Service—6

Statistical Reporting Service—6

SRT St. Regis Paper Co.—9A

SRU Seilon, Inc.—9A

SRY Stanray Corp.—9A

S&S Saratoga & Schuylerville Railroad—1

signs and symptoms—17

SS Schutzstaffel (Nazi elite guard)—12

Secret Service—6

semis (one half)—18

sensu stricto (in the strict sense)—18

senza sordini (without mutes) (music)—19

shortstop—11

Silver Star—28

soapsuds—17

steamship—1

Sunday school—16

supersonic—17

super sports (car)—8

supra scriptum (written above)—18

suspended sentence 26

SSA Soaring Society of America—11

Social Security Act 7

Social Security Administration—6

SSAN Social Security account number—7

SSB single side band (radio)—17

Social Security Board—6

Social Security Bulletin—7, 22

SSC Sunshine Mining Co.—9A

SSD Sacrae Scripturae Doctor (Doctor of Sacred Scriptures)—5

Sanctissimus Dominus (Most Holy Lord)—16

Space Systems Division (of U.S. Air Force)—4

SSE south-southeast—27

SSF standard saybolt furol—17

SSJ Society of St. Joseph (Josephites)—16

SSM surface-to-surface missile 4

SSND School Sisters of Notre Dame—16

SSP Superscope, Inc.—9B

SSR Social Security rulings—7

Soviet Socialist Republic—12

SSS Selective Service System—4, 6

SSP Industries—9B

SST supersonic transport—1

SSU standard saybolt universal—17

SSW south-southwest—27

ST Chicago, Milwaukee, St. Paul and Pacific Railroad Co.—9A

short ton—9

STA A.E. Staley Manufacturing Co.—9A

STADAN Space Tracking and Data Acquisition Network (of NASA)—6, 14

STAQ security trader's automated quotations—9

STAR scientific and technical aerospace reports—14, 17, 22

STB Sacrae Theologiae Baccalaureus (Bachelor of Sacred Theology)—5

Scientiae Theologiae Baccalaureus (Bachelor of Science in Theology)—5

STD Sacrae Theologiae Doctor (Doctor of Sacred Theology)—5

Standard Alliance Industries, Inc.—9B

ST&E Stockton, Terminal & Eastern Railroad—1

STE special (or standard) test equipment—17

Steel Co. of Canada, Ltd.—9B

STEN Shepard-Turpin-England gun—4, 14

STF Stauffer Chemical Co.—9A

STG space task group—17

Sterling Precision Corp.—9B

STH Standard-Thomson Corp.—9B

STI Statham Instruments, Inc. 9B

STJ St. Johnsbury Trucking Co., Inc.—9B

STL space *t*echnology *l*aboratory—17

Standard International Corp.—9B

STM *S*acrae *T*heologiae *M*agister (Master of Sacred Theology)—5

The Stern Metals Corp.—9B

STN J.P. Stevens and Co., Inc.—9A

STO Stone Container Corp.—9A

STOL short *t*ake*o*ff and *l*anding—1, 14

STOLPORT short *t*ake*o*ff and *l*anding air*port*—1, 14

STP *s*cientifically *t*reated *p*etroleum—3

*s*erenity, *t*ranquility, *p*eace (used by LSD-takers)—8

*s*tandard conditions of *t*emperature and *p*ressure—17

STP Corp.—9B

*s*ystem *t*raining *p*rogram—17

STR Star Supermarkets, Inc.—9B

STRAC *St*rategic *A*rmy *C*orps—4, 14

STRAF *St*rategic *A*rmy *F*orces—4, 14

STRATCOM *Stra*tegic *Com*munications *C*ommand—4, 14

STRICOM (United States) *Stri*ke *Com*mand—4, 14

STT Standard Container Co.—9B

STU Standard Prudential Corp.—9A

STUKA *Stu*r*zka*mpfflugzeug (dive bomber)—4, 14

STX Stewart-Warner Corp.—9A

STY Sterling Drug, Inc.—9A

SU Supronics Corp.—9B

SUA *s*hipped *u*n*a*ssembled—9

SUB Suburban Gas—9A

SUBAD *su*b*m*arine *a*ir *d*efense—4, 14

SUC SuCrest Corp.—9A

SUDS *su*b*m*arine *d*etection *s*ystem—4, 14

SUID *s*udden *u*nexpected *i*nfant *d*eath—17

SUM *s*urface-to-*u*nderwater *m*issile—4

SUN Sun Oil Co.—9A

SUNFED *S*pecial *U*nited *N*ations *F*und for *E*conomic *D*evelopment—13, 14

SUNOCO *Sun Oi*l *C*ompany—3, 14

SUNY *S*tate *U*niversity of *N*ew *Y*ork—14, 23

SUO Shell Oil Co.—9A

SUR Saturn Airways, Inc.—9B

SUS *s*aybolt *u*niversal *s*econds—17

SUV *s*aybolt *u*niversal *v*iscosity—17

SUVCW *S*ons of *U*nion *V*eterans of the *C*ivil *W*ar—2

SUW Struthers Wells Corp.—9B

SV *S*ancta *V*irgo (Holy Virgin)—16

*s*ide *v*alves—9

*s*piritus *v*ini (spirit of alcohol)—17

*s*ub *v*erbo (or *v*oce) (under the word)—19

SVB Savin Business Machines Corp.—9B

SVE The Seagrave Corp.—9A

SVM Servomation Corp.—9A

SVO Servisco—9B

SVP *s*'il *v*ous *p*laît (if you please)—19

SVR Silvray-Litecraft Corp.—9B

*s*piritus *v*ini *r*ectificatus (rectified spirit of alcohol)—17

SVS Sav-A-Stop, Inc.—9B

SVT Servotronics, Inc.—9B

*s*piritus *v*ini *t*enuis (proof spirit of alcohol)—17

SVU Super Valu Stores, Inc.—9A

SVZ Sinclair Venezuelan Oil Co.—9B

SW short *w*ave—17

*S*outh *W*ales—27

*s*outh*w*est—23

Stone and Webster, Inc.—9A

SWA Seaboard World Airlines, Inc.—9A

*S*outh *W*est *A*frica—27

SWAK *s*ealed *w*ith *a* *k*iss—8

SWAMI *S*tanford *W*orldwide *A*cquisition of *M*eteorological *I*nformation—14, 17

SWAT *s*pecial *w*eapons *a*nd *t*actics—14, 26

SWC Southwestern Investment Co.—9B

SWD Standard Shares, Inc.—9B

SWF Southwest Forest Industries, Inc.—9B

SWG standard wire gauge—9

SWK The Stanley Works—9A

SWL Swingline, Inc.—9A

SWS Sargent-Welch Scientific Co.—9A

SWX Swift and Co.—9A

SX Southern Pacific Co.—9A

SXP Saxon Industries, Inc.—9B

SY Sperry Rand Corp.—9A

SYB Sybron Corp.—9A

SYE Skelly Oil Co.—9A

SYL Stylon Corp.—9B

SYN Syntex Corp.—9B

SYO Synalloy Corp.—9B

SYP Simplicity Pattern Co., Inc.—9A

SYS Systron-Donner Corp.—9B

SYT Systems Engineering Laboratory, Inc.—9B

T American Telephone and Telegraph Co.—9A

T&A tonsillectomy and adenoidectomy—17

TA tantalum—17A

teaching assistant—23

training analyst—9

Transamerica Corp.—9A

TAA Trans-Australia Airlines—1

Transportation Association of America—10

TAB Technical Abstract Bulletin—14, 22

technical analysis branch—14, 17

Technical Assistance Board—13

TAC Tactical Air Command—4, 14

Take A Child—2, 14

Technical Assistance Committee—13

TACAN tactical air navigation—14, 27

TA&G Tennessee, Alabama & Georgia Railroad—1

TAG Transport Air Group—4, 14

TAI Transports Aériens Intercontinentaux (Intercontinental Air Transport, France)—1

TAL Tally Industries, Inc.—9A

TAM television audience measurement—25

transistor amplifier multiplier—17

Tubos de Acero de México, S.A.—9B

TAN Tandy Corp.—9A

Transportes Aéreos Nacionales (National Air Transport, Honduras)—1, 14

TANZANIA Tanganyika and Zanzibar—14, 27

TAO triacetyloleandomycin—17

TAP Transportes Aéreos Portugueses (Portuguese Airlines)—1, 14

TAPPI Technical Association of the Pulp and Paper Industry—10, 14

TAPS Trans-Alaska Pipeline System—3, 14

TARFU things are really fouled up—8, 14

TAS true air speed—1

TASS Telegrafnoye Agenstvo Sovyetskovo Soyuza (Telegraphic News Agency, Soviet Union)—12, 14, 22

TAT tetanus antitoxin—14, 17

Thematic Apperception Test—14, 23

toxin-antitoxin—14, 17

TA&W Toledo, Angola & Western Railroad—1

TB tailback—11

technical bulletin—22

terbium—17A

trial balance—9

tubercle bacillus—17

tuberculosis—8, 17

TBA to be announced—25

TBC Tasty Baking Co.—9B

TBM *tactical ballistic missile*—4

TBN Tobin Packing Co., Inc.—9A

TBO *time between overhauls*—1
  total blackout—25

TBR "21" Brands, Inc.—9B

TBS *talk between ships*—1

TBT *target-bearing transmitter* (submarines)—4

TC *teachers' college*—23
  technetium—17A
  Tennessee Central Railroad—1
  tre corde (three strings) (music)—19
  Trustee Council (United Nations)—13

  twin carburetor—1

TCA Trailer Coach Association—10
  Trans-Canada Airlines—1
  Trans-Caribbean Airways—1, 9B
  trichloroacetic acid—17

TCB *taking care of business*—8

TCBM *transcontinental ballistic missile*—4

TCCA Textile Color Card Association of the United States—10

TCEU Transportation-Communication Employees Union—21

TC&GB Tucson, Cornella & Gila Bend Railroad—1

TCL Transcon Lines—9A

TCO *termination contracting office*—6

TCP *tricresyl phosphate* (gasoline additive)—3, 17

TCS *traffic control station*—1
  transmission-controlled speed—1, 9

TCU Texas Christian University—23

TD *tank destroyer*—4
  Territorial Decoration—28
  time deposit—9
  touchdown—11
  traffic director—9
  Treasury Department—6

TDE *tetrachlorodiphenylethane*—17

TDM *time division multiplexing*—17

TDN *totally digestible nutrients*—17

TDO *technical development objective*—9

TDY Teledyne, Inc.—9A
  temporary duty—4

T&E *test and evaluation*—9

TE Tampa Electric Co.—9A
  tellurium—17A
  tight end—11
  transverse electric—17

TEAC Tokyo Electro-Acoustical Co.—3

TED The Toledo Edison Co.—9A, 9B

TEE Trans-Europe Express—1, 14

TEF The Epilepsy Foundation—2, 17

TEI *transearth injection* (or *insertion*)—17

TEK Tektronic, Inc.—9A

TEL *tetraethyl lead*—17

TELERAN *television and radar navigation system*—14, 27

TEM *transverse electromagnetic*—17
  triethylene melamine—17

TEMPO Technical Military Planning Organization—4, 14

TEN Tensor Corp.—9B

TEPP *tetraethyl pyrophosphate*—14, 17

TESL *teaching English as a second language*—23

TESOL Teachers of English to Speakers of Other Languages—14, 23

TET Texas Eastern Transmission Corp.—9A

TEUC *temporary emergency unemployment compensation*—7

TEX The Texstar Corp.—9B

TEXACO The Texas Company—3, 14

TEXARKANA Texas, Arkansas, Louisiana—14, 27

TF Tallulah Falls Railroad—1
  task force—4, 26
  territorial force—4
  Twentieth Century-Fox Film Corp.—9A

TFB Taft Broadcasting Co.—9A

TFD Thrifty Drug Stores Co., Inc.—9A

TFT Thriftimart, Inc.—9B

TFX *t*actical *f*ighter, *ex*perimental (airplane)—4

Teleflex, Inc.—9B

TFZ Tastee Freez Industries, Inc.—9B

T&G *T*onopah and *G*oldfield Railroad—1

*T*remont & *G*ulf Railroad—1

TG Texas Gulf Sulphur Co.—9A

*t*ype *g*enus—17

TGE Tucson Gas and Electric Co.—9A

TGIF *T*hank *G*od *i*t's *F*riday—8

TGT Tenneco, Inc.—9A

TH American Thread Co.—9B

Territory of *H*awaii—27

*th*orium—17A

TH&B *T*oronto, *H*amilton and *B*uffalo Railroad—1

THC *t*etra*h*ydro*c*annabinol (active ingredient in marijuana)—17

THE Terminal-Hudson Electronics, Inc.—9B

THFA *t*etra*h*ydro*f*olic *a*cid—17

THI *t*emperature-*h*umidity *i*ndex—17

Thiokol Chemical Corp.—9A

THP *t*erminal *h*olding *p*ower (advertising)—9

THY *T*urk *H*ava *Y*ollari (Turkish Airlines)—1

TI *t*i*t*anium—17A

*T*itle *I*nsurance and Trust Co.—3

TIA *T*rans-*I*nternational *A*irlines—1

TIC Travelers Corp.—9A

TID Technical Information Division (of Atomic Energy Commission)—17

*t*er *in* *d*ie (three times a day)—18

TII Thomas Industries, Inc.—9A

TIK Transcontinental Investing Corp.—9B

TILRA *T*ribal *I*ndian *L*and *R*ights *A*ssociation—2, 14

TIN *t*er *in* *n*octe (three times a night)—18

TIP *t*echnical *i*nformation *p*rogram—9, 14

TIPI *t*actical *i*nformation *p*rocessing and *i*nterpretation—14, 17

TIROS *t*elevision and *i*nfrared *o*bservation *s*atellite—14, 17

TIS *t*echnical *i*ntelligence *s*ystem—4

Tishman Realty and Construction Co., Inc.—9A

TJ *t*urbo*j*et—1

TJB *T*i*j*uana *B*rass—25

TK Technicolor, Inc.—9B

TKA Tonka Corp.—9B

TKO *t*echnical *k*nockout—11

TKR Timken Roller Bearing Co.—9A

T&L *t*hrift and *l*oan—9

TL *t*ha*l*ium—17A

Time, Inc.—9A

*t*ime *l*oan—9

*t*otal *l*oss—9

*t*rade *l*ast—8

*t*rade *l*ist—9

TLC Talcott National Corp.—9A

*t*ender *l*oving *c*are—8, 17

TLI *t*rans*l*unar *i*njection (or insertion)—17

TLO *t*otal *l*oss *o*nly—9

TLS Tel-A-Sign, Inc.—9B

TLX Trans-Lux Corp.—9B

TM *t*actical *m*issile—4

*t*echnical *m*anual (or *m*emorandum)—17

The Technical Materiel Corp.—9A

*t*empo *m*ark (music)—25

Texas Mexican Railroad 1

*t*huliu*m*—17A

*t*ime *m*odulator 17

*t*rade*m*ark—7, 9

*t*ransverse *m*agnetic 17

*t*rue *m*ean—17

TMA Television Manufacturers of America Co.—9B

Toy Manufacturers of America—10

TMC The Times Mirror Co.—9A

TMI Thorofare Markets, Inc.—9B

TMR Tamar Electronics Industries, Inc.—9B

TMRBM tactical medium-range ballistic missile—4

TMS Tidwater Marine Service, Inc.—9A

TMV tobacco mosaic virus—17

TNB Thomas and Betts Corp.—9A

trinitrobenzene (explosive)—17

T&NC Tennessee & North Carolina Railroad—1

TNC Town and Country Mobile Homes, Inc.—9B

TNEC Temporary National Economic Committee—6

TNL Technitrol, Inc.—9B

TNM Texas-New Mexico Railroad—1

TNPN total nonprotein nitrogen—17

TNT trinitrotoluene (explosive)—17

TNY Tenney Engineering, Inc.—9B

TO table of organization—4, 9

Technical Operations, Inc.—9B

theater of operations—4

turnover—9

TOC Tos (q.v.) Operations Center—17

TOD Todd Shipyards Corp.—9A

TO&E Texas, Oklahoma & Eastern Railroad—1

TOPS take off pounds sensibly—2, 14

TOS tactical operation system—4

TIROS [which see] operational satellite (or system)—17

TOW Tower Credit Corp.—9B

TOY Transogram Co., Inc.—9B

T&P Texas and Pacific Railroad—1

theft and pilferage—9, 26

TP TelePrompter Corp.—9B

title page—22

toilet paper—8

township—7

transship—9

turning point (surveying)—17

TPA terephthalic acid—17

TPD tons per day—9

TPF Triangle-Pacific Forest Products Corp.—9B

TPG Tropical Gas Co., Inc.—9B

TPH tons per hour—9

TPI teeth per inch—9

treponema pallidum immobilization test (for venereal disease)—17

turns per inch—9

TPL Texas Pacific Land Trust—9A

TPM tons per minute—9

TPN triphosphopyridine nucleotide—17

TPPC Trans-Pacific Passenger Conference—3

TPR temperature, pulse, respiration—17

TP&W Toledo, Peoria & Western Railroad—1

TQ tale quale (as it comes)—18

TR tempore regis (in the time of the king)—19

Theodore Roosevelt—29

tons registered—1

Tootsie Roll and Industries, Inc.—9A

transmit-receive (or transmitter-receiver)—17

trust receipt—9

TRA The Trane Co.—9A

Thoroughbred Racing Association—11

TRB Trans-Beacon Corp.—9B

TRE Tool Research and Engineering Corp.—9B

TRF thyrotrophin-releasing factor—17

tuned radio frequency—17

TRI Triangle Industries, Inc.—9A

TRIP transformation-induced plasticity—14, 17

TRN Transitron Electronic Corp.—9A

TRPB   *T*horoughbred *R*acing *P*rotective *B*ureau—11

TRS   Transairco, Inc.—9B

TRW   *T*hompson *R*amo *W*ooldridge Co.—3

TRW, Inc.—9A

TS   *t*asto *s*olo (one key alone) (music)—19

*T*idewater *S*outhern Railroad—1

*t*ool *s*hed—9

*t*op *s*ecret—4, 7

*t*ough *s*hit (polite: *s*tuff)—8

*T*rumann *S*outhern Railroad—1

*t*urbine *s*hip—1

TSC   *T*ractor *S*upply *C*o.—3

TSC Industries, Inc.—9A

TSD   *t*ime, *s*peed, *d*istance (type of auto race)—11

TSF   *t*élégraphie *s*ans *f*il (wireless telegraphy)—19

TSI   *t*ons per *s*quare *i*nch—9

TSM   Tri-State Motor Transit Co.—9B

TSO   Tesoro Petroleum Corp.—9B

TSS   *t*urbine *s*teamship—1

TST   *T*hompson-*S*tarrett *I*ndustries—3

TSU   Tobacco Securities Trust Co., Ltd.—9B

T&T   *T*ijuana and *T*ecate Railroad—1

TT   *T*anganyika *T*erritory—27

*t*ee*t*otaler—8

*T*exas *t*ower—4, 9

*T*oledo *T*erminal Railroad—1

*T*ourist *T*rophy (motorcycle racing)—11

*t*uberculin-*t*ested—17

TTA   *T*rans-*T*exas *A*irways—1

TTC   The Telex Corp.—9B

TTD   *t*etraethyl*t*hiuram *d*isulfide—17

TTI   Technical Tape, Inc.—9B

TTS   *T*ele*t*ypesetter—22

TTY   *t*ele*t*ypewriter—22

TU   *t*oxic *u*nit—17

*t*rade *u*nion—21

*t*raining *u*nit—4

*t*ransmission *u*nit—17

TUA   *T*ransit *U*nion *A*malgamated—21

TUC   *T*rades *U*nion *C*ongress—21

*t*ransportation, *u*tilities, *c*ommunications industries—9

TV   *t*ele*v*ision—8

*t*erminal *v*elocity—17

*t*rans*v*estite—8

*t*urn*v*erein (gymnastic club)—11

TVA   *T*ennessee *V*alley *A*uthority—6

TVI   *t*ele*v*ision *i*nterference—17

TWA   *T*rans-*W*orld *A*irlines 1, 9A, 9B

TWF   Trans-World Financial Co.—9A

TWIMC   *t*o *w*hom *i*t *m*ay *c*oncern—8

TWS   *T*imed *W*ire *S*ervice—22

TWT   *t*raveling *w*ave *t*ube—17

TWU   *T*ransport *W*orkers' *U*nion of America—21

TWUA   *T*extile *W*orkers *U*nion of America—21

TWX   *t*eletype*w*riter e*x*change—9

TX   Texaco, Inc.—9A

TXG   Texas Gas Transmission Corp.—9A

TXI   Texas Industries, Inc.—9A

TXN   Texas Instruments, Inc.—9A

TXO   Texas Oil and Gas Corp.—9A

TXP   Texas Power and Light Co.—9B

TXT   Textron, Inc.—9A, 9B

TY   Tri-Continental Corp.—9B

TYC   Tyco Laboratories, Inc.   9B

U   The United Corp.—9A

*u*ranium—17A

UA   United Aircraft Corp.—9A

United *A*rtists—25

UAHC   *U*nion of *A*merican *H*ebrew *C*ongregations · 16

UAL   *U*nited *A*ir *L*ines 1, 9A

UAM   *u*nderwater-to-*a*ir *m*issile 4

UAP United Aircraft Products, Inc.—9B

UAR United Arab Republic—27

UARCO United Autograph Register Co.—3

UAS United Asbestos Corp., Ltd.—9B

UAUM underwater-to-air-to-underwater missile—4

UAW United Automobile, Aerospace and Agricultural Implement Workers of America—21

UB United Brethren in Christ—16

UBC United Board and Carton Corp.—9B

UBO U.S. Tobacco Co.—9A

UBP United Bahamian Party—12

UC una corda (one string) (music)—19

under construction—9

unemployment compensation—7

University of California—23

Upper Canada—27

uppercase—22

Utah Construction and Mining Co.—9A

UCB United California Bank—3

UCC Union Camp Corp.—9A

United Church of Christ—16

Universal Copyright Convention—12

UCD unemployment compensation deduction—7

University of California at Davis—23

UCG Universal Cigar Corp.—9B

UCI University of California at Irvine—23

UCL Union Oil Co. of California—9A

UCLA University of California at Los Angeles—23

UCM Universal Church of the Master—16

UCMJ Uniform Code of Military Justice—4

UCMS United Christian Mission Society—16

UCNY University of the City of New York—23

UCO The Union Corp.—9A, 9B

UCP United Cerebral Palsy—2

UCR Universal Container Corp.—9B

University of California at Riverside—23

UCSB University of California at Santa Barbara—23

UCSD University of California at San Diego—23

UCT United States Ceramic Tile Co.—9B

UCV United Confederate Veterans—2

UDC United Daughters of the Confederacy—2

universal decimal classification—17

Urban Development Corporation (New York City)—6

UDI Unilateral Declaration of Independence (Rhodesia)—12

UDO Udico Corp.—9B

UDS United Dollar Stores—9B

UDT underwater demolition team—4

UE United Electrical Workers—21

UEP Union Electric Co.—9A

UES University Elementary School (Los Angeles)—23

UEX Unexcelled, Inc.—9B

UF United Fruit Co.—9A

UFC Union Financial Corp.—9B

United Free Church of Scotland—16

UFD United Foods, Inc.—9B

UFG U.S. Freight Co.—9A

UFL United Financial Corp. of California—9A

UFO unidentified flying object—8

U.S. and Foreign Securities Corp.—9A

UFPC United Federation of Postal Clerks—21

UFT *United Federation of Teachers* —21

United States Filter Corp.—9B

UFWA *United Furniture Workers of America*—21

UFWOC *United Farm Workers Organizing Committee*—21

UGI UGI Corp.—9A

United Gas Improvement Co.—3

UHA *ultrahigh altitude*—1, 17

UHF *ultrahigh frequency*—17

United Health Foundations—2, 17

UI *unemployment insurance*—7

Universal-International Studios—25

ut infra (as stated below)—19

UIC United Industrial Corp.—9A, 9B

UIP U.I.P. Corp.—9B

United Improvement and *Investment* Corp.—3

UIS Utah-Idaho Sugar Co.—9B

UIU *Upholsterers' International Union* of North America—21

UIV Union Investment Co.—9B

UJA *United Jewish Appeal*—16

UJWF *United Jewish Welfare Fund*—16

UK Union Carbide Corp.—9A

United Kingdom—27

UL *Underwriters' Laboratories,* Inc.—3

Unilever, Ltd.—9A

ULC *upper-* and *lowercase*—22

ULF *ultralow frequency*—17

ULMS *underwater long-range missile system*—4

ULS United States Leasing International, Inc.—9B

UM *underwater mechanic*—4

UMC *Universal Match Corp.*—3

UMF *ultramicrofiche*—3, 22

UMM United Merchants and Manufacturers, Inc.—9A

universal mission module—17

UMT UMC Industries, Inc.—9A

universal military training—4

UMW *United Mine Workers* of America—21

UN Unilever N.V.—9A

United Nations—13

UNAC *United Nations Association Command*—13, 14

UNAU *United Nations Association* in the *United States*—2

UNC *United Nations Command*—13

United Nuclear Corp.—9A

UNCIO *United Nations Conference* on *International Organization*—13

UNCIP *United Nations Commission* in *India* and *Pakistan*—13

UNCLE *United Network Command* for *Law* and *Enforcement* ("The Man from U.N.C.L.E.," TV show)—14, 25

UNCMAC *United Nations Command Military Armistice Commission*—13, 14

UNCSAT *United Nations Conference* On the Application of *Science And Technology* for the Benefit of the Less-Developed Areas—13, 14

UNCTAD *United Nations Conference* on *Trade* and *Development*—13, 14

UNCURK *United Nations Commission* for the *Unification* and *Rehabilitation* of *Korea*—13, 14

UNDP *United Nations Development Program*—13

UNEF *United Nations Emergency Force*—13, 14

UNESCO *United Nations Educational, Scientific* and *Cultural Organization*—13, 14

UNG Union Gas Co. of Canada, Ltd.—9B

UNGA *United Nations General Assembly*—13

UNHCR United Nations High Commissioner for Refugees—13

UNICEF United Nations International Children's Emergency Fund—13, 14

UNIVAC universal automatic computer—14, 17

UNKRA United Nations Korean Reconstruction Agency—13, 14

UNO United Nations Organization—13

UNOGIL United Nations Observation Group in Lebanon—13, 14

UNPA United Nations Postal Administration—13

UNR Unarco Industries, Inc.—9A

UNREF United Nations Refugee Fund—13, 14

UNRPR United Nations Relief for Palestine Refugees—13

UNRRA United Nations Relief and Rehabilitation Administration—13, 14

UNRWA United Nations Relief and Works Agency—13

UNS Unishops, Inc.—9A

UNSC United Nations Security Council—13

UNSCOP United Nations Special Committee on Palestine—13, 14

UNT United National Investors Corp.—9B

UNTSO United Nations Truce Supervision Organization—13

UOP Universal Oil Products Co.—3, 9A

UOS Union Stock Yards Co. of Omaha, Ltd.—9B

UP underproof—17

Union Pacific Railroad—1, 9A

United Presbyterian—16

UPA units per assembly—9

UPC U.S. Plywood-Champion Papers, Inc.—9A

UPD The United Piece Dye Works—9B

UPI United Press International—22

UPJ The Upjohn Co.—9A

UPK The United Park City Mines Co.—9A

UPP United Papermakers and Paperworkers—21

UPS Underground Press Syndicate—22

United Parcel Service—3

UPU Universal Postal Union—13

UPW United Public Workers—21

UPWA United Packinghouse Workers of America—21

URAVAN uranium-vanadium (town in Colorado)—14, 27

URB Uris Buildings Corp.—9A

URBM ultimate-range ballistic missile—4

URC Uarco, Inc.—9A

URD underground residential distribution (of utilities)—9

United States Radium Corp.—9B

UROC United Republicans of California—14, 24

URS URS Systems Corp.—9B

US ubi supra (where mentioned above)—19

United Service—16

United States—27

ut supra (as stated above)—19

USA Union of South Africa—27

United States Army—4

United States of America—27

USAAC United States Army Air Corps—4

USAAML United States Army Aviation Materiel Laboratories—4, 17

USAC United States Auto Club—2, 14

USAF United States Air Force—4

USAFI United States Armed Forces Institute—4, 23

USAID United States Agency for International Development—6

USAMC United States Army Materiel Command—4

USAR United States Army Reserve—4

USARAL United States Army, Alaska—4, 14

USAREUR United States Army, Europe—4, 14

USARP United States Antarctic Research Program—17

USARPAC United States Army, Pacific—4, 14

USARSOUTHCOM United States Army, Southern Command—4, 14

USASCC United States Army Strategic Communications Command—4

USATT United States Atlantic Tuna Tournament—11

USB upper side band (radio)—17

USBGN United States Board of (or on) Geographic Names—6

USBR United States Bureau of Reclamation—6

USC under separate cover—9

United States Code—7

United States of Colombia—27

University of Southern California—23

USCA United States Code Annotated—7

USCC United States Catholic Conference—16

USCG United States Coast Guard—4

USCGS United States Coast and Geodetic Survey—6

USDA United States Department of Agriculture—6

USDI United States Department of the Interior—6

USECC United States Employes' Compensation Commission—6

USES United States Employment Service—6

USET United States Equestrian Team—11

USF U.S. Natural Resources, Inc.—9B

USG United States Government—7

United States Government Railroad—1, 7

U.S. Gypsum Co.—9A

USGA United States Golf Association—11

USGLI United States Government Life Insurance—7

USGS United States Geological Survey—6

USH Uslife Holding Corp.—9A

USHA United States Housing Authority—6

USHL United States Hydrographic Laboratory—6, 17

USI U.S. Industries, Inc.—9A

USIA United States Information Agency—6

USIS United States Information Service—6

USL U.S. Lines Co.—9A

USLTA United States Lawn Tennis Association—11

USM underwater-to-surface missile—4

United Shoe Machinery Corp.—3

United States mail—7

United States Marines—4

United States Mint—6

USM Corp.—9A

USMA United States Military Academy—4, 23

USMC United States Marine Corps—4

United States Maritime Commission—6

USMHS United States Marine Hospital Service—4, 17

USMM United States Merchant Marine—1

USN United States Navy—4

USNA United States National Army—4

United States Naval Academy—4, 23

USNG United States National Guard—4

USNM United States National Museum—6

USNPO United States Navy Project Office—4

USNR United States Naval Reserve—4

USNRF United States Naval Reserve Force—4

USO United Service Organizations—2

USOM United States Operations Mission—6

USP United States Pharmacopoeia—18

The United States Playing Card Co.—9A

USPHS United States Public Health Service—6, 17

USPO United States Post Office—6

USPS United States Power Squadron—11

USR United States Reserves—4

The U.S. Shoe Corp.—9A

USRC United States Reserve Corps—4

USRRC United States Road Racing Club—11

USS United States Senate—7

United States Service—4

United States Ship (or Steamer or Steamship)—1, 4

USSA United States Ski Association—11

USSB United States Shipping Board—6

USSCT United States Supreme Court—6

USSR Union of Soviet Socialist Republics—27

USSS United States steamship—1, 4

UST U.S. Reduction Co.—9B

universal subscriber terminal—9

USTA United States Trotting Association—11

USTC United States Tariff Commission—6

USTFF United States Track and Field Federation—11

USTS United States Travel Service—6

USU U.S. Rubber Reclaiming Co., Inc.—9B

USV United States Volunteers—4

USVI United States Virgin Islands—27

USW underseas warfare—4

United Steelworkers of America—21

USWB United States Weather Bureau—6

UT United Utilities, Inc.—9A

universal time—30

University of Texas—23

UTA Union Transportation Aérienne (Air Transport Union)—1

UTBU "Unhealthy To Be Unpleasant" (theatrical play)—25

UTC "Uncle Tom's Cabin"—25

UTEP University of Texas at El Paso—23

UTP Utah Power and Light Co.—9A

UTR Unitrode Corp.—9B

UTWA United Textile Workers of America—21

UTX Union Tank Car Co.—9A

UTY U.S. Realty Investments—9B

UUA Unitarian Universalist Association—16

UUM underwater-to-underwater missile—4

UV ultraviolet—17

Unadilla Valley Railroad—1

U.S. Smelting, Refining and Mining Co.—9A

UVC Universal Marion Corp.—9B

UVV Universal Leaf Tobacco Co., Inc.—9A

UW unconventional warfare—4

underwriter (or -written)—9

used with—9

UWU Utility Workers Union of America—21

UXB unexploded bomb—4, 8

V vanadium—17A
VA verb active—15
Veterans' Administration—6
Vicar Apostolic—16
vice admiral—4
Order of Victoria and Albert—28
vixit annos (he lived . . . years)—19
volt-ampere—17
VAB vehicle assembly building (at Cape Kennedy)—17
VAL The Valspar Corp.—9B
VAMP [perhaps] Voluntary Association of Master Pumpers—14
VAR vacuum arc resmelting (steel process)—9
Varian Associates—9A
visual-aural range—17
volt-ampere reactive—17
VARIG Viação Aérea Rio Grande (Brazilian Airlines)—1, 14
VASCAR visual average speed computer and recorder—14, 26
VASP Viação Aérea São Paulo (Brazilian Airlines)—1, 14
VASS Van Allen simplified scoring (tennis)—11
VAT value-added taxes—9, 14
VAVS Veterans' Administration Voluntary Service—6
VC Veterinary Corps—4
vice-chairman—28
vice-chancellor—28
vice-consul—28
Victoria Cross—28
Vietcong—8, 12
VCD vice control district—26
VCG vector cardiography—17
VCR Victor Comptometer Corp.—9A
V&CS Virginia & Carolina Southern Railroad—1
VCS vehicle control system—17
VD various dates—9
venereal disease—8, 17
VDC Van Dorn Co.—9B
volts direct current—17
VDH valvular disease of the heart—17

VDM vasodepressor material—17
verbi Dei minister (minister of the word of God)—16
VDS variable depth sonar—17
VE Victory in Europe—8
VEL Virginia Electric and Power Co.—9A
VEM vasoexcitor material—17
VEN The Vendo Co.—9A
VERLORT very-long-range tracking—14, 17
VET Vetco Offshore Industries, Inc.—9B
VF very fine—8
video frequency—17
voice frequency—17
VFC V. F. Corp.—9A
VFR Verein Für Raumschiffahrt (Society for Space Travel, Germany)—12, 17
visual flight rules—1
VFW Veterans of Foreign Wars—2
VG verbi gratia (for example)—19
very good—8
vicar general—16
VHA very high altitude—1, 17
VHC very highly commended—8
VHF very high frequency—17
VI Vancouver Island—27
verb intransitive—15
vide infra (see below)—19
Virgin Islands—27
viscosity index—17
volume indicator—17
VIASA Venezolana Internacional de Aviación, Sociedad Anonimo (Venezuelan Airlines)—1, 14
VIC variable instruction computer—23
Victoreen Leece Neville, Inc.—9B
VIG vaccinia immune globulin—17
VII Venice Industries, Inc.—9B
VIK Vikoa, Inc.—9B
VIL Villager Industries, Inc.—9A
VIM vertical improved mail—7

VIN   Vintage Enterprises, Inc.—9B

VIP   versatile information processor—9

very important person—8

VIS   Visual Electronics Corp.—9B

VISTA   Volunteers in Service to America—2, 6, 14

VITA   Volunteers for International Technical Assistance—2, 14

VIX   Vanguard International, Inc.—9B

VJ   Victory over Japan—8

VKE   Virginia Iron, Coal and Coke Co.—9B

VL   Vulgar Latin—15

VLA   very low altitude—1, 17

VLE   Valle's Steak House—9B

VLF   very low frequency—17

VLM   Volume Merchandise, Inc. —9B

VLR   very-long-range aircraft—1

VLV   Valve Corp. of America—9A

VLX   Viewlex, Inc.—9B

VM   Vuilleumier cycle—17

VMC   Vulcan Materials Co.—9A

VMD   Veterinariae Medicinae Doctor (Doctor of Veterinary Medicine)—5

VMI   Virginia Military Institute—23

VMP   Valley Metallurgical Processing Co., Inc.—9B

VN   verb neuter—15

VNCS   Vietnam Christian Service—16

VNO   Vornado, Inc.—9A

VO   verbal order—4

very old—8

VOA   Voice of America—6

VOC   Vocaline Co. of America, Inc.—9B

VOCOM   voice communication—14, 17

VON   Von's Grocery Co.—9A

VOPO   Volkspolizei (People's Police, East Germany)—12, 14

VOR   very high frequency omnidirectional radio range—1, 17

VOT   Vogt Manufacturing Corp.—9B

VP   verb passive—15

vice-president—28

VPA   vote profile analysis—28

VPI   Virginia Polytechnic Institute—23

VPS   vibrations per second—17

VR   Veeder Industries, Inc.—9A

verb reflexive—15

Victoria Regina (Queen Victoria)—29

VRA   Vocational Rehabilitation Administration—6

VRN   Vernitron Corp.—9B

VRO   Varo, Inc.—9B

V&S   Valley & Siletz Railroad—1

VS   versus—8

veterinary surgeon—28

vide supra (see above)—19

volti subito (turn the page quickly) (music)—19

VSI   VSI Corp.—9A

VSOP   very superior old pale—3

VSP   very special person (or people)—8

VSTOL   vertical and (or very) short takeoff and landing—1

VT   vacuum tube—17

variable time—30

verb transitive—15

voice tube—1

VTC   Volunteer Training Corps—4

voting trust certificate—9

VTL   vertical turret lathe (machine)—9

VTO   vertical takeoff—1

VTOHL   vertical takeoff and horizontal landing—1

VTOL   vertical takeoff and landing—1

VTR   video tape recorder—25

VTR, Inc.—9B

VTS   vanillin thiosemicarbazone—17

VU   volume unit—17

VUL   Vulcan Corp. (Ohio)—9B

VV   percent volume in volume—17

vice versa—8

VVO very very old—8

VW very worshipful—28

Volkswagen—1, 8

VX Vulcan, Inc. (Pa.)—9B

W tungsten (from wolfram)—17A

Westvaco Corp.—9A

WA Wabash Railroad Co.—9A

West Africa—27

Western Allegheny Railroad—1

Western Australia—27

WAA War Assets Administration—6

WAAC Women's Army Auxiliary Corps—4

WAAF Women's Auxiliary Air Force—4

WAAS Women's Auxiliary Army Service—4

WAC Western Athletic Conference—11

Women's Army Corps—4, 14

WAF with all faults—9

Women in the Air Force—4

WAFS Women's Auxiliary Ferrying Squadron—4

WAG Walgreen Co.—9A

WAK The Wackenhut Corp.—9B

WAL Western Air Lines—1, 9A

WAN Wang Laboratories, Inc.—9B

WAR Warner Co.—9A

WASP white Anglo-Saxon Protestant—8, 14

Women's Air Force Service Pilots—4, 14

WATS wide area telephone service—3

WAVES Women Accepted for Voluntary Emergency Service—4, 14

WB Wachovia Corp—9A

warehouse book—9

water ballast—1

water boiler—9

waybill—9

Weather Bureau—6

westbound—1

wideband—17

wing back—11

WBA World Boxing Association—11

WBB Del E. Webb Corp.—9A

WBC Western Bancorporation—9A

white blood count—17

WBF Westbury Fashions, Inc.—9B

WBL Welbilt Corp.—9A

WBS Warner Bros.-Seven Arts, Ltd.—9B

WC water closet—8

Weiman Co., Inc.—9B

Wesleyan Chapel—16

without charge—9

WCA wind correction angle—27

WCB Whitaker Cable Corp.—9B

WCC Wilson Pharmaceutical and Chemical Corp.—9B

World Council of Churches—16

WCP West Chemical Products, Inc.—9B

WCS White Cross Stores, Inc.—9A

WCTU Women's Christian Temperance Union—2

WD War Department—6

Ward Foods, Inc.—9A, 9B

when distributed—9

withdrawn—9

WDC War Damage Corporation—6

WDL Woodall Industries, Inc.—9B

WDS Woods Corp.—9A

WE Westec Corp.—9B

Western Electric Co.—3

WEC Wadell Equipment Co., Inc.—9B

WED Walter Elias (Walt) Disney—29

WEI White Eagle International, Inc.—9B

WEN Wentworth Manufacturing Co.—9B

WEU Western European Union—12

WEY Weyenberg Shoe Manufacturing Co.—9A

WF West Feliciana Railroad—1

wrong font—22

WFNA white fuming nitric acid—17

WFP World Food Program (of the FAO)—13

WF&S Wichita Falls & Southern Railroad—1

WFTU World Federation of Trade Unions—21

WFUNA World Federation of United Nations Associations—2

WG water gauge—9

weight guaranteed—9

Willcox and Gibbs, Inc.—9B

wire gauge—9

WGA Writers' Guild of America—10

WGAW Writers' Guild of America—West—10

WGL Washington Gas Light Co.—9A

WH watt-hour—17

The White Motor Corp.—9A

WHCA White House Communications Agency—6

WHD Weatherhead Co.—9A

WHIP white people (or person)—8, 14

WHL The Wheelabrator Corp.—9B

WHO World Health Organization—13

WHR Whirlpool Corp.—9A

WHT Whitehall Electronics Corp.—9B

WHX Wheeling Pittsburgh Steel Corp.—9A

WI West Indies (or Indian)—27

when issued—9

WIA wounded in action—4

WIC Waltham Industries Corp.—9B

WID Wean United, Inc.—9A

WIE Wieboldt Stores, Inc.—9A

WIH Western International Hotels Co.—9B

WII Wolverine Industries, Inc.—9B

WIL Wilson and Co., Inc.—9B

WILCO will comply—8, 14

WI&M Washington, Idaho & Montana railroad—1

WIN Winn-Dixie Stores, Inc.—9A

WIP Work Incentive Program—7

WIS Wisconsin Power and Light Co.—9B

WIT Witco Chemical Corp.—9A

WITCH Women's International Terrorist Conspiracy from Hell—2, 14

WIX The Wickes Corp.—9A

W&J Washington and Jefferson College—23

WJ Watkins-Johnson Co.—9A

WKR Whittaker Corp.—9A

WKT Wayne Gossard Corp.—9A

WKW Workwear Corp.—9B

W&L Washington and Lee University—23

WL water line—1

wavelength—17

WLA Warner-Lambert Pharmaceutical Co.—9A

WLB War Labor Board—6

Wilson Brothers—9B

WLC Wellco Enterprises, Inc.—9B

W&LE Wheeling and Lake Erie Railroad—1

WLE Wheeling and Lake Erie Railway Co.—9A

WLM R.C. Williams and Co., Inc.—9B

W&M College of William and Mary—23

WM Western Maryland Railroad—1, 9A

Worshipful Master—28

WMB Williams Brothers Co.—9A

WMC Wallace-Murray Corp.—9A

War Manpower Commission—6

WMH Williamhouse-Regency, Inc.—9B

WMI Wabash Magnetics, Inc.—9B

WMK watermark—22

Weis Markets, Inc.—9A

WML Weil-McLain Co., Inc.—9B

WMO World Meteorological Organization—13

WMU Women's Missionary Union (of the Southern Baptists)—16

W&N Wharton & Northern Railroad—1

WNI Webster's New International Dictionary—22

WNK Winkelman Stores, Inc.—9B

WNU Western Nuclear, Inc.—9B

WNW west-northwest—27

Wood Industries, Inc.—9B

WO wait order—9

War Office—4

warrant officer—4

without—9

WOA World Airways, Inc.—9A

WOB washed overboard—1

WOC Wilshire Oil Co. of Texas—9B

without compensation—9

WOM Wometco Enterprises, Inc.—9A

WOMPI Women of the Motion Picture Industry—2, 14

WOP without papers (refers to Italian immigrants)—8, 14

without pay—8, 14

WOR Western Orbis Co.—9B

W&OV Warren & Ouchita Valley Railroad—1

WP weather permitting—1

Western Pacific Railroad—1

wild pitch—11

wire payment—9

working pressure—17

worthy patriarch—28

WPA Works Progress Administration—6

WPB War Production Board—6

WPC Wisconsin Electric Power Co.—9A

WPM West Point Pepperell, Inc.—9A

words per minute—9

WPP Whippany Paper Board Co., Inc.—9B

WPS Wisconsin Public Service Corp.—9A

WPT Westates Petroleum Co.—9B

WR wardroom—1, 4

warehouse receipt—9

war risk—9

wide receiver—11

WRA War Relocation Authority—6

Western Railway of Alabama—1

WRAC Women's Royal Army Corps—4

WRAF Women's Royal Air Force—4

WRC Warnaco, Inc.—9A

WRD Wards Co.—9B

WREN Women's Royal English Navy—4, 14

WRG Wells, Rich, Greene, Inc.—9B

WRNS Women's Royal Naval Service—4

WRO Welfare Rights Organization—2

Wichita Industries, Inc.—9B

WRS The Western Pacific Railroad Co.—9A

WRSSR White Russian Soviet Socialist Republic—12

WRT Wright-Hargreaves Mines, Ltd.—9B

WRU Western Reserve University—23

WS Wadley Southern Railroad—1

The Warner and Swasey Co.—9A

weapons system—4

West Saxon—15

WSA War Shipping Administration—6

Worker-Student Alliance—2

WSB Wage Stabilization Board—6

WSC Wesco Financial Corp.—9A

Winston Spencer Churchill—29

WSG Wilson Sporting Goods Co.—9B

WSJ Wall Street Journal—22

WSMR White Sands (N.M.) Missile Range—4, 17

WSO Watsco, Inc.—9B

WSP West Penn Power Co.—9A

W&SR *W*arren & *S*aline *R*iver Railroad—1

WSS Washington Steel Corp.—9A

*W*inston-Salem *S*outhbound Railroad—1

WSW *w*est-*s*outh*w*est—27

White Consolidated Industries, Inc.—9A

white *s*idewalls (tires)—1, 8

W&T *W*rightsville & *T*ennille Railroad—1

WT *w*atch *t*ime—27

*w*ater*t*ight—1

F. W. Woolworth and Co., Ltd.—9B

WTA Welded Tube Co. of America—9B

WTC Westcoast Transmission Co., Ltd.—9A

WTG Whiting Corp.—9B

WTR *W*estern *T*est *R*ange (of NASA)—17

WTX West Texas Utilities—9B

WU *W*estern *U*nion Telegraph Co.—3, 9A

WUI *W*estern *U*nion *I*nternational—3, 9B

WUR Wurlitzer Co.—9A

WV *w*eight in *v*olume—17

*W*est *V*irginia—27

WVDC *w*orking *v*oltage, *d*irect *c*urrent—17

WVS *W*omen's *V*oluntary *S*ervice—4

WVU *W*est *V*irginia *U*niversity—23

WW *W*alter *W*inchell—29

Walworth Co.—9A

*w*eight in *w*eight—17

*w*ith *w*arrants—9

*W*orld *W*ar (I and II)—8

WWD *W*omen's *W*ear *D*aily—22

WWP The Washington Water Power Co.—9A

WWW *W*olverine *W*orld-*W*ide, Inc.—9A

*w*orld *w*eather *w*atch—17

WWY William Wrigley Jr. Co.—9A

WX *W*estinghouse *E*lectric Corp.—9A

WY Weyerhauser Co.—9A

WYL Wyle Laboratories—9B

WYO *W*yandotte *I*ndustries Corp.—9B

WYS Wyomissing Corp.—9B

X U.S. Steel Corp.—9A

XBT *ex*pendable *b*athy*t*her-mograph—17

XC *ex* (without) *c*oupon—9

XCL *ex*cess *c*urrent *l*iabilities—9

XD *ex* (without) *d*ividend—9

XDIS *ex* (without) *d*istribution—9

XDS *X*erox *D*ata *S*ystems—3

XE *xe*non—17A

XF *e*xtra *f*ine—8

XIN *ex* (without) *in*terest—9

XL *e*xtra *l*arge—8, 9

XLO *E*x-*C*ell-*O* Corp.—9A

XM *e*xperimental *m*issile—4

XMD *ex*cused from *m*ilitary *d*uty—4

XO *e*xecutive *o*fficer—4

XPR *ex* (without) *p*rivileges—9

XQ (cross) *q*uestion—9

XR *ex* (without) *r*ights—9

XRT *ex* (without) *r*igh*t*s—9

XRX Xerox Corp.—9A

XSM *e*xperimental *s*trategic *m*is-*s*ile—4

XTR Xtra, Inc.—9A

XU *x*-ray measuring *u*nit—17

XUV *e*xtreme *u*ltra*v*iolet—17

XW *e*xperimental *w*arhead—4

ex (without) *w*arrants—9

XYL *ex* (former) *y*oung *l*ady (wife)—8

Y Alleghany Corp.—9A, 9B

*y*ttrium—17A

YAF *Y*oung *A*mericans for *F*reedom—2

YB yearbook—9
ytterbium—17A
YC yacht club—8
YCL Young Communist League—24
YD Young Democrats—24
YES Youth Employment Service—6
YGP yards gained passing—11
YGR yards gained rushing—11
YHA Youth Hostels Association—2
YIP Youth International party (yippies)—2
YL young lady—8
YMCA Young Men's Christian Association—2, 16
YMHA Young Men's Hebrew Association—2, 16
YO year old—9
YOB Youth Opportunities Board—6
YOC Youth Opportunity Centers—7
YP yield point—9
YPF Young People's Fellowship—2, 16
YPSCE Young People's Society of Christian Endeavor—16
YPSL Young People's Socialist League—24
Y&R Young and Rubicam, Inc.—3
YR Yonkers Raceway, Inc.—9B
Young Republicans—24
YRA Yacht Racing Association—11
YRU Yacht Racing Union—11
Y&S Youngstown & Southern Railroad—1
YS yield strength—9
YSB Yacht Safety Bureau—11
YSD The Youngstown Steel Door Co.—9A
YST Yukon standard time—30
YT Yukon Territory—27
Yukon time—30
YTD year to date—9

YTEP Youth Training and Employment Project—6
YU Yale University—23
YWCA Young Women's Christian Association—2, 16
YWHA Young Women's Hebrew Association—2, 16

Z F.W. Woolworth Co.—9A
ZA American Zinc Co.—9A
ZAL Zale Corp.—9A
ZB Crown Zellerbach Corp.—9A
zum Beispiel (for example)—19
ZCMI Zion's Cooperative Mercantile Institution—3
ZD zenith distance—27
ZE Zenith Radio Corp.—9A
ZEEP zero energy experiment pile—14, 15
ZF zone of fire—4
ZG zoological gardens—17
ZGS zero gradient synchrotron—17
ZI zone of the interior—4, 17
ZIM Zi Mischari (merchant fleet) (Israel)—1, 14
Zimmer Homes Corp.—9B
ZIO Zion Foods Corp.—9B
ZIP Zone Improvement Program code—7, 14
ZN zinc—17A
ZOA Zionist Organization of America—16
ZOS Zapata Norness, Inc.—9A
ZPG Zero Population Growth (organization)—2
ZR zirconium—17A
ZRN Zurn Industries, Inc.—9A
ZRO Zero Manufacturing Co. —9B
ZY Zayre Corp.—9A
ZZ zigzag—8